3rd Edition

Involving Parents in their Children's Learning

A Knowledge-Sharing Approach

Margy Whalley

& the Pen Green Centre Team

SAGE

Los Angeles | London | New Delhi
Singapore | Washington DC | Melbourne

Los Angeles | London | New Delhi
Singapore | Washington DC | Melbourne

SAGE Publications Ltd
1 Oliver's Yard
55 City Road
London EC1Y 1SP

SAGE Publications Inc.
2455 Teller Road
Thousand Oaks, California 91320

SAGE Publications India Pvt Ltd
B 1/I 1 Mohan Cooperative Industrial Area
Mathura Road
New Delhi 110 044

SAGE Publications Asia-Pacific Pte Ltd
3 Church Street
#10-04 Samsung Hub
Singapore 049483

Editor: Jude Bowen
Assistant editor: George Knowles
Production editor: Victoria Nicholas
Marketing manager: Dilhara Attygalle
Cover design: Wendy Scott
Typeset by: C&M Digitals (P) Ltd, Chennai, India
Printed by CPI Group (UK) Ltd, Croydon, CR0 4YY

First edition published 2004. Second edition published 2008. Reprinted 2009, 2010, 2012 and 2015.

Library of Congress Control Number: 2016955968

British Library Cataloguing in Publication data

A catalogue record for this book is available from the British Library

ISBN 978-1-47394-621-7
ISBN 978-1-47394-622-4 (pbk)

To my daughter Natasha, now aged 36 and very much a
'shining light powerful beyond measure'.

Contents

Author and contributor bios

Margy Whalley has a 36-year-old daughter and three gorgeous grandchildren, Molly, Tom and Harriet. She has worked for over forty-four years in education and community development projects in England, Brazil and Papua New Guinea. She is a qualified teacher with an MA in community education and a doctorate in leadership within early years settings. She was Director of the Pen Green Integrated Centre for Children and Families for thirty-three years and set up the Research, Training and Development base in Corby. Margy is a passionate advocate for children and families.

Cath Arnold is an education consultant at the Pen Green Centre for under fives and their families. She has almost forty years' experience in both private and public sector childcare and education. She is a qualified teacher, has a Master's degree in education and a PhD. Cath is a parent to three children and grandparent to six. She has published books about her two eldest grandchildren, who are now adults, as well as articles and chapters case studying other children.

Jo Benford has worked in early years for twenty-seven years, and has been part of the Pen Green team for sixteen of those. Initially responsible for the development of the Creche Provision within the centre, Jo soon found her passion for children extended to the adults she was working with. In recent years Jo has written and validated the Foundation Degree and BA Top-up in Integrated Working with Children and their Families in the Early Years, and is currently the Programme Leader. Working with the Early Years Workforce nationally is one of the ways Jo feels able to share her experience and contribute to the ever-evolving understanding of how young children learn and develop.

Trevor Chandler trained as a social worker. He worked at Pen Green for twenty years, originally as Deputy Head and subsequently as Head of Centre. He has completed an MA in education with care. Trevor has two children, Rachel and David.

Tracey Cotterell started working with families and young children after having her fourth child. This was through the setting up and running of a large nursery, which she ran for ten years. This also involved setting up one of the first Forest Schools in the Country in 2000. Tracey then carried out research with a focus on the outdoors, and how this can inspire storytelling and writing while she ran Forest School sessions for a primary school for children from reception through to year 4. This led to a Master's degree in education. Since then, Tracey has worked as an early years teacher in primary schools in Somerset and North Somerset and is currently working in Bristol as a lead teacher, a Centre Lead for the Children's Centre and Assistant Head for the school.

Annette Cummings is the Assistant Head of Pen Green Centre and a member of the Centre Leadership Team. She originally came to Pen Green as a parent of two children, Alexandria and Olivia. As a parent she became involved in the research work of the Centre and returned to university in 1996/97 to gain a PGCE. Annette has undertaken a number of practitioner research projects with staff in the Research Base at Pen Green and has a Master's degree in early education with care.

Marcus Dennison was a family worker at Pen Green for seven years and also worked as a researcher in the Pen Green Research Base for a further three years. He ran groups at Pen Green for parents during the day and in the evening. Marcus has four children, and he left to care for his youngest daughter.

Julie Denton worked for many years as a mental health nurse specialising in working with those with alcohol problems and homelessness concerns. She is the proud mum of two children and became a childminder following the birth of her second child. This was twelve years ago. She brought with her from nursing an enduring interest in emotional wellbeing and believes deeply in the significance of working with parents.

Kate Hayward trained to be a teacher after being involved in the early education of her three children, Tom, Hannah and Emily. Previously she worked in community development projects and health programmes in Britain, Kenya and Papua New Guinea. She worked at Pen Green for eleven years as a researcher, leading on pedagogical support and professional development programmes including PICL and Making Children's Learning Visible (MCLV) and the MA in Integrated Provision for Children and Their Families (Early Years). She is currently working to support Pen Green with projects with which she had been involved before going off to travel.

Hannah and **Darren Howe** have attended Pen Green Centre for children and families for over eight years with their two sons. Hannah works as an administrator in her family craft business and also for Home-Start Corby and Darren works in the security industry. During their time at Pen Green they have both become increasingly interested in child development and particularly parents' involvement in their children's learning. Hannah and Darren have recently participated in research projects as parent researchers, alongside Penny Lawrence.

Penny Lawrence is a Senior Lecturer in Early Childhood Studies at The University of Roehampton. Her research interest is observing and documenting multi-modal interactions between children, in broadcast television, in education 0-6 in Reggio Emilia in Italy, in participatory research with children and parents at the Pen Green Centre, and most recently with two-year-old children making decisions.

Andrea Layzell works in Bradford in the north of England, and is passionate about the professionalisation of the early years workforce. She has worked with the Pen Green team since being involved in a local project with them and is currently part of the team offering the Pen Green Foundation Degree at St Edmund's Nursery School and Children's Centre in Girlington, Bradford. The principles and values that underpin the work of both St Edmund's and Pen Green affirm her personal commitment to the knowledge that parents are the major force in the lives of their children, in any community. Andrea works to support practitioners to create effective, meaningful partnerships with mothers, fathers and carers.

Sarah Marley became a Family Worker at Pen Green Children's Centre ten years ago after being a student based in the Baby and Toddler Nest. She felt the ethos of the centre reflected her beliefs about how children learn and the importance of parents as partners in their children's learning. Sarah has since completed her BA Hons in early years while working as a Senior Family Worker in the Couthie (under threes' provision). She has also had the opportunity to be a part of several research studies including Being in Relation. She really enjoyed the opportunity to look in depth at the subtle ways in which children communicate their intentions and how relationships develop between children and the adults around them.

Sandra Mole is a mother of four very intelligent and independent teenagers, having been heavily involved in their education for the past decade and a half, who is now proudly sitting back and enjoying watching them make their mark on the world. She first discovered Pen Green when her children were all babies and was lucky enough to find opportunity after opportunity for herself as well as for her family. She progressed through volunteering to paid employment and completing her Master's. She is currently working in community development helping ensure that services in the Centre remain reflective of the needs/wants of the community.

Angela Prodger is a qualified teacher with an MA in integrated provision for children and families. She has worked as an Early Years educator at Pen Green Centre since 1989. As joint head (with Tracy Gallagher) of a fully integrated centre, Angela has lead responsibility for the nursery. She strives for the highest quality early years education with care. Angela is passionate about working with children 'at risk of social exclusion' and their families. She has worked on projects engaging parents in their children's learning and working with fathers. More recently her work has been focused on children with Special Educational Needs and Disabilities and working with the traveller communities to strengthen the inclusive practice in the Centre. Angela believes in parent participation and supporting parents to have a voice in shaping services and driving the Centre forward.

June Smith began her career in early years as a parent volunteer in her eldest son's infant school. For the past thirty years she has worked in a variety of roles in early education, including the setting up and running of early years provision in both the private and maintained sectors, and the management of a trailblazing Sure Start Local Programme. She is currently Head of a Maintained Nursery School and

Children's Centre and Director of the recently designated Teaching School. June's passion for high quality early years provision has remained constant throughout her career and she now has the added pleasure of watching the development of her five young grandchildren.

Colette Tait is a Principal Researcher at the Pen Green Research Base in Corby. She lectures on the Foundation Degree, BA and MA in Integrated Working with Children and their Families. Prior to this she worked at Pen Green for twelve years before leaving to lead a phase two Children's Centre in the county. She has two children, Georgia and Harry, who both attended the Pen Green Nursery, and who are now grown up.

Preface

This book was just one of the outcomes of a five-year research and development project at the Pen Green Centre for children and their families. In the first and second editions we described the rich and challenging dialogue that can develop when early years practitioners engage collaboratively with children and their families. The Pen Green practitioner research community works within a democratic research paradigm (Fletcher, 2014, page xi; Whalley, 2014, page xxi) where everyone's participation is equally valued.

Small-scale innovative projects such as this one, with its focus on parent participation, have a major contribution to make, not just to the community that they serve, but also to the wider early years community (Oliver, Smith and Barker, 1998). Practitioner research can inform the wider debate about the ethical dimension of research and can demonstrate how effective it is to work in a genuine research partnership with those who have traditionally been the objects of research (Holman, 1987).

The original research project involving parents in their children's learning was set up in 1995. It was partly funded during 1996 by the Teacher Training Agency and subsequently fully funded from 1997 to 2000 by the Esmée Fairbairn Charitable Trust. We are very grateful to our funders for giving us the opportunity to work so closely and thoughtfully with parents and children. The full research report is available from the Pen Green Research, Training and Development Base (www.pengreen.org). At the end of the project a video was made with four case studies illustrating this approach. It was produced and disseminated with support from the Department for Education and Employment (DfEE). An updated version of the video is now distributed as part of a continuous staff learning and development programme delivered by researchers, practitioners and parents at the Pen Green Centre.

Early years educators rarely have sufficient non-contact time to thoroughly develop their skills as reflective practitioners. When we embarked on this research and development project in the mid-1990s, our vision for the future was that there would be many integrated centres for children and families across the public, private and voluntary sector where staff could develop innovative projects with the same kind of support that we had received:

> Imagine early years centres where all staff are beginning to be assertive, self-critical and supportively critical of each other, where the staff are deeply attached to each other, work co-operatively, respect each other's strengths, and celebrate each other's successes and failures. Centres in which the adults, parents and staff are rigorous thinkers,

> focused and analytical, and yet aware of the rhythms of the organisation and their personal lives; where the work is rooted in the local community but staff also reach out, make their views known and challenge local and central government over important issues. These would be centres in which children's rich emotional lives were acknowledged and supported, where children were encouraged and cognitively challenged and their learning was promoted. In such centres children could truly become the managers of their own possibilities.
>
> (Whalley, doctoral study, 1999: 336)

This vision was an invitation to imagine an integrated service for children and families, full of democratic characteristics. In the fifteen years since we wrote the first edition of this book (2001) the field of parental involvement has become a much more contested site for study and debate and we have needed to reflect this in our third edition.

Whilst there is an even greater recognition of the critical importance of home learning and the need for strong links to be made between home and early childhood or school settings, it is the approach that professionals take to bridge that schism that has been problematised by academics and early childhood practitioners across the world.

When we chose the title for the first edition we knew exactly what we meant. Our understanding was that as practitioners we were only doing half our job if we failed to engage with all the important adults in the children's lives, as co-educators. We wanted to engage our colleagues in early childhood settings in the same learning journey. We naively made the assumption that our starting point wouldn't be open to interpretation. Interestingly, the continuing professional development (CPD) materials we produced as a result of this research project were entitled 'Parents' Involvement in Their Children's Learning' because we were describing and celebrating the many specific ways in which parents engage with their children successfully as their first educators. Parents, practitioners and colleagues generally refer to this as the PICL approach, not the Pen Green approach.

Participation is at the heart of all our work with parents and children and it is key to the success of the project and this approach. It is the very antithesis of 'doing things to people' and you can find its antecedents in the powerful de-schooling literature of the 1970s produced by Freire, Kohl and Illich, as well as by contemporary giants such as Athey, Shaw and Easen.

So we have added to the title 'the knowledge-sharing approach' to make it clear to any doubters that the project and this approach depend upon the full participation of parents as their child's first educators and the early years practitioners who have the privilege of caring and educating children during the day. It is about two sets of knowledge that, when put together, make everything possible.

Note: Whenever a case study was sensitive, we have suggested to parents that we use a pseudonym, bearing in mind that children will grow up and read what has been written in the future. Where stories are less sensitive, we have given parents the choice to use their real first names or a pseudonym of their choice.

Acknowledgements

At Pen Green we are very aware of the 'giants' upon whose shoulders we stand. We owe a huge debt of gratitude to Chris Athey who directed the Froebel Early Education Project 1973–8 and became a mentor and friend for many years.

We want to acknowledge and thank the other pioneers who have inspired, supported and advised us over the last thirty-three years:

- Professor Tony Bertram
- Professor Colin Fletcher
- Professor Ferre Laevers
- Professor Chris Pascal
- Professor Teresa Smith
- Professor Colwyn Trevarthen

We also want to acknowledge the Teacher Training Agency, who funded our pilot project, the Esmée Fairbairn Charitable Trust, who funded our three-year project, and the many staff, parents and children at Pen Green who became so deeply involved in the projects.

The Pen Green team want to express their thanks to Dr Cath Arnold for co-ordinating the third edition and once again encouraging and cajoling us to 'get our act together'.

Companion website

This new edition of *Involving Parents in their Children's Learning* is supported by a wide range of online resources, which you can access at **https://study.sagepub.com/whalley3e**

Visit the website to:

- access a selection of free SAGE journal articles supplementing each chapter
- follow weblinks which direct you to useful websites
- watch videos to help link theory to real life Pen Green practice.

1

New forms of provision, new ways of working

The Pen Green Centre

Margy Whalley

The Pen Green Centre opened in 1983 as one of a small number of pioneering integrated centres offering children and their families both nursery education and a wide range of support services. It was established after a comprehensive research project undertaken in the late 1970s on under fives services in Northamptonshire, with a clear intention to bridge the traditional divide between day-care and child protection services provided through social services-run day nurseries and early education as it had traditionally been provided in nursery classes and nursery schools.

The centre had a joint advisory group with strong political representation from both education, social care and health and the project was jointly managed by the Education and Social Services Departments and the local Health Authority. From the start the centre was staffed by a multidisciplinary team; in 1983 there were six staff working with 50 children and providing a range of services for 300+ younger children and their families. The staff included a social worker, early educators, a teacher and an unqualified community worker from the local area, with health visitors 'on loan' from the local health visiting team.

Pen Green was one of the first six Early Excellence Centres in 1996, became a trailblazer Sure Start programme in 1999 and was one of the first children's centres in England in 2006. By this time we were employing more than 120 staff including teachers, early educators, social workers, play workers, midwives, health workers and support staff, working on an annual basis with over 1400 families. Today, there are now three nursery areas (for children from 2 to 5 years) and two baby nest areas (for children from 9 months to 3 years) working daily with 340+ children. We also have indoor and outdoor environments for children and families that are used 48 weeks a year, five days a week and into the evening, and on Saturdays and Sundays between 9am and 1pm. We still engage with over 1500 families from across the whole town.

Corby, where the centre is based, became a steel town in the 1930s with a teeming population of steelworkers who had come down from Scotland to find work. A high proportion of the town's population were first generation Scots and the Scottish culture is still very strong with kilts, bagpipes, highland gatherings, ceilidhs and large followings for Celtic and Rangers football clubs. This migration has been summed up in the local adage '80% of the population are Scots and the rest are jealous'. The town also has a large Irish community with their own clubs and social centres and cultural traditions and in the immediate pre- and post-war years many families also migrated to Corby from Eastern Europe. The town's school registers represented this shift, so along with the Camerons, McKenzies, Wallaces, O'Malleys and Dochertys we began to see the Dejaralovics, Konsbergs and Merniaks.

In the 1980s, when the Pen Green Centre opened, the steelworks had closed, the local council housing estates were boarded up and shops were barricaded with wire grills; 43 per cent of the male population were unemployed and 50 per cent of children attending the centre when it first opened were from single parent families. Poor nutrition, inadequate housing and high infant mortality rates were all major factors influencing the lives of young families. There were minimal public services for parents and young children and very few of the traditional voluntary organisations for families facing social economic challenges or to support children at risk of social exclusion.

In Corby in the early 1980s there was no choice of services for parents wanting nursery education, childcare or 'time out' to study. There was no partnership between the public, private and voluntary sectors because there was little provision for family support or early education. There was only one private day nursery, a small number of registered childminders and a few volunteer-led playgroups. The part-time nursery education that was available in nursery units attached to local primary schools was hugely oversubscribed, and these short nursery sessions did not help parents who wanted to attend college or go back to work. There was also a social services children's centre in Corby, which was perceived by local parents as a resource exclusively for 'problem families'.

The Pen Green Centre was set up in what was formerly a comprehensive school built in the 1930s by the Stewarts and Lloyds steelmaking company to provide an education for the children of the steelworkers. The houses that surround the centre were built specifically to be homes for the 'steelworkers'. Sixty feet away stood the last of the blast furnaces that had transformed a small Northamptonshire village into a thriving steel town (Whalley, 1994). In the first year that the centre opened we witnessed the detonation of the last 'Corby candle'.

Problems and contradictions

Corby in the 1980s exemplified many of the problems and contradictions inherent in education and day-care/childcare services in the UK at this time. The issues that staff at Pen Green had to face then remain problematic some thirty-three years later in 2016.

1. *Simplistic demarcation lines*: crude divisions remained in the 1980s between those who saw themselves as providing for the educational needs of the children i.e. the local education authority, and those supporting the child in terms of welfare and childcare i.e. social services, and in a very limited way, the private sector.

   In 2016 these divisions still remain. The main provider for 3-and 4-year-olds is the local authority through provision in nursery classes in primary schools across Corby. Most of these offer limited access to breakfast clubs or after-school provision and they do not open during the school holidays. Childcare support for the 3-and 4-year-olds of working parents is therefore very limited. The evidence from the Effective Provision of Pre-School Education (EPPE) study of the standard of early learning and development in nursery classes also shows that they do not currently demonstrate the same good outcomes for children as nursery schools (EPPE Study; Sylva et al., 2004).

   Corby now has a plethora of private childcare services, some of which are still run on the old playgroup model of school hours and school year. There has been a very significant take-up of 2-year-old provision in Corby in the private sector, however, only two primary schools in the town make that kind of provision. There are particular difficulties for families with young children with disabilities and special education needs in accessing high-quality services. The 'crude divisions' in 2016 in Corby would be between the various academy providers, as most of the primary schools and all of the secondary schools are now academised. We have six different academy chains involved in the delivery of education across the town. Currently 59 per cent of the schools are in Special Measures.
2. *Separatism*: in the 1980s there was no tradition of working in a fully integrated way with other services such as health visiting, midwifery, child and family guidance (CAMS) or Adult Education, all of which had a critical role in working with children and their families.

   Paradoxically we can look back on the 1980s as halcyon days for multidisciplinary working in Corby. Because of the closure of the steelworks, public service engagement and collaboration between health visiting and social care were outstanding. Whilst there have been an enormous number of policy directives on multi-agency partnership working the level of co-operation that we had with health visiting, midwifery and other services was at its very best in the years up to and including the Sure Start intervention years. Since then joint working has become increasingly eroded with constant reorganisations in health and social work in Northamptonshire; the long anticipated shift of health visiting from Public Health England into the local authority has become a very protracted journey. Whilst there have been some powerful interventions such as Family Nurse Partnership for the most vulnerable young mothers in Corby, there is no seamless integration of services between midwifery and health visiting or full data sharing between social care and education. Indeed the pressures on all these services are such that we are struggling to maintain the level of joint working that we had in past years, with up to 60 per cent of social workers employed by agencies.

The direct work of health visitors and midwives at Pen Green has been outstanding and hard fought for and has demonstrated a deep commitment from individual workers. Even when departments were reorganising, health visitors and midwives held onto their commitment to community-based services within an integrated centre for children and families. Health visitors and midwives work directly with our across-town family support team, and Home Start which is based at Pen Green, to co-ordinate new birth visits and referrals. Data sharing can still be problematic across agencies, but in the area of SEN and disability we have made some major breakthroughs with very early notification and identification and highly effective joint working.

3. *Over-professionalisation of services and under-representation of the voluntary sector*: this was a key issue in the 1980s and continued to be so into the 1990s whilst early childhood services were perceived by government as the panacea for all social ills. The contribution of the voluntary sector was and is still underestimated and Pen Green's commitment to voluntary groups such as Home Start has prevented their closure on several occasions.

   The concept of the Pen Green Centre was about co-constructing local services with local people. It has to be said this was largely the result of an action group against the centre, which was established in 1982 when the local authority first developed the idea of a new early years service for Corby. Local people took matters into their own hands and made it clear that they did not want another 'problem family' centre in Corby. What they really wanted was an institution that would be flexible and responsive and driven by local need.
4. *Inability to learn from history or the rest of Europe*: when setting up the early childhood services in Corby in the 1980s there was very little reference to early interventions at the beginning of the century; for example Margaret McMillan's work in Deptford and Bradford, the family centre movement in social care or radical community interventions in health in this country. Nor was there any effort made to learn from other European countries, such as Scandinavia or Italy, where fully integrated services for young children have a long history.

   In subsequent years we have worked collaboratively with projects across the UK, Western Europe, Australia and New Zealand.
5. *The narrow view of evidence-based models*: the only 'models' generally recognised as successful in the 1980s were those transplanted from the USA. The insistence on using medical models to provide the evidence base was particularly unhelpful for small-scale local projects. There was very little recognition in the 1980s of the importance of a local 'diagnosis' of need and this remains true today.
6. *Compensatory models*: in 1980 the prevalent professional perspective on working with parents assumed a 'deficit' model of parenting. This could be seen in almost all policy and much practice. There was an assumption that parents could become more effective by being taught a set of 'parenting skills' and this remains true to this day.

   In 2016 former Prime Minister David Cameron spoke about life chances and once again presented us with the notion of parents who require 'treatment' to improve their performance. There was and remains very little acknowledgement or celebration of 'difference' in terms of parenting approaches. The assumption is still that there is only one way to be an effective parent, and that is to have produced a compliant 'school ready' child.

7. *Political will*: it was clear in the 1980s that the early years workforce was relatively inexperienced in engaging in political debate and unaware of the inherently political nature of early years work. What has been most significant in subsequent years is the huge shift in delivery of early years education and care services from the public sector into the private sector where most provision for 0–3s now takes place (Gallagher and Arnold, forthcoming). Even in areas of very significant socio-economic deprivation like Corby, the private sector has become the preferred provider for the local authority and public sector provision, particularly in nursery schools, has been marginalised (Gaunt, 2016). The delivery of services such as preventative family support, which used to be found in both the public and voluntary sectors, is now predominantly delivered exclusively through large national voluntary organisations which are highly dependent on government funding. In Corby, the nursery schools and primary schools still do continue to deliver the children's centre offer. Pen Green's experience is that, without local borough council and county council support, settings such as ours would have been cut back on successive occasions. It has been the political will of the local community that has been most significant in retaining Pen Green as a local service that is much loved and well supported by families and the wider community.
8. *Lack of public accountability*: in the 1980s this was manifested as a general lack of awareness of the changing needs of young families, and the need for services to be increasingly flexible and responsive to the realities of family life. Families in Corby had fought hard to get their critical concerns recognised throughout the 1980s and 1990s as active stakeholders in public services. Corby is a town that is prepared to march and Corby families marched in the 1970s to save the steelworks and many times over the last few years to save *their* centre for children and families. With the marked exception of pre-election rhetoric, successive governments have failed to recognise the concerns that children, parents, families and the wider community have for services that really support family life in the twenty-first century; services that recognise parents' need to work and study and children's right to a rich early childhood experience with the added provision of accessible and effective family support within their locality.
9. *Poor conditions of service and training*: in the 1980s our studies had shown that although early childhood educators were capable of powerful advocacy on behalf of children and families, they were relatively passive in relation to their own pay and conditions of service. Staff were accustomed to working long hours, with inadequate training, little supervision and no non-contact time to plan and reflect on children's learning and development.

There has been relatively little improvement in pay and conditions in the private sector. In 2016 the government still appears to see Early Childhood Education and Care (ECEC) as a Cinderella service, assuming staff will work for less than the living wage. In the public sector significant improvements have been made. Well-qualified staff at Pen Green have pay that is commensurate with their incredible commitment and hard work. All staff have continuous professional development opportunities and we work with a 76–84 per cent graduate workforce across the three nursery spaces and two baby nests. Most senior staff have Master's degrees and all staff have some non-contact time to home visit and to dialogue and document children's learning and development.

Working with the community

Pen Green, as a centre for children and families, developed from a perspective 'which regards early childhood services as a need and right for all communities and families, and as an expression of social solidarity with children and parents' (Moss, 1992: 43; Moss and Penn, 1996). However, this social solidarity was born, in the first instance, out of conflict.

When the centre was set up, staff had to work with a very vocal and often hostile group of people. The most well-organised volunteer group in the local community was a local action group *against* the centre. This group was made up of local residents who felt that there had not been enough consultation between those setting up the new early years service and those who were expected to use it. They were afraid that the local authority planned to set up a centre for 'problem families', a day-care/child protection service exclusively for families where children were perceived to be 'at risk'. This was not what local residents wanted. The Local Action Group (LAG) was clear that what was needed in their local community was a radically new kind of service.

From December 1982 to July 1983 the purpose and principles behind the services that were to be set up at Pen Green were carved out by this 'local action group', local politicians, local authority officers, the centre leader and newly appointed staff group. The LAG's 'big idea', their vision for the future, was that in this small community there should be a service for children under five and their families, a service that would honour the needs of young children and celebrate their existence. It would also support families, however they were constituted within the community.

This vision for the newly established Pen Green Centre in 1983 was underpinned by the belief that:

- the most effective way of delivering coherent early education, health and social services to young families was through an integrated centre which would be easily accessible (i.e. at pram-pushing distance);
- services should be flexible and responsive to the needs of all local children and their extended families;
- education and care were indivisible; the early years curriculum offered in these services should be developmentally appropriate for children aged up to five years and should recognise the central position of play in early learning (DES, 1990).

- services should respect and value children's and parents' individual differences and celebrate ethnic, linguistic and cultural diversity;
- education begins at birth, and services must recognise the key role parents play as their children's first educators, and parents' commitment to their children's early education and development;
- adult community education should be made available to parents *within* services for early childhood education and care;
- all the staff working in these settings need to be highly trained, reflective practitioners with equitable conditions of service, adequate pay, appropriate non-contact time, in-service training, supervision and support, opportunities for promotion, and to engage in reflexive practice and practitioner research;
- workers in early childhood settings need to be concerned with power-sharing, community participation and local regeneration.

Hindsight

From our perspective in 2016 it is becoming easier to see that the greatest single determinant in terms of the development of the centre was probably the LAG and the energy for change in the local community. When we first began to develop the Pen Green pilot project, as it was described by the local authority, the energy and commitment of local parents were palpable. It is fair to say that in our experience all Corby parents want more for their children than they had themselves and consistently demonstrate their commitment to achieving the best possible outcomes for their families. It is not insignificant that at all times in the centre's history more than 50 per cent of staff working in the setting have started their learning journeys as parents who have volunteered, taken on training and become workers in the setting where their children were also being educated and cared for. Our intention was to engage parents on their terms and in their own timescale and it has worked. Pen Green has been judged 'Outstanding' at each and every Ofsted over the ensuing thirty-three years and Ofsted have commented on many occasions about the strong family ethos of the centre:

> Senior Managers show outstanding commitment to the children and their families and the local community. They are instrumental in maintaining the strong family ethos and make a considerable contribution to community cohesion within the nursery and beyond.
>
> Staff work tirelessly with families, children and a range of agencies both in the children centre and beyond to sustain children's excellent achievement and wellbeing. Outstanding links with parents ensure that they understand how staff are supporting their children's learning and are able take part in the process.
>
> (Ofsted, December 2009)

Whilst the vision has not changed in 2016 we have to communicate our local project within a global Early Childhood Education Context.

Figure 1.1 Pen Green estate when the steelworks was thriving

It wasn't until the centre had been going for about twenty years that parents and staff had the opportunity to travel and were invited to visit settings in Denmark and Italy and in Australia and New Zealand. One very young parent governor on returning from a visit to Denmark was heard harassing our Chair of Governors (who was also the opposition leader of the County Council) because she had discovered that in Denmark there had been one hundred years of integrated service development while people in England were, in her words, 'still stuffing children up chimneys'. She wanted to know why there hadn't been a wholesale buy-in to the notion of integrated services in this country. She didn't get an answer, but she did go on to take senior responsibility as an active volunteer and further her own adult education and development, as well as supporting her children's learning and development right through the education system. We are clear that when governments fail to respond to the needs of families and prioritise other issues the only way for early childhood services to survive periods of oppression is to be aware of the innovation and expansion of services that may be happening nationally, internationally and globally, because that gives heart to our endeavours.

Principles

The staff group appointed to work at Pen Green in the early 1980s were committed to engaging parents as decision-makers in the planning and implementation of work at the centre. They knew that working in this way was not about 'compensating for disadvantage'. Instead it was about acknowledging the impact of poverty on the lives of local children and their families, and encouraging families to take an equal and active role in developing high-quality, fully integrated responsive services.

The principles that underpin the work at Pen Green are the principles of community education. That community education should:

- be concerned with individuals' capacity to be self-directing;
- help individuals to gain more control over their lives;
- be about raising self-esteem;
- promote learning as a lifelong experience;
- be about equal opportunities;
- be about pushing boundaries;
- be about constructive discontent and not having to put up with things the way they are;
- encourage people to feel they have the power to change things;
- be about self-fulfilment.

(adapted from Whalley, 1994)

We were strongly influenced by Paulo Freire's (1996) work when we first developed services at Pen Green, as senior staff had also worked in Northern Brazil. We were very concerned that we should understand and respect the strengths of the local community and its very specific history (www.youtube.com/watch?v=BkFlOiRkuew). Clearly the project has thrived and survived for thirty-three years. We have had to learn much more about the changes socially and culturally in the local community during this period. We have a very significant increase in the number of families migrating to Corby from Russia, Poland, Bulgaria and Portugal, as well as Latvia and Croatia, all bringing their very different cultures, values and languages which strengthen the Corby community. In 2016 we still buy into the principled approach that we adopted in 1983 but we would probably articulate it differently. Today we are concerned with *co-constructing services* with the children and the families. We resist imposing new models of working and new interventions unless they build on respectful and reciprocal relationships with stakeholders. We have tried to build up our own evidence base on what works and why it works in this local community (see Chapter 2 for more on how we secure national validation for local interventions).

A 'one-stop shop' (Audit Commission, 1994)

Chris Athey, one of the greatest pioneers of early childhood education in this country, and a mentor to Pen Green staff for many years, describes the conceptual gulf that exists when groups of people who lack shared experience begin to work together (Athey, 1990). Whilst we knew that the 'Pen Green project' was not an entirely new concept, since there was nothing new about putting baby clinics next to a community nursery inside a family centre where day-care was on offer, Margaret McMillan was working in this way in Deptford at the beginning of the century (Whalley, 1994). What was new, however, was that we adopted a way of working which was based on an intense collaboration between parents and workers – 'a radical notion of self help as personal growth and the development of a sense of community responsibility' (Hevey, 1982, personal communication). We knew that we needed to work in an integrated way and that we also needed to adopt inter-agency strategies to achieve this. The newly appointed staff at Pen Green in 1983 adopted an 'open-door' approach, which helped to bridge the gap between these local parents and the new service. Parents were invited into the centre before the concrete was even dry. They shared the experience of transforming a derelict comprehensive school, one which many of them had attended as students, into a stimulating and secure environment for very young children and their families. They shared the responsibility for establishing priorities, allocating space and developing the work.

From 1983–1997 the centre developed the following strands of activity, which are still fundamental to the work of the centre in 2016:

Early years education

Extended hours, extended year provision to support families

Inclusive, flexible, education with care for children in need and children with special educational needs

Adult community education and family support services

Voluntary work and community regeneration

Training and support for early years practitioners

Research and development

The Audit Commission in 1994 described the 'one-stop shop' for families with young children as implicit in the local community approach that we had adopted. What we at the centre provided for children and families was as follows:

- A high-quality, developmentally appropriate, early childhood education with care provision for young children from 0–5.
- A place where children could meet, learn and grow; where staff worked hard to meet children's affective and cognitive needs; where there was appropriate provision for children in need.
- An inclusive service for children with special educational needs/special rights.

- A seamless provision for parents, with accessible adult education, health and social welfare services all on one site; a focus for lifelong learning in the community.
- A centre where parents were engaged in an equal, active and responsible partnership, and shared their concerns about their children's development.
- A centre where workers engaged with parents and shared power and responsibility.
- A centre where knowledge and information were shared about children's development and learning.

The changing political and educational agenda 1996–2016

The concept of a 'triangle of care' was conceptualised in the Start Right report (Ball, 1994), which described a new kind of partnership between parents and professionals. Through this equal and active partnership, a secure, warm and stimulating environment could be created for children. Parents, probably for the first time in a government report, were described as having their own proper competence, and their deep commitment to their children's learning was finally acknowledged.

The Start Right report made it clear that the key issue for early childhood educators in education and care settings was to develop a strong relationship with parents as the child's first and enduring educators. The role of early childhood settings was to support parents through:

- exemplifying good practice;
- providing information about current research;
- offering appropriate parent education and professional support;
- helping parents to develop and sustain their sense of self-esteem and self-efficacy.

Somewhat disingenuously the main author of the report, Sir Christopher Ball, made his own recommendation that if parents were non-compliant and failed to engage in parent education programmes they should have their benefits reduced. Words like 'parent support' and 'parent education' have to be 'troubled' when they represent the iron fist of the state dressed in a velvet glove, and this is as true in 2016 as it was in the 1980s and 1990s.

By 1997, the need to involve parents actively in their children's education was high on the political agenda of the newly elected Labour government. The role of parents as their children's first and most consistent educators seemed to be firmly established, at least in policy directives (Barber, 1996: 244). The link between parents' own experiences of the education system, their attitudes and expectations, and their children's achievement was acknowledged as a factor of even greater significance than school improvement (OECD, 1997).

In 1997, the government recommended that there should be a fully integrated approach to early years education and care across the public, private and voluntary sector. 'Supporting' parents and 'training' parents were identified as major tasks for all early childhood educators in all settings (DfEE, 1996, 1997) although still conceptualised on a deficit model rather than as an equal and active dialogue between parents and professionals.

Early Excellence Centres 1997

In December 1997, the government launched its Centres of Excellence programme (DfEE, 1997), offering financial support and defining standards for those individual centres or networks where flexible, high-quality, early years education and care were offered alongside education and training for parents. This government initiative acted as a catalyst, inspiring many local authorities to bid for funding to improve existing services or initiate projects.

Pen Green was one of the first centres designated by the government as an Early Excellence Centre. The additional financial support the centre received meant that we could increase our educational services to both children and their parents with new after-school programmes for school-aged children and for family community education. The government acknowledged the work of the centre in providing local and national training: 'The centre is ... a focal point for training early years educators in the public, private and voluntary sectors and is playing a major role in the dissemination of good practice in early years provision' (DfEE, 1998: 19). Under the Early Excellence Programme, Pen Green was allocated funding for new family education premises, which provided badly needed accommodation in which to set up research, training and development work.

Corby Sure Start 1999

In 1999, the government introduced another major initiative, the Sure Start local programme (DfEE, 1999). These programmes were designed to offer comprehensive support to families with children under four in disadvantaged neighbourhoods. A Sure Start Unit accountable to both the Minister for Health and the Minister for Education was established at Westminster. Identified communities were invited to prepare proposals for innovative multidisciplinary work at a local, community level. The programme had a strong community development strand, and there appeared to be a real expectation that local residents would be involved in developing these locality bids. In practice, local consultation was severely restricted as the consultation period for the Sure Start pilots was, as always, across the summer holidays.

Pen Green became the lead partner for Corby Sure Start and worked in close collaboration with all the other statutory and voluntary agencies concerned with family support across that summer. A particular feature of the Corby Sure Start programme was the very large numbers of parents involved in conceptualising local outcomes and programmes of work. Parents who had been involved in Pen Green for several years became powerful advocates for other parents living in the extended catchment area that was to become the 'Sure Start reach area'. A 'parent-led' needs assessment was immediately set up to assess the effectiveness of local services for the 103 new families whose children were born in the previous year. Parents were recruited and trained in interview techniques. They constructed an interview schedule collaboratively with staff and then were paid to conduct informal interviews (Pen Green Research Base Report, 2000; McKinnon, 2005). This provided rich data for the new Corby Sure Start programme, data which were then shared with health visitors, midwives and social care professionals. Parents presented the data at local seminars, and professionals were able to use the constructive feedback they were given very creatively. Within a few months, professionals were already beginning to think differently and make services more accessible and responsive to families. Retrospectively, it is possible to see how devising and developing new approaches to 'research from the underside' (Holman, 1987) was critical in terms of the development of our research in practice base at Pen Green. We developed innovative ways to identify local need and responded with home-grown, tried and tested interventions and we were able to embrace all four of Labour's major programmes (McKinnon, 2014).

A learning community

Pen Green benefited enormously from Labour's Neighbourhood Nursery programme in 2001, in that it made it possible for us to open our first baby nest provision (Gallagher and Arnold, in press). We developed our NNI baby nest as a research in practice project over several years. Pen Green now has two baby nest projects onsite and two offsite provisions are being developed in parts of the town facing specific challenges.

The additional funding and capital build that we attracted when we became one of the first children's centres in 2004 made it possible for us to realise significant family support coverage across the whole of the town with four children's centres working on an integrated locality-based model, led and managed through a Community Interest Company. We profoundly regretted the title 'children's centres' and rarely used it. The title 'Pen Green' comes from the name of the street in which we are located and we have always been described as an integrated centre for children and their families. The concept of a Centre for Children and Families seemed very important to us and in 2006, when we took on the legal status of a nursery school, the hundreds of parents who attended the consultation event insisted that we should not become an outward facing school but be rooted in the community and committed to working with families.

By 2006 what we had created at Pen Green was an environment in which:

- children, parents and staff were encouraged to be good decision-makers, able to question, challenge and make choices;
- there were opportunities for staff to become highly trained reflective practitioners, with good levels of support and supervision, in an environment where they

could build powerful relationships with other agencies and with families, where they felt valued personally and professionally;
- staff consult with, and see themselves as accountable to, all stakeholders – children, parents, staff, the local community, and local authority;
- parents have become passionate advocates for their children and are sharing their understanding of their children's learning at home with nursery staff.

Over thirty-three years, we had been able to develop a comprehensive parent partnership programme. Many thousands of local parents had been involved (Whalley, 1997b), and staff had established a model of co-operative working that respects both the learning and support needs of parents, and their children's right to high-quality early years education with care.

Our work with parents continues to be underpinned by the belief that all parents have a critical role to play as their child's primary educators. Working as we do increasingly with foster parents and adoptive parents reminds us that we must engage effectively with *all* the important adults in a child's life. We are very aware that young children achieve more and are happier when early years educators work together with parents and share views on how to support and extend children's learning and this belief is supported by powerful international research (Athey, 1990; Meade, 1995; Arnold, 2010; Blanden, 2006).

Setting up a research base in a centre for children and families

The involvement of parents in the Froebel Early Education Project (1973–8) provided strong evidence of deep commitment on the part of parents, who were consulted on professional concerns rather than 'peripheral issues' (Athey, 1990: 206). Dissemination of Athey's work has taken many years and her rallying call for a proper parent professional partnership in all early childhood settings has yet to be realised:

> Parents and professionals can help children separately or they can work together to the greater benefit of children.
>
> (Athey, 1990).

Building on our long tradition of parental involvement, we decided in 1996 to establish a practitioner research base at Pen Green in partnership with parents, early years educators and researchers in higher education. We realised we had underestimated the enthusiasm which parents demonstrated for a deeper and more extended dialogue about their children's learning. We began to see that teaching and learning and curriculum issues, which had previously been the fairly uncontested domain of professional staff, needed to be opened up for a wider discussion with parents in the early years community (Hughes and MacNaughton, 2000; Pushor, 2007).

What we needed was a rich and relevant dialogue between parents and nursery staff, which could be sustained over time – a dialogue that focused on the children's learning and achievements and our shared pedagogic practice. We wanted to deepen our understanding about the impact of engaging parents to share their knowledge about their child's learning at home. We also wanted to see how a knowledge-sharing approach could help us to best support children's learning and development in the nursery.

2

Developing evidence-based practice

Margy Whalley

Introduction

In this chapter we describe the development of a research community at Pen Green. We outline the critical stages in our TTA- and Esmée Fairburn-funded research projects, Involving Parents in their Children's Learning (1995), and show how we developed a shared language to describe children's development in the home and in the nursery setting. Case studies are included to demonstrate how involvement in the project impacted on the children and their parents.

> I would like to see the research world opening its doors much more fully to practice and practitioners, embracing the messy chaotic world of the young child and trying to work with it in order to understand it more fully.
>
> (Pascal, 1996: 5)

As a committed group of reflective practitioners concerned with both organisational development and professional development, staff at Pen Green had naturally developed a commitment to the research process. Because the service we were offering was innovatory, there was a great deal of interest in the centre, from social scientists and educationalists in universities and research institutions both in the UK and overseas. Staff, parents and children grew accustomed to being the 'object' of other people's research programmes. These research exercises helped us to become better-informed practitioners. At Pen Green, the staff, as with early childhood educators in Reggio Emilia and in Sweden (Edwards, Gandini and Forman, 1998), are convinced that 'pedagogic practice demands continuous adaptation and reflection if it is to evolve' (Dahlberg, 1998, Pen Green seminar). Although these research exercises helped us to become better-informed practitioners, being the objects of research, rather than participants in it, proved to be problematic at times.

Our early years curriculum has evolved dynamically over the years and is very much concerned with the 'researching child' capable of performing 'heroic feats' (Dahlberg, 1998). We worked hard to encourage the children to become effective decision-makers, able to reflect deeply on their own experiences. We also encouraged staff to become both reflective and reflexive (linking practice to theory and theory to practice) practitioners. Increasingly, staff took on small-scale action research projects linked to the undergraduate and postgraduate course that we run in our own Research, Training and Development Centre, addressing their own questions and concerns. These research questions were often concerned with children's development and parental involvement (Arnold, 1990, 1997b; Malcolm, 1993). Staff learnt a great deal from these small-scale research projects about children's well-being, their learning strategies and the importance of observation. They also developed a deeper understanding of the kinds of intervention that women valued as parents and why fathers often found it harder to engage with settings. The fact that all staff consistently received high levels of support and supervision made it possible for them to receive critical input from parents, colleagues and visitors, and to be positively self-critical without feeling overwhelmed by guilt when things were not going well.

At this stage the decision was made that we should formalise our research partnerships with our critical friends from higher-education institutions and with the children and their parents (Hargreaves, 1996). We decided to start taking ourselves more seriously as practitioner researchers. During 1995–6, we established a small-scale, research development and training base with two key research posts. Funding, in the first instance, came from income generated by training and development work, and, subsequently, the Early Excellence Centre pilot (DfEE, 1997), and from research grants. Over the next ten years, the research base developed significantly (Fletcher in McKinnon, 2014). With DfES support, we were able to construct a leadership, training and development centre and research base on the same campus as the integrated centre for children and families and the nursery school (www.pengreen.org). The research base accommodates our growing number of MA students and our comprehensive professional learning route from Diploma to Foundation Degree, BA, EYITT and Initial Teacher Training (ITT) training programmes and the evolving leadership programme (Whalley, 2005).

Our aims in the Initial Teacher Training Agency and Esmée Fairbairn-funded research projects in 1995–7 were to:

- develop an effective dialogue with parents about their children's learning at home and at nursery;
- develop a style of working with parents that empowers rather than deskills;
- develop a greater understanding of how parents were encouraging their children to learn at home;

- compare and contrast the styles that nursery staff and parents adopt when engaging children in learning experiences;
- produce materials to assist parents to get actively involved in recording and understanding their children's development.

Equal and active research partners

Building on our own previous experience, we felt it was important that the research was not about doing things to people. We wanted to develop a research methodology where the forms of investigation were enabling and participative. Young families and early years practitioners are both marginalised groups, often living on low incomes. In the 1980s and 1990s a large number of the families using Pen Green had no choice but to depend on welfare benefit and use welfare services. In 2016 Corby is still a town of the working poor, characterised by low income, zero-hours contracts and agency working. Bob Holman, a radical community worker, makes the point that research in the social sciences is largely about, on or for the poor and is rarely designed or written by, or with, the poor. One of the central concerns of our research at Pen Green was that it would help families living in poverty. Throughout the life of the project, we were concerned with involving parents as equal and active partners in the research process. We adopted a timescale and methodology that were acceptable to them. In this way, our research project fitted the category that Holman defined as 'research from the underside' (Holman, 1987).

We also made it clear to parents that the research was not undertaken with the view that the parenting they were demonstrating was in any way a 'deficit model'. Our experience was that the parents using the nursery at Pen Green had a passionate commitment to their children. Their deep insight into their own children's development had often provided nursery staff with essential data on which to build a rich curriculum. In this way parents had helped us to develop a more effective pedagogical approach, and more relevant and responsive interventions.

Our shared code of ethics was as follows:

Research at Pen Green should always:

- be positive for all the participants;
- provide data that are open to, accountable to and interpreted by all the participants;
- focus on questions that the participants themselves (parents, children and staff) are asking;
- be based on a relationship of trust where people's answers are believed;
- produce results which are about improving practice at home and at nursery, or at least sustaining it.

First attempts at involving parents in the research process in 1995

Our initial dialogue with parents about their involvement in their children's learning was fairly unfocused. During this period nursery parents were encouraged to keep records of their children's play and development at home, using diaries and video cameras. Small numbers of parents got involved. Often parents found it difficult to decide what was noteworthy. While a few parents made insightful observations of their children playing at home that were very useful for nursery staff, other parents simply recorded amusing incidents or family events such as birthday parties. Parents behaved like nursery staff when they first used the camcorder and tended to go for quantity rather than quality. That summer we had more than 30 hours of videotape to watch and analyse. Parents were also hungry for feedback. Although these vignettes of family life helped parents to maintain a creative dialogue with nursery staff and gave us useful information about the children's rich social lives (Pollard, 1996), they did not help us to consistently support and extend the children's learning in the nursery.

Having a second 'shot' 1996: parents and early childhood educators sharing knowledge about children's learning and development

With new funding from the Teacher Training Agency (TTA) we spent five months looking closely at the different ways that nursery staff and parents engaged with the children in the nursery (Whalley and Arnold, 1997a). Initially, we worked with a group of ten families who had already shown an interest in their children's development through discussions with their family workers in nursery. The families involved were all going to be using the nursery during the summer holidays and throughout the following academic year, and all were able to commit time to the project. The cohort included employed and unemployed parents, single parents, reconstituted families where one parent was a step-parent, and married and unmarried couples. Eight of the families were white European and two parents were from minority ethnic groups.

At the first informal meeting between parents, nursery staff, and the research team the parents were asked if they were willing to be videotaped settling their children into nursery and playing alongside their children at the beginning of the day. The parents were also asked if they would keep a diary (or make a video tape) about how their children played at home. We discussed with them their willingness to either let staff video them at home or help them set up the video at home so that they could film themselves interacting with their child. It was very important that the parents made their own decisions about the nature and level of their involvement.

Developing a shared language

> Teachers of young children could make a revolutionary move forward in developing a pedagogy of the early years if they recorded how they conceptualised and shared their professional concepts with parents.
>
> (Athey, 1990: 206)

It seemed to us that if parents were to be able to enter into a dialogue about their children's learning, then nursery staff and parents needed to have a shared conceptual framework. We felt it was essential to spend time developing this framework for thinking with parents, not because there is only one way to think about learning and teaching but because it is critically important to develop a shared language with parents (Drummond, 1989; Dahlberg, Moss and Pence, 1999). Using a shared language, we could discuss the ways in which children learn and how adults can effectively intervene to support and extend children's learning. When adults intervene either at home or in the nursery setting, they adopt a particular pedagogical approach, and this approach is underpinned by a particular philosophy. At Pen Green, we share the view that early childhood educators are social constructivists (Athey, 1990; Bruce, 1997). Early childhood educators base their interventions on close observations of the children; they spend time watching children, working alongside them and supporting and extending their learning. Staff sensitively teach skills when appropriate, and they reflect deeply and make links between child development theory and their own practice. When we observe children in the nursery we analyse our observations using a conceptual framework. We decided to share these key concepts with parents as they underpin the way that we work. We set up training sessions to help parents find a focus for their observations of their children at home, sharing with them our understanding of the work of Susan Isaacs at the Malting House (Isaacs, 1936). Susan Isaccs' open-ended observations and celebration of children's cognitive competence had made a real impact on our staff group. Clearly the observations were made many years ago but were written in such a way that they still illustrate the children's key concerns and affirm their strong disposition to learn (in Chapter 8, this approach is described in more detail).

Deep-level learning

In one of the training sessions, we explained to the parents how we used the Leuven involvement scale when observing children in the nursery (Laevers, 1994a) and shared our understanding of how best to use it at home. Laevers' rating scale was not designed to make summative judgements of children's performance. It was designed as a tool to access whether the provision and pedagogy a setting offered were sufficiently stimulating to support and extend the children's learning and development:

> The child's closely focused attention usually suggests that a good match has been made between an adult's stimulus and some particular or general concern in the child.
>
> (Athey, 1990: 63)

When a child is 'deeply involved' she scores 4–5 on the scale. This rating would indicate that the provision is appropriate and the pedagogical approach is supportive. When the child is scoring at a low level, Laevers proposed that something is wrong with the provision or the adult may be intervening inappropriately or the child's well-being may be low.

Parents found these sessions fascinating and quickly picked up on the idea that if their children were deeply involved at home then it would be appropriate to record what they were doing, using the camcorder or their home/school diaries. Chris Athey commented on how the parents in the 1970s Froebel Early Education Project responded in a similar vein: 'Nothing gets under a parent's skin more quickly and more permanently than the illumination of his or her own child's behaviour. The effect of participation can be profound' (Athey, 1990: 66).

Adult engagement styles

The parents became equally absorbed in a subsequent training session on adult engagement styles (Pascal and Bertram, 1997). The adult engagement style is a methodology designed to assess adults' ability to engage children effectively in a learning situation. It is described in detail in the work of Pascal and Bertram, who directed the Effective Early Learning Project (1997). Staff at Pen Green, who had been involved in the EEL project since 1993, were accustomed to recording the way that adults in a nursery interact with children in terms of the degree to which they stimulate the children and the sensitivity with which they engage them. We wanted parents to have the same kind of information and understanding as staff about these pedagogical approaches.

In Chapter 4, Cath Arnold describes in much more detail the training sessions that we set up and suggests how these concepts could be shared in other settings.

What we all learnt

Parents were given a lot of time and space to express their anxieties about the research project in general, and the training programme in particular. All ten parents got involved on their own terms. Some could only commit to a few fairly evenly spaced meetings in the evening. Others were keen to keep diaries, make video recordings and work with staff on a daily basis. Our job was to use the time that parents had to spend with us to good effect.

We learnt not to make simplistic judgements about parents' commitment to the project on the basis of how often they showed up or by the quality of the material that they brought with them. *All* the parents were deeply concerned about their children and fascinated by their progress. We soon realised that we had to plan meetings very carefully around parents' work shifts; running meetings in the evenings worked *if* there was a crèche. This meant parents had no anxieties about childcare, and we provided a meal, which helped to ensure conviviality and maintain energy.

For some of the parents, this was the first time that they had become deeply engaged with staff in the centre. Mubashera, Zaki's mother, had spent enormous amounts of time with her son in the nursery and had become a regular parent/helper (she went on to train as a paid crèche worker, a home visiting volunteer and subsequently became the librarian in the research base). Abid, Zaki's father, was unable to spend much time in the nursery because of his work as a senior manager. Abid had a deep interest in his son's learning and joined a group of fathers attending an evening course focusing on early literacy issues. During the research project, Abid was able to get very involved and attend evening meetings, sharing his views and frequently using the camcorder at home. Some of the richest video clips that parents brought us were of Zaki and his father chatting in Urdu and English whilst mixing up paste to decorate their kitchen (Figure 2.1). Abid clearly understood the importance of Zaki's 'rotation' schema and was feeding his interest in 'stirring things' with appropriate curriculum content (Athey, 1990: 203).

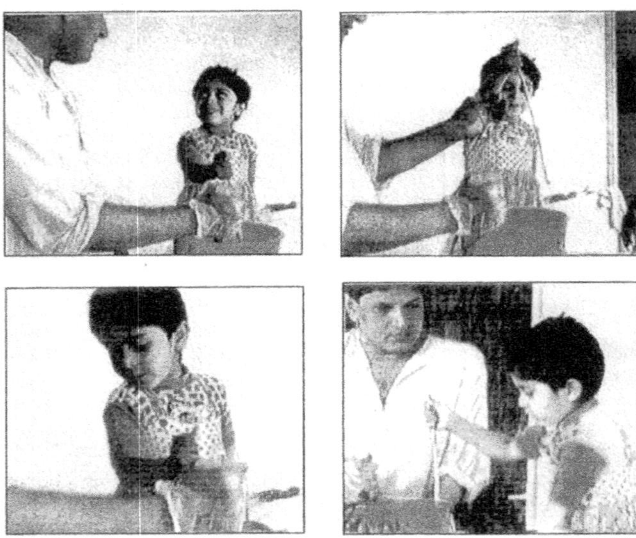

Figure 2.1 Zaki filmed at home

Mubashera and Abid's video sequence shows Abid encouraging Zaki, then 3½ years old, to rotate a screwdriver and attempt to repair a door hinge; Abid encourages Zaki to mix the paste (Zaki refers to this as 'making the dinner') and allows him to disassemble and then repair a trolley by unscrewing and then screwing back on all of its eight wheels. Each of the beautifully video-filmed learning sequences made by Mubashera show Zaki on his own or, more often, deeply engaged in activities with his father (Zaki now has a degree in engineering and is much sought after for his skills and knowledge).

When we completed this project, nine out of ten of the original families had sustained their involvement over the entire five months. Despite the fact that three marriages had broken down in this period, only one couple felt that they had to withdraw from the project as a result of marital conflict or domestic pressures.

Working collaboratively with staff with a strong focus on their children's learning and development enabled parents to develop strong personal relationships with nursery staff and gain new insights into their children's learning. Athey describes this as 'Parents participating with professionals with an articulated pedagogy' (Athey, 1990: 50).

The nursery curriculum also became much richer and more relevant because it increasingly acknowledged and built on the children's learning at home. We had previously made home visits, and knew a great deal about the children's social and emotional lives, but for the first time the research focus was on cognition. We began to know much more about what excited and interested the children, and could then plan to support and extend their interests in the nursery to great effect.

The importance of video material as data that can be discussed

Using videos of the children

Evening meetings were always well attended by parents, particularly when video clips of their own children were to be viewed and discussed. In Chapter 7, we look closely at the way in which parents developed insights into their children's learning and shared their understandings with staff through attending study groups and making and watching tapes.

Videos of the adults (staff and parents) engaging with the children

Parents and nursery staff wanted clear boundaries set with regard to watching videos that had been made of adults interacting with children in the nursery and in home settings. Parents were clearly anxious that staff might watch the videos and make judgements or formulate opinions about the parents' pedagogical interventions without having heard the parents' perspective. Nursery staff had the same kind of anxieties. They were very happy to agree that the analysis of the video should be a shared activity. Once again, we had completely underestimated how much video footage the research project would generate. During this period we made 24 hours of footage, and this included, for the first time, video material of the children in their own homes.

The quality of these tapes was very high and they made rich and rewarding viewing but every hour of tape required many hours of viewing and analysis. The children were almost always learning at a deep level. Parents seemed to have put to good use their training sessions on the Leuven involvement scale and made well-informed decisions about what was worth videoing. In subsequent filming they made informed decisions about what kind of provision to make for their children in the home.

Since we were committed to offering training to all parents who expressed an interest in getting more involved in their children's learning we decided that it would be useful to produce a CD-ROM as a training tool. By carefully selecting video clips from home and nursery and matching them with a simple text, it was possible for us to communicate and share complex and dynamic ideas with parents (Whalley and Whalley, 1996). The CD-ROM demonstrated both the complexity and the intimacy of the relationships between parents, nursery staff and children, and the rich dialogue that had been established in a fairly short time between all the partners in this project. It was used in-house regularly by parents, particularly fathers, nursery staff and visitors who wanted to deepen their understanding of schematic play.

One riveting sequence on the CD-ROM was made by staff who were allowed to film Sean (aged 3) and his father John at home. John, a single parent, allowed staff to film at first, and then taught himself how to set up the camcorder. He made some gripping home movies of Sean learning to subdivide space by cutting up bread with a fairly sharp knife. Through John's tapes, we began to appreciate the extent to which he was living out his role as his child's first educator 24 hours a day, seven days a week. This helped us to put into perspective the significant but relatively small contribution that we make to any child's life as early childhood educators.

When Sean was not in the nursery he was still learning all the time; his father took him on long walks each day to the park with his dog. John carried Sean in a pannier and went on cycle rides to visit derelict manor houses, and to tea dances with the old folks at the care home. He took Sean on trade union marches. Challenged by other project parents as to how safe it really was to take his son to the park, which was full of 'winos', dog faeces and refuse, John responded that his son knew all the 'winos' by name and that he was bringing him up to be a socialist soldier.

Mainstreaming the research project: extending the approach to engage all nursery parents, 1997–2000

We had learnt a great deal, and all the nursery staff were deeply committed to sustaining a dialogue with parents. We knew that it would be important to develop an approach that could become part of everyday nursery practice. Working with the parents, we negotiated the aims of the extended project.

Our aims for the children were to:

- value each child's individuality, enhance each child's self-esteem and identify the cognitive concerns of all the children in the nursery;
- generate stimulating curriculum content, particularly in areas that are sometimes neglected in the early years, such as mathematics and science;
- extend the impact of the research and development work to younger siblings in the home.

For the parents, our aims were to:

- encourage parents to observe and understand how and what their children are learning at home;
- acknowledge the skills and competencies of parents and build on these to enhance our own pedagogical strategies;
- encourage parents to feel equal and active in their involvement, and to develop an information exchange as a two-way process;
- provide accessible and relevant routes into involvement so that *all* families using the nursery felt informed about their children's development – fathers as well as mothers, isolated vulnerable parents, and parents who are traditionally seen as 'hard to reach'.

For the nursery staff and other early childhood educators, our aims were to:

- make it possible for all the nursery staff to become 'practitioner researchers' able to debate issues among themselves, to articulate their understanding of theory and practice, and to develop a genuine dialogue with parents;
- share the parents' and nursery staff's knowledge and experience with as wide an audience as possible.

The children's perspective

The philosophy of our nursery has always been that the curriculum should encourage children to have high self-esteem and a strong sense of self-efficacy, since 'children's expectations may be more influential in their learning than their ability' (Smiley and Dweck, 1994). Like Rutter (1997), we believe resilience should be seen as an outcome of education.

Children can become very effective decision-makers. They need to be able to plan and translate their plans into actions (Laevers, 1995). They also need to hypothesise and experiment. If we are to help them develop this sense of mastery, it is critically important that we take children's central cognitive concerns as a starting point for our nursery curriculum (Sylva, 1994). Children's thinking is characterised by their ability to 'conceptualise and consolidate' (Handy, quoted in Scott, 1996: 4):

> Parents and nursery staff, who are important adults in young children's lives, need to be centrally concerned with the provision of a rich and challenging curriculum. 'The development of co-ordinating complexities of thinking must be cultivated and fleshed out from birth in the home and in the school.'
>
> (Athey, 1990: 206)

Nursery staff worked hard to match their observations of the children with those of the parents. Each member of staff took responsibility for reading and reviewing the diary entries that parents brought in from home and the video vignettes that some parents offered us. All nursery staff met together each week and matched the parents' observations with those made in the nursery by the staff team. With both sets of information, curriculum planning in the nursery became much more focused, and we were able to respond quickly to individual children. Staff developed the workshop environments within the nursery so that children could 'service themselves' and access almost all the materials independently.

Scholium

Critically Pen Green staff during this period (1997–2006) had five hours of non-contact time a week, which gave them the opportunity to home visit and work in small reflective practice groups to share data and dialogue at a deep level. Today (2016) there is pressure to offer extended nursery sessions five days a week 8am to 6pm and to be open on Saturday and Sunday for the wider community. Staff still have individual non-contact time and home visiting time but struggle to find sufficient time to enter into dialogue as a team.

Autonomy

Nursery staff were convinced that developing a sense of autonomy was important for children. We worked closely with the parents and the children to develop a shared understanding of autonomy:

- an action that has been freely chosen,
- where the child willingly self-regulates,
- for which the child accepts full responsibility, and
- which is based on personal conviction, and is not simply about obedience (Burk-Rodgers, 1998).

The Pen Green nursery team and the parents became 'autonomy supporting educators'. We shared the belief that offering children choices was critically important and that the choices 'should be geared to the children's level of involvement' (Burk-Rodgers, 1998: 77). We knew different members of the nursery staff encouraged children to be autonomous in different ways and to different degrees (Bertram, 1995). We also knew that there were big differences between rules, boundaries and the level of choice offered to children at home and at nursery (Nucci and Smetana, 1996). Staff set up groups to establish parents' views on autonomy and to find ways to encourage children to make decisions and choices in nursery. These focused discussions provided rich material for debate in staff meetings and continue to do so in 2016. Over the last few years we have deepened our own understanding of autonomy, mastery orientation and self-regulation through new research projects focusing on children's relationships with each other.

Boys being boys

Over a number of years nursery staff had noticed that from January to March, a small group of 4-year-old boys would emerge who appeared to be less engaged and whose behaviour was seen as problematic in a predominantly female environment. This was often the case even when the boys concerned had previously shown consistently high levels of involvement. Each year, staff tried different strategies to engage these boys but without much success, and their behaviour had been interpreted by nursery staff as some kind of 'rite of transition' and 'exploration of liminality', or a need to test out boundaries before entry into primary school. By January 1998, at the end of year one of the 'mainstreamed' project, for the first time staff noticed that this pattern of behaviour did not occur or at least the nursery team were interpreting their behaviour differently. The group of 4-year-old boys due to move on to primary school in September remained deeply involved. We speculated that this was because we were matching their cognitive needs with a much richer curriculum content heavily weighted, probably for the first time, towards mathematics and science and design and construction (engineering). Subsequently we invested hugely in our garden area as a rich provision for exploration and challenge and created increased access to our Forest School.

Becoming scientists and mathematicians

Over the five years of the project, the children's hypothesising became increasingly complex. Although our nursery head at that time was a mathematician, most of us as early years educators needed further in-service training in the areas of mathematics and science and we seriously lacked confidence in these curriculum areas. As our understanding of children's home interests and nursery interests developed, we continued to make greater provision for science and mathematics in the nursery. We set up in-service training days, which focused on these aspects of the curriculum, so that staff felt better able to respond to children's fascination with levers, pulleys, gravity, rotation, spheres and trajectories. In Chapter 8, we see the impact this had on girls as well as boys.

Pen Green discovery area

By 1999 nursery staff were working with architects, designers, manufacturers and educational consultants to develop a new science discovery area. This was funded in part by the DfEE and through our own fundraising efforts. Our decision-making process was heavily informed by watching the nursery children in a number of different settings. We took the children with their parents to the Science Museum in London, where they investigated water channels and wheat chutes, and used conveyor belts. Today these regular visits are seen as part of the children and families' enrichment entitlement. Subsequently, we gave the children opportunities to experiment with a range of equipment in schools and parks. For example, we took a small group of children to Chatsworth Park to experiment with a range of outdoor play equipment; our children found the Archimedean screw too hard to turn, and staff discovered that the flow of water from the local stream fed insufficient water into the system for it to present any challenge to children. Time was well spent in reconnaissance.

Perhaps the most important part of this planning stage was time spent in discussion with each other as a nursery team. We knew from our extensive observations of children in nursery that what was needed was a stimulating and challenging environment, where, through effective interactions with staff and their peers, children's thinking and hypothesising could be supported and extended. Initially, we focused on concepts that the children were already exploring in the nursery and identified aspects of the new provision that might enhance their learning. We wanted the children to feel that they were in control of the new equipment and that they could make independent decisions about how it was used:

> Returning to the bedrock education principles, children need to actively learn, physically through movement. If they can't make equipment work by themselves, they become frustrated and the curriculum becomes one of 'can't do'. Self-motivation is damaged. Autonomy turns to dependency on adults for help.
>
> (Bruce, 1999)

Figure 2.2 Discovery area

The physical environment was designed in such a way that through sound, light, texture and colour, children's aesthetic, kinesthetic and emotional needs were satisfied (Ceppi and Zini, 1998). In this way we celebrated our pedagogy and our understanding of children's learning styles through the architecture. The discovery area offered children a much enhanced provision, including a very deep and large gravel pit with a conveyor belt, and horizontal and vertical pulleys with visible workings. It also contained a complex system of water chutes that could be dammed and flooded, and the children could direct the water flow. We invested in closed-circuit television (CCTV) cameras so that we could record the use of this equipment, study the way that this new provision supported and extended children's learning, and consolidate and reflect on our pedagogical approaches (Pen Green Centre/DfEE, 1999).

By 2016, after visiting a New Zealand kindergarten, staff had designed and developed a magnificent 'beach', which became the Pen Green equivalent to a Reggio nursery piazza or open meeting space where children, families and staff like to congregate. It has become a site for construction, engineering, science and fantasy play.

Supporting siblings

In 1996 and 1997, the project parents noted that the insights they had gained both from child development theory and sharing ideas with other parents about their own nursery children's learning had a direct impact on younger siblings in the family. This impact on siblings was a strong feature of the original Froebel Early Education Project (Athey, 1990: 56). As a staff group, we knew that 'rich experiences really do produce rich brains' (Nash, 1997: 37; Blakemore, 1998), and that is why it seemed critical to us that we should be making direct links with children from birth to 3 years old as well as with nursery-aged children: 'The early months, never mind the early years of a child's life, are critical to their life chances' (Barber, 1996: 244).

In 1998, by popular demand, two baby and toddler study groups were set up, and they were co-led by parents and staff who had been involved in the nursery parents' study groups. Both groups were called 'Growing Together' groups and then, as now, are always full. Unlike the nursery parent study groups, parents attend the Growing Together groups *with* their babies and toddlers. These parents were offered the same training sessions in child development concepts as the nursery parents, and an additional training session on using the video camera or phone application.

Within each session, parents were encouraged to observe and support their children's learning. The provision included treasure baskets (Goldschmied, 1991) and heuristic play materials as well as water, sand and playdough.

Parents became increasingly confident in using the camera to record important learning moments at home, and they brought these video vignettes to the session. Within the sessions, staff videoed interesting learning sequences and printed them out through the computer so that parents could take them home to show to partners or grandparents (see Figure 2.3). In Chapter 11, there is a full account of the work undertaken in Growing Together groups.

The parents' perspective

Parents using the nursery had demonstrated a deep commitment to supporting and nurturing their children in the pilot project. They had shown us that it was possible for parents who had everything stacked against them in terms of socio-economic status, lack of educational achievement and low levels of family support, to become very effective advocates for their children. Since 'Parents' expectations are the most powerful predictor of children's later school success' (Bredekamp and Shephard, 1989: 22; Blanden, 2006), we knew that it would be important to sustain and extend the research project.

Different parents: different approaches

Since parents are all very different, we were aware that we needed to offer them a range of 'ways in' to the project. Some parents had time during the day and valued the opportunities we offered to share problems and anxieties with other parents in study groups that ran for a year or more. In these groups they would discuss their children's cognitive concerns and share problems and perceptions regarding their child's social and emotional needs. Parents' diary entries, nursery observations and video vignettes of the children in nursery were used to inform these sessions. Sometimes parents would bring in the videotapes they had made at home. By 1999, 33 per cent of parents had borrowed the video camera and brought in vignettes of their children playing and learning at home, and nursery staff had made ten videotapes and sent them out to parents when parents or partners could not come into the nursery.

Other parents attended a monthly evening meeting. We tried to make each of these evening sessions a self-contained discussion group. During the day, parents were asked to fill in a reply slip to say whether they would be attending that night or not. If we knew they were coming, then video vignettes of their children were made in the nursery. These short video clips formed the basis for sharing information in the evening session about their child's learning needs.

Chapter 3 outlines the many strategies we developed to encourage parents to take part. The nursery team made no assumptions about commitment on the basis of attendance at meetings. We observed parents who, after attending only one training session, managed to maintain high levels of involvement, keeping home diaries, sharing this information with nursery staff, and video filming at home even when they could not physically attend meetings at the nursery on a regular basis. The issue of attrition was critically important to us, and we wanted to encourage parents to sustain their involvement over time. However, we knew that the pressures of parenting, tiredness, anxiety, work commitments, and practical difficulties like access and babysitting would often create problems for parents.

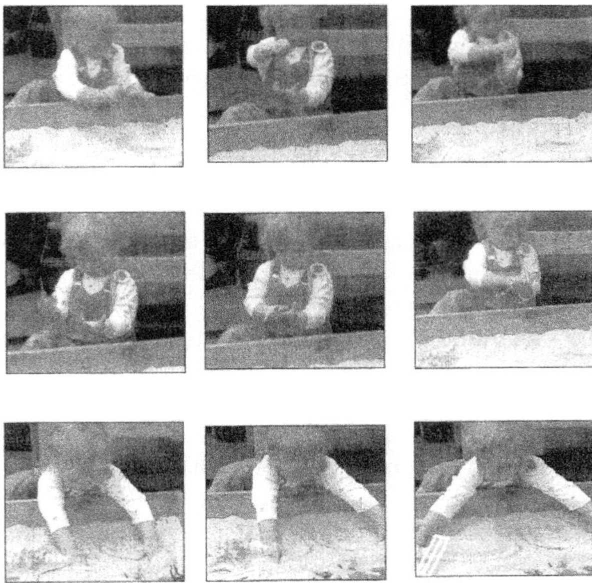

Figure 2.3 Lucy's learning sequence

Involving fathers

Getting in touch with fathers was sometimes a problem. We have always had a policy of regular home visiting before the child starts nursery, and then three times a year as a general rule. However, many of the nursery children were living in reconstituted families, and in some cases fathers had limited or no contact with their children. In some cases, when parents had separated acrimoniously, fathers were not informed about what was happening in their children's lives at nursery. Often staff did not have fathers' addresses, and all contact was through the child's mother. Additionally, even where mothers and fathers were living together, some mothers told us that they censored information coming from the nursery because they thought it would not be important, or appropriate, for the child's father to be involved. We clearly could not afford to be gender neutral in developing this project.

Involving fathers or male carers is, however, a complex issue. Staff at Pen Green have had some degree of success in engaging fathers in practical ways in the past (Whalley, 1998). Encouraging fathers to sustain their involvement over time has been more problematic (Chandler, 1997). In Chapter 5, we consider in more detail the new ways in which staff have worked to sustain engagement with fathers.

Direct work with parents who are isolated, vulnerable or distrustful of 'the system'

We were aware in the early stages of the pilot project that some women attending sessions had an overwhelming need to talk about themselves and what was going on in their lives even when the group had as its primary focus children's development and learning. Since there are many groups at the centre that offer support to isolated, depressed and vulnerable families, these parents sometimes simply 'dropped out' of the research project and joined a therapeutic or support group where the focus was, more appropriately, on their adult needs (Whalley, 1997b). There was also a small number of mothers who did not appear to benefit from the experience of meeting and sharing with others information about their children's development. These women, although initially enthusiastic, tended to withdraw after two or three sessions. Most of these women had been excluded from school and had left school before the age of 16 (Whalley et al., 2012).

We sensed that it might be particularly important to engage both these groups of women, since they often had older children who were struggling and failing in the primary or secondary phase. However, if these parents were to accept any form of intervention, it had to be offered initially on an individual basis. Some of these women were experiencing extremes of poverty or social isolation because of drug usage, or because there were professional concerns about child protection issues. Others were suffering from depression, perhaps as a result of emotional or sexual abuse in childhood. Janet Shaw (1991) describes in detail the effectiveness of individual work with such parents and the importance of sustained home visiting. Shaw's work makes it clear that it is possible, and indeed essential, to encourage parents in these circumstances to become involved in their children's learning. In Chapter 6, Cath Arnold describes, at some length, interventions that worked with women who were fairly distrustful of the 'system'.

The impact on parents' engagement with their children

All the parents involved in this project were asked to fill in a questionnaire concerned with the impact of the project on their relationship with their child. *Most* parents reported significant changes in the way that they responded to their child. *All* the parents commented on their increased understanding of the learning potential there was in everyday experiences. *Most* reported that being involved in the project had changed the way that they selected books, toys, and Christmas and birthday presents for their children.

The following account is an extract from one parent's feedback on the impact of the project.

Case study

LOUISE C'S STORY

At home Philip (real name) is very demanding. I have to be no more than a few inches away from him most of the time, and when I do get to be in a different room from him, he checks on me every few minutes. Since taking part in the research project, I try to find things that interest him, so that when I'm washing up or making the beds or just cooking dinner, he has things to do that hold his interest long enough for me to do what I've got to do.

Since the project started, I've learnt to be a bit more tolerant about the mess philip and his brother make (most of the time). They have learnt that there are places where they can paint and draw (in the dining room), and that as long as they keep to the few rules that I try to make them keep, I allow them a bit more leeway; i.e. I won't tidy up the table if they are halfway through colouring or drawing a picture. I'll leave it until they get home from school.

When Allan and I were trying to work out what they would get for Christmas, we did try to link with what Philip did in nursery – we bought him a fishing game (which he plays with most days), playdough, lots of cutters. He also got a small parcel with stickers, Sellotape, glue, scissors and paper shapes. Allan wasn't sure about these, but they were a big hit. We also bought things they had particularly asked for but these haven't been played with as much. It has also made me realise that toys are not always the most obvious things for him to play with. Philip will often empty the drawer with all the plastic dishes, and play with them for a long time. One of the 'toys' he likes best, is the egg timer he wanted me to buy. He has had a lot of fun with that and it is never far away from his favourite toys.

Having the videos has helped to keep family and friends up to date. His grandma feels she misses such a lot since he started full-time nursery, it's nice to show her videos of what he's doing.

For me, it is good to know that Philip is no better or worse behaved than many other children. It is nice to know that other people have the same problems, and to know that your child is developing normally. I hope that he will continue with these friendships he has already made.

It has made me think about the things I do with the boys – I would never have thought to take Philip to the Science Museum, but he had a great time, and took in more than I would have expected him to. Keeping his diary has helped to show me how he has developed and grown and changed – although it is only by going back and reading it that I can see it.

It just seems a shame that there will not be a similar project at school – it would be interesting to see how he develops, but I can appreciate that there are too many children and not enough teachers to tailor a child's education.

For me it has been good to know that other parents get cross, upset and annoyed at their children and all that any parent can do is love their child always – unconditionally.

A catalyst for training and adult learning

Many parents who have been involved in the research and development project have also gone on to undertake accredited training in childcare/early education/ social work. Some, like Louise, have joined the nursery team at Pen Green and have become early years educators, having undertaken their diploma course at Pen Green and then the Foundation Degree and BA Hons.

There were ten parents in the original Tuesday afternoon study group; of these, the following eight parents have gone on to undertake training or to run education and care services in a voluntary or paid capacity; five parents had children who went on to study at university, the first in their families to be awarded degrees.

Rosanna – worked as a volunteer co-leading a weekly baby massage group, undertook paid work as a research worker for the Sure Start Project, went on to run groups for the Sure Start Project and is currently employed as a Family Worker in a local primary school.

Dave – worked voluntarily in the Pen Green nursery and undertook his NVQ level 3 in childcare. He also worked full-time at night.

Lesley – completed the NVQ level 3 in childcare, became an NSQ assessor, and now works full-time in one of the Pen Green baby nests. She has a BA in Early Years.

Carole – gained an A grade in A-level English, having studied at Pen Green whilst her child was in nursery, and undertook supply work in the Pen Green nursery. She now has paid work as an administrator in a local primary school.

Louise – completed her NVQ level 3 at Pen Green and went on to do her Foundation Degree and BA Hons. She is now working full-time in a senior role in the nursery team.

Eloise – worked as a volunteer co-leading a weekly parent and toddler play session and still has paid work as a member of the kitchen staff.

Tracey – studied at Pen Green and passed A-level English and works part-time outside the centre.

Karen – was a centre volunteer at Pen Green and went on to be a Higher Level Teaching Assistant (HLTA) in a local secondary school. Her daughter Natasha gained a 1st class honours degree in 2015 and Stephanie her older daughter is studying for a Foundation Degree.

Sustaining and embedding the research project: the nursery team perspective

Our key concern as the research project developed was to see whether what we had achieved could be sustained and consolidated across the integrated centre for children and families. For example, by 1998 we had 84 per cent of nursery families involved in the programme. Not only were these parents involved, but their involvement had also continued throughout the time their child was in nursery, and their commitment to their children's learning was sustained on transition into the infant school. Attrition, an acknowledged problem in many parent intervention programmes, was not a significant feature of this research and development project.

In the first year of the Parents' Involvement in Their Children's Learning (PICL) project, much of the research and development work had been undertaken by the research team and a small core of the nursery staff, although all staff were involved in a practitioner research training programme. From 1998–2000, we wanted to encourage *all* staff to become more deeply engaged in the project so that much of the research work could become 'mainstreamed'. We wanted the key concepts of training for parents, and the sharing of information on children's development from home and from nursery, to become part of the everyday activity of the community nursery. Only in this way could we be sure that these important activities could be sustained beyond the lifetime of the research project.

At various stages in the project, staff needed to raise concerns over the increase in their workload as a result of the new ways of working. Sometimes they needed to discuss their anxieties when parents were hard to engage. It was also clear that certain staff were particularly excited by the project, and it was important that they had 'time out' to become more actively involved and also become what we call 'PICL champions'. Other members of staff, because of family commitments, pressures relating to other aspects of their work or personal inclination, were somewhat less engaged.

Having time to think and reflect on the work they do is critical if early childhood educators are to become increasingly rigorous and insightful in their practice. It is also important that the staff who work in the nursery know how to articulate their experiences (Drummond, 1989). When teachers do not have a clearly articulated pedagogical approach or a deep understanding of children's development, they may find it difficult to share information with parents and may perceive parents' questions as a challenge to their professionalism (Athey, 1990).

All nursery staff were allocated some additional time to make an extended home visit to interview the nursery child's parents, and to develop portfolios of the children's learning. Needless to say, the 'time out' allocation was never enough and was often at the end of an already very long day. When staff were involved in running study groups, they were replaced in nursery. Towards the end of the project, nursery staff, who had all also trained to work with adults, were able to be paid to run the evening study groups through the local further education college.

All nursery staff were offered additional training in:

- video techniques;
- staff issues around being video recorded;
- ethical frameworks for interviewing;
- interview techniques;
- styles of engaging parents;
- producing portfolios of children's learning.

The impact on staff

Members of the nursery staff who were asked to fill in questionnaires about what kind of an impact they felt the research project had made commented on the richer provision, the increasing in-depth nature of nursery planning sessions, and the greater relevance of the experiences we were offering to children.

Angela, a senior family worker (now Joint Head of Pen Green), reflected:

> I feel that the research project has given a focus to some parents and helped them to understand their children's learning and it has given us an opportunity to extend their learning. Parents have been able to discuss and challenge our teaching styles and our practice in an open and non-threatening way. The families in my group who have kept diaries have recorded many of their children's interests and this information was invaluable to me when I returned to work after maternity leave. I feel most parents who have been involved are able to talk about their child's learning positively and with confidence. I feel that the children have gained and that they are having their needs addressed and catered for.

Trevor Chandler, the former head of centre, commented:

> Through attending the weekly research group, parents have shown their deepening level of understanding of their children's learning at home and the nursery. Through sharing this knowledge and experience in the group they have provided play and learning opportunities for their children based upon their child's dominant schemas. One mother who has a child with special needs described their holiday where her daughter experienced so many different sensory experiences. Her mother proudly celebrated her child's learning. The knowledge shared within the group has been regularly fed back to the nursery staff and informed the nursery's planning which, in turn, has enriched the child's experience.
>
> At the evening meetings, more fathers have been involved and they have felt included, and this has enriched their understanding of their child's play and learning opportunities. One father said, following an evening meeting, that it has had a profound effect on his understanding of his child's play and behaviour, and he sees his son very differently now.

The perspective of other early childhood educators and the research community

As a centre we are committed to supporting and training early childhood educators from the public, private and voluntary sector both locally and nationally.

For example, staff at Pen Green were involved in training over 5,000 practitioners in 1999 (Bertram and Pascal, 2000).

Setting up a dissemination project for this work has become increasingly important as the project has developed. Both parents and staff from Pen Green have been involved in offering training to others. For example, local playgroups asked for and received training in child development concepts with the video materials that the research team developed for use with parents. Local teachers in primary schools in Corby have decided to set up small-scale projects, and staff and parents from Pen Green have worked alongside them. In Chapter 12, Kate Hayward describes the impact of some of this work in other settings.

What we have established at Pen Green is a multifaceted intervention project with, as its principal focus, parents' involvement in their children's learning. Small-scale projects like this one rarely have the staff time or funding to establish and maintain a database, and record the research process. At a cross-departmental review of provision for young children (1990), Marjorie Smith from the Thomas Coram Research Unit and John Bright from the government's Social Exclusion Unit both made the point that it was essentially this kind of *process information* that was often not included in reports (Smith, 1990; Bright, 1998; Oliver, Smith and Barker, 1998). Yet this sort of information was of particular interest to organisations seeking to replicate good practice. This is why we decided to write up and publish the research and development project in an accessible format so that it could be used by a range of early years professionals. Through a series of national conferences and seminars, other educators have also been offered training so that they can set up similar programmes in diverse locations. In February 2000, a new Parents' Involvement in Their Children's Learning (PICL) video and training pack was completed. These contained vignettes of parents engaging with children in their own homes, and parents and workers engaging with children in the nursery.

Over a period of six months, a team of practitioners, researchers and parents co-constructed professional development materials, which were designed and developed in-house and then produced for dissemination across a range of settings. In 2001–7, the Pen Green research team began working with 25 local authorities in England and have disseminated this approach across the UK. Staff have also undertaken training and dissemination work in Ireland, Italy, Portugal, New Zealand, Australia and Brazil. These materials were updated and reprinted when we ran a DfE-funded project across four local authorities, known as the Early Learning Partnership (ELP) Project. These were revised once again in 2016 (for more information visit the Pen Green website: www.pengreen.org).

With the advent of the Children's Centre initiative in 2006 central government and local authorities began, once again, to address the issues of transformation and change for children and families across localities. Our great hope was that involving parents in their children's learning would be seen as the most critical aspect of this work (Blanden, 2006). With 3,500 children's centres it seemed possible that 'Pen Green's silver bullet', harnessing parents' energy and capacity to advocate for their own children throughout the education system, could be achieved. Our hope was that the staff teams in all these centres would be committed to developing the social and cultural capital within their local communities. Instead from 2012–16 we have seen the demise of children's centres as powerful and enabling universal services.

As early years educators we have to hold on to the belief that the construct of fully integrated services for children and families will once again become a central strand of government policy. The critical intervention in all such centres will be a shift from a conventional model of teaching and learning to a new approach where parents and staff work together as co-educators.

Moving on – 2016 and beyond

Staff at Pen Green are committed to a strengths-based approach, always valuing what people within the community offer, and building on it. Pen Green staff see parents as their child's best educators, and we are committed to encouraging parents to be passionate advocates on behalf of their children – from their first day in a parent and toddler group or when they start in the nursery, right the way through their primary, secondary and tertiary education.

In the 1980s, when we first opened the centre, professionals often talked about 'hard to reach families'; they failed to recognise the fact that in many cases it was services that were hard to access. Today, it is still hard for some parents to access services in ECEC settings. Mari, one of the parents who uses the services in Pen Green, lives on a New Age Travellers site. About ten families live on the site, which is fairly local to the Pen Green Centre. She recently undertook a study of the pedagogical impact of parents, on the Travellers site, on their children's learning; she celebrated the way that parents were working with their children in her own community. Mari had to draw our attention to the issues that sometimes made it difficult for other members of her community to use Pen Green's services. As a consequence, we had to change our professional practice.

If nursery schools, early years settings and children's centres are to engage effectively with all parents, then staff will need to challenge traditional ways of working. All ECEC settings will need to become learning communities engaging with people respectfully and creating services that are so relevant and responsive that all families will want to use them (Whalley, 2006).

This research and development project has raised important issues for all of us. As we work hard to develop even more effective ways of working with children and parents, we need to recognise:

- the great untapped energy and ability of parents and their deep commitment to supporting their children's development;
- the importance of developing a mutual understanding based on shared experiences;
- the need to have a clearly articulated pedagogical approach – when we are clear about our own beliefs, we can share them with parents;
- the need to employ staff who are confident, articulate, well trained and excited about working with adults as well as working with children;
- that it takes time to establish an equal, active and responsible partnership where parents decide what interests them; parents may write beautiful 'baby biographies' for a year at a time or just attend one session on understanding

their children's educational needs – parents need to get involved in their own time and in their own way;
- that working with adults in this way is always political; in the words of Paulo Freire, the great educator and philosopher, it is about opening up for parents a 'language of possibilities' (Freire, 1970: 68).

Increasingly we have had to demonstrate that the PICL approach makes a difference to both the children and their parents. In what follows Kate Hayward, in her capacity as Deputy Director of the Research Base, sets out her findings, showing how we were able to achieve this within current constraints.

The drive for an 'evidence base': demonstrating that we make a difference by Kate Howard

Findings

Over the last ten years there has been a government-led desire for all interventions intended to support children and families to be 'evidence based' (Allen, 2011). This has resulted in a heavy reliance on what is often called 'scientific evidence' or 'hard evidence' in the form of random control trials. This approach to measuring outcomes for children and families had resulted in a more standardised 'teaching' of set skills and knowledge in short-term parenting programmes (Barrett, 2009).

Pen Green's work with parents has always been context specific. We have been guided by a firm set of principles and have based our work much more on relationship-building between parents and professionals, with a shared focus on how to support children to learn in the home as well as in the ECE nursery or setting.

We have been keen to illustrate the ways in which parents and workers support children through the PICL approach by detailing case studies and child and parent narratives. We know our work stands on a strong evidence base and many of the narratives within this book illustrate not just the effectiveness of the approach, but also the complex nature of the work required.

In order to encourage other settings and local authority commissioners to engage with the PICL approach, we were faced with ever-growing pressure to represent our work on a list of 'evidence-based' programmes. In order to score at all on the 'evidence-based' points system set up initially by the Parenting Academy, we needed to fund an external evaluation. We approached an external agency, the Institute for Public Policy Research (IPPR), and engaged them in an evaluation of PICL. At the same time we worked up a submission to validate our own local practice through C4EO (the Centre for Excellence and Outcomes, www.C4EO.org.uk) and we were successful in having both the PICL approach validated by C4EO and also our 'Making Children's Learning Visible' assessment approach.

(Continued)

(Continued)

Parents have always been involved in the design and development of services at Pen Green so one of the first actions in the evaluation process was to set up a parent steering group. Researchers worked with parents to review some of the standardised measures used in other evaluations. Corby parents were very sceptical about external observers measuring parents' capacity to 'parent' their children in the home. They questioned the idea of 'before' and 'after' measures and wondered how ethical or realistic these processes were. They were very clear that an evaluation of PICL was not going to be achieved by measures that exclusively focused on 'school readiness'. If there was going to be a scale to measure a parent's shift in their engagement with their children, then they wanted to create something that had meaning for them and related to their experience.

Parents who had experienced the PICL approach said that after in-depth conversations with their child's family worker they felt they could understand their child better and were more confident in their ability to support their child's learning. They also felt they were able to be an advocate for their child; most parents were able to go on to talk to their child's teacher in school.

After trialling reflection on these themes, parents talked about an increase in confidence and well-being. Five key strands emerged that were then developed into the self-evaluation tool:

- CONFIDENCE
- WELL-BEING
- BEING WITH
- UNDERSTANDING A CHILD'S INTERESTS
- BEING AN ADVOCATE FOR MY CHILD

These strands were set out in a user-friendly parent booklet on a ten-point scale so that parents could look back and indicate where they felt they were at the beginning of their time with Pen Green and where they felt they were when they left. There is also room in the booklet for personal stories and reflections so that it becomes a vehicle for discussion and reflection.

Parents and staff have found this to be a useful tool when used retrospectively. Parents claimed that they were able to be more honest when looking back than when faced with a 'before' scale at a time when they had not built up trust with professionals in the centre. At an organisational level, the data also meet the need for hard evidence to demonstrate the impact for the parent of being involved in the child's learning. The shift in each strand can be demonstrated through inputting the data on an Excel sheet and graphs of 'parental shift' can be generated to illustrate the impact of a particular group or intervention or a range of services.

Suggestions for your own practice

- If you are already using video documentation as a way of observing and documenting children's development and learning, how might you share this material with parents?
- How might you support fathers not living in the family home who might want to share knowledge about their child's interests?
- Is it possible for you to use the video documentation to dialogue with parents who work during the day but are keen to know how to support and extend their children's learning?
- Is it possible for your setting to buddy with another setting, which is already using these techniques, so that staff gain confidence from other staff who know that this approach really works?
- Have you made sure that all staff in your setting are trained in 'e safety' and that you have a policy on the use of video and mobile phone applications which all staff and parents understand?

Key points

- Child development experts have, for a hundred years, undertaken child studies of their own children.
- Parents are also natural 'baby biographers' and want to share knowledge and understanding with their child's early years educators.
- It is vital that we engage with all the important adults in a child's life, not just the person who brings the child to nursery and collects them at the end of the session.

Recommended reading

Arnold, C. (2003) *Observing Harry*. Maidenhead: Open University Press.
Athey, C. (1990) *Extending Thought in Young Children: A Parent–Teacher Partnership*. London: Paul Chapman.

3

The many different ways we involve families

Colette Tait and Angela Prodger

Introduction

In this chapter we want to look at the many different ways that staff try to encourage parents to become involved in their children's learning. Over many years we have developed a range of 'models of engagement' so that as many different nursery parents as possible get involved in this shared approach. Initially we will share how staff 'get to know' the families they are working with and will describe the different engagement approaches we have developed over twenty years. We will discuss how we have monitored the uptake of the service by parents and identify some of the problems we have encountered and, finally, focus on where involvement leads to for those parents and children who become very committed to this approach.

> Pen Green's image of the child is rich in potential, strong, powerful, competent and, most of all, connected to adults and other children.
>
> (Adapted from Malaguzzi, 1993; cited in Edwards, Gandini and Forman, 1998: 42)

Family life in Corby

Staff recognise the fact that parents are not a homogeneous group; family values, and family composition may all be very different and the approach to engagement that works for one family will not necessarily work for another. In our experience, the one thing that unifies all families in Corby is the aspirations that parents have for their children. All parents want their children to be happy and fulfilled. What this project offers additionally is a strong focus on children's progress throughout the education system. The demographics in Corby have changed significantly over the last 33 years. Now, in 2016, 31 per cent of the children in the nursery are multilingual learners, with 18 different languages spoken across the Centre. Due to recent changes to the benefit system, in many more families both parents are having to take up employment or access training. For us to be effective in engaging as many parents as possible, we need to really 'get to know' the families and understand the challenges that they face. We also need to be prepared to adapt the ways we work in order to accommodate diverse families' needs. We have to recognise the continually changing needs of families as children grow older and some families break up and re-form.

In one nursery year, whilst we were carrying out our practitioner research into parental involvement, local families using the nursery experienced major changes in their lives. In 2016, these and other major life events still impact on some families (see Table 3.1 for the most recent version). Corby is a town made up predominantly of the 'working poor' and poverty is still a major factor in the lives of many families using services at Pen Green.

Over the past three years, children in the nursery have experienced huge stressors; one of the children's parents died and several children have been removed from their families and taken into care. We have added these categories to the 'major life events in the family' chart since the last edition of this book. Most of the family workers in the nursery will now be the lead person on an Early Help Assessment (EHA) for a specific child where specific family interventions have been identified and parents have agreed to having an EHA in place. Through Team Around the Child meetings, family workers and parents often work closely with Pen Green's family support team to make sure the most appropriate services are put in place to help the family achieve co-constructed outcomes.

Table 3.1 Major life events in the family

Event	Number reported	% sample
Change of job	16	32.7
Major illness	15	30.6
Change of address	12	24.4
Separation	12	24.4
Divorce	6	12.2
Someone moving out	6	12.2
Access difficulties	7	14.3
Someone moving in	10	20.4
Birth	9	18.4
Recent unemployment	9	18.4
Serious accident/illness	4	8.2
Other major events	9	18.4

Whilst 23 per cent of families using the three nursery spaces and the baby nest have an EHA in place, the reasons for the EHA are very different. Some of the families may be experiencing marital breakdown with contact and access issues, others will have very different issues such as support for the family where one of the parents is experiencing mental health problems or where a family needs support in place for a child with SEN or disability. Family workers need to be trained, skilled and prepared to deal with any of the many challenges that children and families face in the twenty-first century. Appropriate support and supervision also have to be available for staff when dealing with these complex family situations, and staff are offered opportunities for reflective practice sessions to help them work effectively in their teams.

Coping with transition

At Pen Green, we have a maintained nursery school with three pedagogical spaces offering 120 full-time equivalent places for 3-and 4-year-olds. Additionally, we offer 24 2-year-old places. In the nursery approximately 50 per cent of the children are referred for nursery places; these referrals come from partnership agencies, self-referrals, family support staff and nursery workers. The referrals can be for children with special educational needs and/or disability (approximately 24 per cent currently), Looked After Children (LAC) or other vulnerable children at risk of social exclusion (approximately 26 per cent currently). We also have two baby nest settings for children from 9 months to 3 years (the Nest and the Couthie) with 80 children on the roll.

The majority of children who start in the baby nest spaces will move through to nursery when they are ready. To meet the needs of all parents, and working parents in particular, the nursery and baby nest settings are open 50 hours per week, 48 weeks per year. We encourage the parents to use their free entitlement flexibly and we are able to offer a limited number of sessions for parents to purchase additional hours if appropriate.

As a team, we are very aware that children may spend their time with different carers, for example grandparents and childminders, as well as using their nursery entitlement. On home visits, family workers will ask parents where their child spends time each week, to help establish a picture of who cares for the child and how many transitions the child makes throughout a week. This information can be very useful and helps family workers to put the child's life experiences in context.

It is important that we are aware of the varying working patterns of the families who use the Centre. Corby is a working-class town with a long history of shift working in the steelworks, Weetabix, Solway Foods and other factories.

Families who are currently using the nursery have many different shift patterns and collecting this information is invaluable; it helps the nursery staff to plan meetings, arrange home visits and book groups at times that are appropriate for each of the families that engage with the centre. Recent employment challenges include the common use of zero-hours contracts; parents are required to work flexibly and reactively each week to meet the needs of the employer. This makes it extraordinarily difficult for parents to arrange consistent childcare or commit to attending groups each week, but with support they can manage it.

Table 3.2 A child's week

	Monday	Tuesday	Wednesday	Thursday	Friday	Saturday	Sunday
Morning	Mum or Dad's girlfriend drops child off at Grandma's house in the morning. Grandma takes child to nursery	Mum drops child off at Grandma's house and Grandma takes child to nursery	Mum drops child off at Grandma's house and Grandma takes child to nursery	Grandma drops child off at nursery	Mum drops child off at Grandma's house and Grandma takes child to nursery		
Afternoon	Child picked up from nursery by Grandma and go to Grandma's house	Child picked up from nursery by Grandma and go to Grandma's house	Child picked up from nursery by Grandma and go to Granma's house	Mum picks child up from nursery and takes child home	Child picked up from nursery by Grandma and go to Grandma's house	Child stays at home with Mum and Mum's boyfriend or stays over at Dad's house with Dad's girlfriend	Child stays at home with Mum and Mum's boyfriend or stays over at Dad's house with Dad's girlfriend
Evening	Mum picks child up from Grandma's house and takes home	Mum picks child up from Grandma's house and takes home	Child stays overnight at Grandma's house	Child stays at home with Mum and Mum's boyfriend	Child stays at Grandma's house until Mum or Dad's girlfriend arrives to take them home		

*The children's dad is in prison so they spend alternate weekends with dad's girlfriend at his house

Providing a flexible and responsive service

When children are allocated a nursery place at Pen Green, they are also allocated a family worker (key person). A family worker will now have between 12–16 children in his or her family group, some children attending in the morning and some in the afternoon and a few would be full-time. This is a huge and relatively recent challenge for our nursery team. Between 1983 and 2006 most family workers would have had between 9 to 12 children and many more places would have been full-time sponsored places through the local authority social care budget or through Sure Start funding. In 2006, the exigencies of ratio changes (we became a school in 2006 and our ratio moved from 1 to 8 to 1 to 13) and budget cuts mean that staff teams are very stretched.

Family workers would aim to work with and get to know the whole family, not just the child attending nursery and all the important adults in a child's life including fathers not living in the family home. Before the child even begins nursery, the family worker would visit the family in their own home, taking with them a first home visit/registration pack, which contains consent and medical forms and gives the family some written information about Pen Green. This first visit is the ideal opportunity to start building up a good relationship with the whole family and this takes priority over the completion of medical forms and the gathering of specific information about the child and the family. Finding out about the child's interests and any family interests or hobbies can really help the family worker to plan for the child when they start in the nursery and make sure there are familiar objects and play things for them during that challenging transition period. Children will often bring with them 'transitional objects' or 'objects of transition' and staff endeavour at all times to make sure that these objects are not lost or mislaid.

Transitional objects and objects of transition

Transitional object (Winnicott, 1991)

A transitional object is used by a child when they are away from their main carer/secure base. Transitional objects provide children with some security and help the child to cope with the separation; transitional objects are often a special blanket or soft toy.

Objects of transition

An emotionally significant and familiar object that is carried and used by the child to help them to make a transition and feel secure when away from their main carer/secure base. These objects of transition are conceptually different from transitional objects, as they can be different each day and may not be soft or possess the scent of the carer.

Family workers will also ask parents about their hopes and aspirations for their child and what they want their child to get out of coming to nursery. As Corby's population becomes increasingly diverse, families bring with them very different expectations of the education system.

An example from practice

A Latvian family challenged staff in the nursery about allowing their child to play with water when it was cold outside. This family was anxious about their child's health and didn't want their daughter to get wet unnecessarily, as they believed this would lead to her becoming unwell. Nursery staff talked with the parents about the challenge of keeping their child out of the water; they said that they would always change their daughter's clothing if it was wet. The parents and staff discussed cultural differences and expectations and agreed a compromise, which meant that their daughter could access the water *inside*, but staff would change her clothes as soon as she had finished and dry her wet clothes ready for going home.

An example from practice

All children in the nursery have a special box where they can keep their most precious things and each box has a photograph of the child on the front. A mother from the Sikh community using the nursery requested that her child's photographs should not be displayed on his 'special box'. This request was a challenge to staff, who assumed that it might be because of particular cultural beliefs. In fact the parents were concerned about the safeguarding of their child. The Family Worker subsequently worked with the child to choose an image that he would like to represent him on his box.

Family workers continue to regularly 'home visit' all families in their family group at least three times across the nursery year. The amount of home visits each family receives does differ depending on the specific needs of the child and their parents. For some families, close working with the Pen Green family support team may mean that more regular home visits take place with either a member of the family support team or a Home Start volunteer, to support parents who are experiencing real challenges. This integrated collaborative approach to working with families can really help to support the child alongside other family members. When families are split and children regularly spend time with both parents, the family worker will arrange a home visit to share the child's learning and find out about the child's experience in their second home.

We have to find out about the family context and the working patterns of both mothers and fathers if we are to offer equal opportunities for engagement with both parents. Each family worker gathers this information for the families in their group and these data are then collated centrally for each of the nursery spaces; because of the nature of employment in the town, and the use of zero-hours contracts, this information needs updating on a term-by-term basis, which is time-consuming but important.

Each family worker gathers information about:

- the nursery child's name, date of birth, address and family worker's name;
- the mother's name, address and working hours;
- the father's name, address and working hours;
- the parent's partner's name, address and working hours (where appropriate, if a new partner is living in the child's family home).

Many families do not easily fit into a standard template; what about families where there has been a divorce or separation? If either mother or father has a new partner, are we able to commit to engaging all these adults or should we concentrate our efforts on the child's biological mother or father? Once birth partners separate and create reconstituted families, just who should we be sharing information with about the child's development and educational achievements?

Table 3.3 Families' work patterns

Shift pattern		Factories/workplaces
Three-shift pattern:	6 a.m. – 2 p.m 2 p.m. – 10 p.m 10 p.m. – 6 a.m	Golden Wonder Weetabix
Continental shifts (including weekends)	4 days on, 2 days off 8 days on, 4 days off	Oxford University Press Quebecor
Twilight shift	5 p.m. – 10 p.m.	RS Components Finnegans Famous Cakes
School hours	10 a.m. – 3 p.m.	CityFax Asda
Part-time	9 a.m. – 2 p.m. 1 p.m. – 6 p.m. 5 p.m. – 10 p.m.	RS Components and many other local factories
Weekend shift	Friday night shift and Saturday night shift Saturday day shift and Sunday day shift	Solway Foods

Parental responsibility: the Children Act definition

The issue of parental responsibility (PR) can be contentious at times and we needed to find out where we stood legally. In the initial months of the research project in 1995 we arranged for a local solicitor to come and hold a training session for staff about PR under the Children Act 1989 (Department of Health, 1991; updated December 2003). We needed to know if we were under any obligation to contact both parents regarding their child's development and learning. We also needed to know if there were situations in which it would be inappropriate for us to contact particular parents. We felt very strongly that local parents also needed to know the facts about PR and this training session was incredibly informative. Parents raised critical issues and gave us examples of how families could be constituted in complex and different ways.

Establishing who has PR can be a big issue when families have separated acrimoniously. Family workers often have to clarify the law and explain that the divorced or separated father does have PR if his name is on the birth certificate and still has the right to be involved and consulted about his child's education, even when the mother says she doesn't want him to be involved. This can create anxiety for staff; how can we be fair to *both* parents and ensure the best interests of the child are at all times central to the decision-making process? There have been instances in the past where a mother has wanted to 'punish' a partner, perhaps because maintenance payments were problematic and she has told centre staff that the father is no longer allowed access to their children and cannot collect them from nursery. In this case the biological father actually did have PR. In these situations it was critical for us, as a staff group, to be clear about where we stood both morally and legally. We produced an information sheet for parents (Figure 3.1) explaining to them what PR is, who would automatically have PR, the consequences of not having PR, and perhaps most importantly, how to obtain PR. Family workers then reported back to families, armed with this information to clarify each individual situation. Where there are challenges in a family around parental responsibility and contact, centre staff may suggest the use of an EHA to help the family address the issues and reach a good resolution. If this is not possible then we would encourage parents to seek legal advice.

PARENTAL RESPONSIBILITY (PR)

Who has parental responsibility?

Parental responsibility (PR) was established in the Children Act 1989 and updated December 2003. Not all parents have parental responsibility.

These people have parental responsibility:

- The natural mother of the child.
- The natural father of the child provided he was married to the mother when the child was born, or he subsequently marries her.
- The natural father if he registers the birth of the child alongside the mother, or is listed on the birth certificate (after a certain date, depending on which part of the UK the child was born in).
- Anyone who has a Residence Order which is currently in force in respect of the child.

These people do not automatically have PR:

- **The father of the child if he and the mother have not been married and he has not registered the birth alongside the mother.**
- Grandparents or other relatives.
- Step-fathers.
- Guardians of the child appointed by will.

What does this mean for my child in nursery?

- This means that at nursery consent forms can **only** be signed by parents with PR.
- That children can be collected by parents who do not have PR **but staff should have written consent** from the parents who has PR.

How do parents get parental responsibility?

Parental responsibility can be acquired by formal **written** agreement with the mother or by order of court. If you want to find out more, many solicitors offer a short consultation free of charge.

Figure 3.1 Parental responsibility (PR) information sheet

A note about who has PR for each individual child is always added to the nursery database. We will still, on some occasions, have to call a local solicitor to clarify a situation, but generally all staff members and families using the centre are much clearer about PR and its implications. This has made it possible for us to deal with difficult and sensitive issues in the best interests of the children. For families coming into this country from abroad this can be a challenge, as they may not understand the concept of PR or the English law in general. We keep all family details on a secure centre database, which is constantly updated by our very committed administrative team.

Using the database, we are able to map and track parents' involvement in all aspects of the life of the centre, for example, whether they use the nursery exclusively or whether they use the adult and community education programme or family support groups as well. We have also developed a nursery tracking tool where information is stored about each child and their family's engagement in the PICL approach. In each pedagogical space, we have a named PICL Champion whose responsibility it is to collate all of the data. We use this information to reflect on our practice and we also evaluate how popular or useful parents find the interventions we offer and then plan for future engagement opportunities.

Using the nursery tracker

We analyse the information on the centre database early in the nursery year. We use it to find out how involved parents already are, and begin to look at possible barriers to involvement and ways of encouraging more families to engage. We also plan and develop new services or groups that might appeal to a wider range of parents. We need to look at what is already happening within the centre and begin to build up a picture of the parents' involvement in their child's learning because we know from research that this is the silver bullet that makes all the difference (Blanden, 2006).

Building up a picture – the settling-in process

When children start nursery at Pen Green, there is a requirement that they are 'settled in' for the first two weeks by either a parent or an adult carer, perhaps a grandparent who does not have the same work commitments as many of our nursery parents. This important adult in the child's life stays with the child in the nursery for the agreed two-week period, flexibly moving between the nursery and the Family Room where they can get a cup of coffee and relax for a few minutes before taking the child back with them into the nursery. As well as enabling the child to become accustomed to nursery routines, this also gives the parent or carer a chance to see how the centre works and what other groups and activities are going on that may be of interest to them. Family workers get to know the adult that settles the child and they will seek to build relationships with other parents and carers where the opportunity arises. The two-week period really enables family workers to get to know families closely and build a deeper and more trusting relationship with them. It gives us time to really listen to parents' concerns around separation; we always make a point of ringing parents and giving them feedback about how a child has settled post-transition.

We make videos of the children's experience as they are settling in and these become the property of the parent and the child.

Parents tend to book their settling-in period around their own holiday period across the summer and into September. We try to have only a small number of children coming into nursery for the first time on any one day. Although we have a large intake in September each year, we now have children starting at the beginning of every term due to the change in 3-and 4-year-old free entitlement funding.

When children are transitioning within the centre, that is from the Nest or Couthie into any of the three spaces, a joint home visit will be arranged by the child's *current* family worker in one of the baby provisions and the *new* family worker from the nursery so that relevant information can be shared with parents. Staff do encourage parents or adult carers to stay with the child once again for two weeks after moving from the Nest or Couthie into one of the other nursery spaces; this means children are well supported within the new settings. Although parents may be convinced that the child is already 'well settled' this transition can also bring challenges with different key workers, different expectations and slightly different cultures in each of the spaces. Both the baby nests open out onto larger nursery spaces and both have small gates that the children can open. The more confident 2 and 3 year-old children may well have been accessing nursery spaces for 3-and 4-year-olds for some time, although only for short periods.

Once all the children are settled in nursery we hold training sessions for parents on key child development concepts so that staff and parents have a shared understanding about children's development and learning. The sessions are as follows: Well-being and Involvement (Laevers, 1997), Schema (Athey, 1990), and Pedagogic Strategies (Whalley and Arnold, 1997a; Lawrence and Gallagher and The Pen Green Team, 2015). A fuller explanation of how these sessions are offered is in Chapter 4.

These are the core concepts that underpin the daily practice in the nursery; nursery staff engage with and observe the children and then document their learning journeys and use these concepts to help them analyse how children are learning and what they are learning. These data help family workers to consider whether the nursery provision matches the interests of individual children. These key concepts have become 'tools' that help staff to understand and refine their pedagogical approaches. They help us to increase staff awareness about how particular children learn and any challenges they are experiencing and to communicate this information to parents. All of the training sessions are offered morning, afternoon and evening, so as to accommodate the parents' working patterns with a free crèche. Once again, we monitor who attends the sessions and at what time of day, and this information is recorded on our database so that we understand family preferences. By 2016, these sessions had to be repeated three times per year to reflect the fact that children are transitioning each term into the nursery. These key concept sessions are also offered in Polish as this is the second largest language group in the nursery; whenever possible we bring in translators (volunteers) to support other parents who are not confident English speakers.

At each transition point staff are beginning to build up a picture of the important adults in each child's family as we already know the working patterns of mothers and fathers. This enables us to hold groups or training sessions at times that we know parents are free to attend. At this point we also know whether adults in the nursery child's household have PR and which parents have attended the key concept training sessions.

Parents' experience and aspirations

Although our current database gives us basic information about each family's composition, it does not give us any information about the parents' own educational experiences or their aspirations for their children. We know from the research that parents' own experience of schooling will have an enormous impact on outcomes for the children (Sylva et al., 2004; Blanden, 2006). In previous years we had undertaken semi-structured interviews with parents using a prompt sheet that covered the following areas:

- at what age the child's parents left full-time education;
- whether they had undertaken further education (FE) or higher education (HE);
- what they hoped their child would get from the nursery experience;
- what they believed their child was actually getting from coming to nursery.

These 1½ hour interviews helped research staff and nursery staff to find out data which were critical for the development of our adult community education programme where parents could embark on learning and undertake vocational and non-vocational training. More recently due to shift working, time constraints and increased numbers of children in the nursery, it has not been possible for nursery staff to carry out these interviews. Because parents' educational attainment does have a significant and lasting impact on children's life chances we still want to ask these questions so that nursery staff can talk to parents about these issues when they are on the initial home visit and subsequent home visits.

The quantitative data

From the quantitative data gathered from interviews during the initial research, we had a much clearer idea about the numbers of nursery parents who had experienced schooling as either a positive or negative experience. If the parents have grown up in our community and had a negative experience at school, they may find it hard to use the centre at all because it is in a somewhat daunting, 1930s comprehensive school building. It was and remains important that staff are approachable and that the atmosphere is welcoming at all times. We make a conscious effort to ensure that the rooms in which parents may attend groups or meetings are comfortable and informal, more like a sitting room than a classroom. The easy chairs are usually arranged in a circle or semicircle, and there is always tea and coffee available and parents can help themselves.

One of the ways we try to make it safe for parents to become involved in their children's learning, in reclaiming their own adult education, and in the life of the centre generally, is by offering them a range of different 'ways in'. *They* are in charge of the whole process and *our* job is to ensure that interventions and services are equally accessible to all.

The nine models of engagement

At this point we need to describe some of the ways parents at Pen Green can become involved in their children's learning in the nursery setting and share knowledge with their family worker about how their children are developing and learning at home.

1. Attendance at initial key concept training sessions

These sessions are run at the beginning of the nursery term and are concerned with the four key concepts that family workers use to inform their work within the nursery; the groups are open to all parents and adult carers of nursery children. They run three times a day, with a free crèche for each session. It is critical that groups are run in this way and that we are responding to the varying shift patterns in which some of our parents' work. The free crèche is also very important, as paying for childcare becomes prohibitive for parents on a low income. Attending the key concepts sessions is often parents' first experience of how groups are run at Pen Green.

2. Attendance at a long-term study group (Parents' Involvement in Their Children's Learning – PICL)

All nursery parents have the opportunity to join a 'Parents' Involvement in Their Children's Learning' (PICL) study group; they can attend this weekly group across the whole of the child's nursery year. Once again the group is offered every week in the morning, afternoon and evening, for parents and carers to attend and discuss with nursery workers their child's development both at home and at nursery. We also offer an additional PICL study group once a week for Polish speakers. Parents are encouraged to make written notes, or upload photographs, video vignettes or observations onto a secure online journal about what their children are doing at home. They are encouraged to describe what their children are doing when they are *deeply involved* in play or when they are displaying *schematic* behaviour. We have to consider the challenges for families that we work with who are multilingual learners and may not yet be fluent in English and for families

(Continued)

(Continued)

where literacy is an issue. Because we already know our families well we can generally pre-empt either of these issues creating problems for attendance, using a secure online learning journal to upload photographs and video vignettes, which can be less threatening for parents. In the early days of the research project the technical challenges of camcorders were a problem for some parents but today most of the parents are very confident in using mobile phone apps. In the sessions, family workers show the group short clips of video taken of the child playing, exploring and investigating in the nursery; this is followed by a group discussion exploring precisely what is happening in the video and using the key concepts to develop a shared language between home and nursery.

3. Attendance at an evening PICL study group

These groups run in just the same way as the weekly long-term study groups; originally they were only run once a month for those parents unable to access the daytime groups. Initially these evening groups were set up as part of a focused intervention to engage fathers, and sessions were advertised as 'meetings' rather than ongoing groups as the fathers seemed to prefer one-off sessions. However, we now run this group on a weekly basis and have done so successfully for many years. The group is no longer exclusively for fathers or couples but fathers often do attend.

4. PICL study group for Polish-speaking families

In the nursery we have a very large number of children whose home language is Polish. Former Polish-speaking nursery parents had told us that they often wanted to participate in the PICL study groups but felt there was a language barrier; discussing conceptual concerns in a second language was a real challenge and they felt some embarrassment about having to keep asking for clarification. They felt that they wanted to make a personal contribution to the group but were not able to. We have run Polish PICL sessions very successfully for the last two years; these sessions are co-led by two native Polish speakers who explore childcare concepts in some depth; parents relish sessions where they can watch videos of their own children and discuss the educational implications of what the children are doing.

5. Individual sessions for parents combining personal support, key concept training and home to nursery information exchange

We think it is always important to be prepared to offer individual sessions for those parents who prefer to engage in a one-to-one situation. Not all parents will enjoy being part of a group; sometimes Pen Green parents perceive parents who attend groups as 'being different' and having all the right answers, and feel that they may be 'othered' by the dominant members of the group. Sometimes families are feeling so overwhelmed by their daily life that focusing directly on their child's development, without taking time to talk about their own issues, is impossible. This model of engagement gives parents time to initially talk about themselves and their own family challenges; subsequently they begin to discuss the development of their child, both at home and at nursery (Shaw, 1991).

For some families this process has involved having a trusted family worker working with them in the nursery or family room, looking at video, sharing their child's celebration of achievement file and raising key child development concepts. The parent and family worker then jointly think about the child's learning and development and begin to plan together how the child can be supported more effectively at home and in the nursery.

Other families that are working with Pen Green's family support team, or with social care, may be unwilling to be involved in case other professionals view their engagement as an acknowledgement that they are not yet 'good enough' parents. Families have, in some cases, worked with a family support worker from the family support team rather than their nursery worker; they have met in the parents' own home in the evening and together reflect on their child's learning and how they can support the child's interests at home. Later, these parents have shared their observations with their child's key worker in nursery.

6. Home/nursery books

This is a very simple way of exchanging information with parents; a home/school book may include photos of the child in nursery with notes added by the family worker explaining and exploring what is happening in the photos. The family worker may ask for comments from the parents about similar things the child is doing at home, and vice versa. This type of home/nursery book may also be used when parents are working opposite shifts or the child is brought to nursery and collected by different adults. The book is, of course, something the child can show to grandparents, aunties and uncles, and friends. It represents the child's achievements and they are proud to see what they have accomplished and to see it presented in this way.

7. Home/school DVD or upload to a secure online journal

This is an ideal way for any parent and especially working parents to become a 'fly on the wall' in their child's nursery (Epstein et al., 1996). The family workers video the child in the nursery when they are deeply involved in an activity and add some

(Continued)

(Continued)

comments themselves to the film to initiate a dialogue with the parents about the nursery child. This video is then sent home for the family to watch. As all family workers in the nursery have iPads, the children become accustomed to being filmed and see it as 'the norm' in nursery. Parents are encouraged to send in videos or photos from home, so this can easily become a two-way exchange, with the nursery staff able to see the child exploring and playing at home.

In 2015–16 we introduced a secure online journal for documenting *all* childrens' learning in the nursery. Staff use this tool to share observations, photos and video taken in the nursery, and to engage parents in their children's learning through shared documentation of teaching and learning opportunities at home and in nursery. Through access to the secure online journal information exchange can be almost immediate from nursery and home, and parents can access the documentation at a time that is convenient to them, in the comfort of their own home.

8. Subject-specific evenings

Some parents feel less pressure if they are asked to attend one-off events. These events may focus on science, mathematics or early literacy, and they tend to be run as interactive workshops so they are often quite a 'hands-on' experience for parents. Interestingly, these events have proven to be particularly popular with fathers/male carers. In the nursery we always have a craft session and tree decorating session at Christmas and these sessions attract lots of families.

9. Trips to the Science Museum

Parents whose children are in their final year at nursery are offered the chance to go on a trip to the Science Museum in London. Groups of parents, children and nursery workers travel to London by train or coach and spend the day at the museum, particularly using the outstanding science discovery area. This trip attracts many fathers and male carers who might not otherwise have become involved in their child's nursery life. Once again several trips are arranged over a course of weeks, to encourage as many parents as possible to engage in this experience.

How do we know what's working and what is making the most difference?

We know that it is vital to offer parents more than one way into the PICL approach, but how do we know what's actually working? This is where we have to go back to the database.

Each time an event occurs (for example, a key concept session), a record is made of which family member attended, and this is recorded by the child's family worker and added to the nursery database. As well as recording attendance at events, we also record when home/school books, DVD or information from home via a secure online journal are exchanged. All family workers use a monitoring spreadsheet for their family group and this is updated on a monthly basis. We can see at a glance who is accessing services and which services are proving most popular.

During the first year of the original research project (1997–2000) when we carried out this monitoring exercise we realised, almost immediately, that not many fathers/male carers were becoming directly involved. We decided that rather than second-guessing the reasons for this, the best thing to do would be to ask some of the fathers/carers why they were not getting involved.

It appeared, given the conversations we had during the research project, that in order to get involved fathers felt they needed a 'reason for coming'. Very few fathers were dropping off or picking up the children from nursery; they did not have the basic everyday encounters that mothers experienced. All the fathers we spoke to said that of course they would attend their children's open evening once they were attending mainstream school 'because it's important for their education', but saw attending nursery as somewhat different. These fathers did not generally identify with the idea that they might want to 'share ideas about their child's learning' or stop and have a chat and a coffee, which is the way in which we would generally advertise these groups for mothers. *These fathers wanted to know how they could make a difference to their child's education by participating*.

In 2016, we now have many fathers bringing their children to nursery and collecting them at the end of the day; most take the opportunity for a daily dialogue with their child's family worker and this is a relaxed and genuine opportunity for fathers to share their experience of their child's learning at home and in nursery. However we need to make sure that *all* fathers feel able to approach nursery staff and that this time is fairly calm and unhurried.

Developing a deeper understanding of the value of parental involvement

Each year, we monitor the percentage of families of nursery children who get involved in some way. This has, of course, raised many questions for us, for example:

- How do we define the nature of each parent's involvement?
- Do we distinguish between the gains for the children when parents regularly sustain attendance at one of the study groups across a whole year or those parents who make use of a home/school book or parents who attend a single event?
- What about the parents who engage in a group or service for themselves e.g. therapeutic or adult education groups or become involved as community activists in the centre?
- What about the small number of families we are still unable to engage?

During the research project we established criteria for monitoring parental engagement and we have continued to use these in the nursery when looking at parental engagement:

- *Involvement*, for us, *is the sustained use of any of the models of engagement*. This would include the parent who, for example, only attends groups sporadically, but makes notes or uploads to a secure online learning journal on a regular basis, and discusses the child's learning with members of the nursery staff.
- We don't feel it is appropriate to distinguish qualitatively between types of involvement because parents are not a homogeneous group. Not every model of engagement will be suitable for every family. Even within one family, one parent may come to a study group, but the other parent may not be at all ready or interested in that type of commitment. Other parents may be very interested in technology and may enjoy sending and receiving uploads via a secure online learning journal involving their child, or coming to issue-specific evenings.
- We struggle with the fact that we have not been able to engage some families. This has been a relatively small percentage, however this really matters to staff. In the original research project the group of parents we found the hardest to reach were in those families where both parents were working incredibly hard to earn enough to build a better life for their children. Technology has made it easier for those parents to participate even if it is late at night. Traveller parents have often been the parents who most vociferously engage in debate about their children's learning and development; the head of the nursery and nursery staff spend considerable amounts of time on the traveller sites because these parents want to engage very much on their own terms and in their own space.

Parents who do not get involved

In the original project our aspiration was to engage 100 per cent of families, and although we did not achieve it this should still be our objective. Over the last twenty years the following factors may have impinged on participation:

- marital status
- the parents' employment status
- language barriers
- family pressures
- whether the child has been one or two years in the nursery
- whether the parent had a previous child in the nursery
- parents' apparent hostility to *any* intervention – lack of trust in the system
- parents' previous educational experiences or literacy levels
- the family worker's personality and capacity to engage parents
- serious changes in family life (e.g. sickness/pregnancy)
- whether the child has special educational needs and SOL or disability or there were other children in the home with special educational needs and SOL or disability.

We have always been clear that parents have the right to get involved in their own time and in their own way; nevertheless, within the organisation we continue to challenge ourselves with issues of non-engagement. We recognise the fact that if we have been responsive, flexible and persistent in offering these families different ways in and they still did not want to be more involved, then we have to respect their wishes. Of course we would continue to have informal chats with these parents, and share information about their children's learning in the nursery when we could. We would also make sure that all new staff have access to training to enable them to work effectively with parents and that all staff within supervision and reflective practice groups get the chance to actively reflect on their own capacity to engage with parents.

What follows is one parent's story.

Case study

LEANNE'S STORY

(Leanne is a nursery parent and has two children, Demi and Logan. Tracy is her family worker.)

I have worked with Tracy for seven years as she was my daughter Demi's family worker, so Tracy knew Logan when he was a baby. Logan was given a place in the nurture group due to difficulties at home. I had a good relationship with Tracy so therefore when Logan was ready to move into nursery he went into her group.

Logan has always had an interest in cars. He loved *Cars* the movie. He liked lining his cars up and connecting them together. There was always some kind of pattern to his play. He has always liked books when he was in nurture group, he enjoyed looking through them on his own, finding a quiet, snuggle area. He was read to regularly by his nurture group workers and seemed to enjoy the close contact and sharing of stories. Logan has a good imagination and has always asked lots of questions.

We didn't have lots of books at home but we would always borrow books from Pen Green. Logan liked to choose books from the lending library and he still does this now.

Logan struggled to settle into nurture group and nursery; he would become clingy and not want me to leave. He would want me to pick him up and then it would be hard to prise him off me. Perhaps he found the size and noise in nursery too much or he was trying to work out why his mummy and daddy now lived in different houses. Maybe he was anxious about who would pick him up at the end of the session.

When Logan started in the nursery he was given five mornings, I'm not at my best in the mornings! To make sure Logan was getting the full benefit of his

(Continued)

(Continued)

nursery time, Tracy suggested that we swapped his sessions to (lunch plus) afternoons. Again this was another change for Logan and he needed time to adjust to this, his well-being dipped. He had lost his close friendship with Dylan. Tracy and I worked together to try and encourage Logan to find a new friend. Close friends are really important for Logan during transition times.

However Logan still struggled to settle when he came into nursery. Tracy and I again came up with strategies we could put in place to support Logan's transition from home to nursery.

In hindsight, and looking back to when my older daughter Demi was in nursery, I made best use of her full-time place and often used the family room to get support. With Logan, he is a different little character; he likes to snuggle on the couch and often loses himself in his play with cars, puzzles and Lego. He is really good at occupying his own time. Therefore, I would allow him to keep playing and not take him to nursery. Tracy did speak to me about bringing Logan to nursery regularly as this does affect his emotional well-being and friendships. We decided that it was probably best to give Logan longer sessions and he started to come in for lunch. This gave him more time to spend with his friend and gave me more time to do the things that I needed to do. We have a CAF (Common Assessment Framework) in place and I was involved in VIG (video interactive guidance) with Demi. This took place every week in our home.

The extra sessions were much better as Logan took time to adjust during lunch but then enjoyed the whole of his afternoon session. I think it just takes Logan a little bit of time to feel comfortable in his surroundings. He often stands back and observes or needs the support of a trusted adult before he will be ready to play.

At home Logan has always asked me to take a photo of what he had made, he is proud of his achievements and knows we then have a record of his work. As well as collecting cars and having lots of Lego to build with, Logan started collecting sticks as we walked to and from nursery. Although I thought this was quite random, the shape of the sticks represented something to him. He has a 'dagger' and a 'basher'. He made his own stick collection in nursery. When he left nursery in the summer he asked me what was going to happen with his sticks. We decided together that we would take photos of his collection so he could have a record of them, although his collection is still in the garden. At home he was interested in collecting toilet roll tubes and kitchen roll tubes. He puts them on his arms and pretends to be a robot. Numbers, shapes and colours have always been his thing. He does lots of work on numbers with his dad. His dad is a maths whizz. Logan would play on my phone, he played a game collecting dragons. Logan started to collect cars and he would put them in groups. He has a collection of rescue vehicles. He would arrange them by size or colour.

Logan will persist with a challenge, he often sets his own challenge and will become frustrated if it does not turn out as he had planned. He doesn't like not being able to do something. Logan loves Lego and will spend long periods of time building models with hundreds of pieces. Although my house is cluttered, if I move any of Logan's constructions or pieces of Lego, he notices and will have to reconstruct. He has an eye for design and a fantastic imagination, bringing his prior knowledge together and creating his own new world. There is often a strong connection schema and when he is allowed to wallow in his play his well-being and involvement are high. He becomes totally absorbed in his play.

I had too much going on in my life to get involved in a group but this did not mean that I wasn't interested in Logan's learning.

(Logan's story continues and is told from the perspective of the organisation in Chapter 8.)

As you can see, although Leanne did not formally attend a PICL study group, she is very knowledgeable about her son's interests, his strengths and his vulnerabilities. She also knows a lot about key child development concepts that staff at Pen Green use and have shared with her and can identify his schemas and describe how she supports and extends his learning at home.

Figures 3.2 and 3.3 Logan's stick collection as an installation in the nursery garden

Family workers have different strengths

When we analysed the data it became clear that certain family workers were more or less successful in engaging the parents in their family group. We did not want to make onerous comparisons about different family workers' performance in this area but what we wanted to do was to celebrate their achievements and support their struggles when they were finding it hard to get parents to become involved. Family workers were clearly better able to get parents involved in groups where they were personally co-leader in the group or where they had a particular commitment to an activity and could work alongside the parents from their own family group. There were training implications for all nursery staff around this project; some staff are very attracted to engaging parents in their children's learning, other staff are interested in other kinds of group work. Because we believe that it is vital for all parents to be able to engage in knowledge sharing about how children are learning at home and that all parents have a right to equally access study groups and Science Museum trips we had to ensure, through our training programme, that workers were able to impress upon parents that their role was critical and that they were valued as co-educators by all the nursery team.

The impact of 'getting involved'

For parents who do become involved in their children's learning, there are many benefits, relating to both the deeper understanding of their children and their own raised self-esteem and self-actualisation. For some parents, like Carla in the case study below, it was really important to fully engage and complete a portfolio of her child's learning and have her work accredited through the Open College Network (OCN). For other parents the dialogue, the study trips and events, and the daily conversations that deepened their relationship with their child's key worker, were precisely the level of participation that they wanted.

Case study

CARLA'S STORY

(Carla is a nursery parent, Alfie is her son and Tracy is his family worker.)

I believe that Alfie's and my relationship started with Tracy long before he actually started in nursery. Tracy always spoke to Alfie as we passed through to go into the Nest. She showed an interest in him and the things that he cared deeply about. Alfie chose Tracy as his family worker, as he would talk about her at home and look for her as we passed through the nursery. I could see they were already forming a relationship. When Tracy came to do the initial home visit, she already knew about Alfie's interests. Alfie was so excited when Tracy came to our house, he couldn't wait to show her his toys and his bedroom. I felt happy and relaxed with Tracy, as

I could see how comfortable Alfie was with her. On the first home visit, Tracy told me about the PICL group. I had just had my second child and we were all trying to find our way, and I thought this would be an ideal opportunity for me to spend time thinking about Alfie. I enjoyed the group, especially watching videos of Alfie in the nursery, and sharing ideas with other parents and nursery staff really gave me a deeper understanding of Alfie and how I could support his learning. We would all exchange ideas about what could be next for our children. I now co-lead a PICL group and value parents' contributions as they do know their children best. Tracy always made me feel like my contribution and voice really mattered and she valued what I had to tell her about Alfie at home. The great thing about having video of Alfie in nursery each week was that we could watch this together as a family and Alfie could show his dad what he had been doing.

(Continued)

(Continued)

Alfie has a strong connecting schema. In these photographs, Alfie can be seen connecting objects, people and himself.

Alfie's dad works all week but he did like to go into nursery on his days off, he also used the Centre at weekends. Brian built numerous pulley systems at home for Alfie to use as he knew that he was interested in this. He also introduced Alfie to climbing clips to extend his play. Alfie took the clips into nursery to show to Tracy and to use in his play.

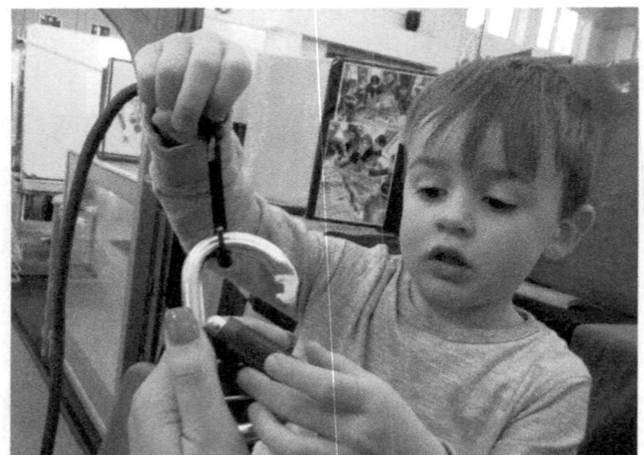

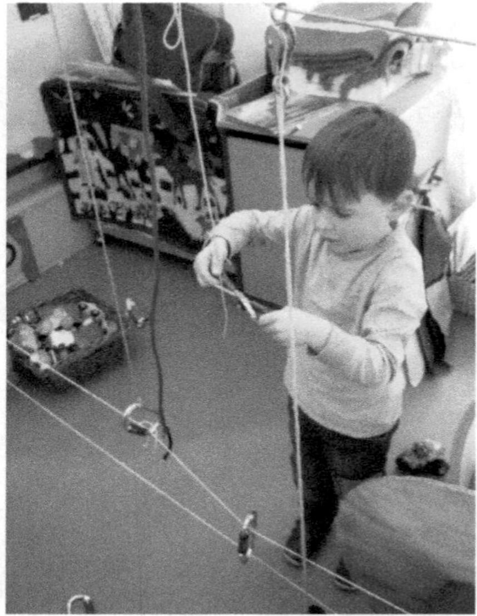

Alfie uses the climbing clips to create his own pulley system in nursery.

Suggestions for your own practice

- Recognise what children are fascinated by and curious about in your setting Feed back to parents either verbally or through a secure online learning journal regularly
- Try to value what parents tell you about their children at home and demonstrate this through your documentation and dialogue with them
- Gather information about parents' working patterns, the important people in children's lives, parental responsibility and major life events
- Use this information to make your services more flexible, responsive and accessible

Key points

Over many years of involving parents in their children's learning, we have learnt that we must try to:

- ensure that there is gender differentiation, both in the way groups are run and advertised, and in the types of trips and outings offered to parents/carers;
- work flexibly and responsively, responding to the expressed needs of parents;
- ensure that there are many 'different ways in' for parents;
- address staff training needs before they are asked to get involved with parents and offer continuous professional development and supervision.

It is important for us to reflect on our practice, looking at what is working, and what is not, and we have to be responsive. The nursery team have a very strong belief that parents are committed to, interested in and excited by their children's learning. It is our job to continue to find innovative ways to engage families.

Recommended reading

The following papers can be found on the Early Intervention site www.eif.org.uk/publication.

Early Intervention Foundation (2015) *The Best Start at Home: What Works to Improve the Quality of Parent–child Interactions from Conception to Age 5 Years.*

Early Intervention Foundation (2016) *What Works to Enhance Inter-parental Relationships and Improve Outcomes for Children.*

Early Intervention Foundation (2016) *Foundations for Life: What Works to Support Parent Child Interaction in the Early Years.*

Websites

Early Intervention Foundation: www.eif.org.uk
Joseph Rowntree Foundation: www.jrf.org.uk
National Children's Bureau: www.ncb.org.uk
National Foundation for Educational Research: www.nfer.ac.uk/publications
Pen Green Centre and Research and Development Base: www.pengreen.org

4

Sharing ideas with parents about key child development concepts

Cath Arnold

Introduction

This chapter considers ways in which parents can become involved in curriculum issues; describes the sorts of language and concepts the staff at Pen Green have been sharing with parents over a period of years; and looks at how to run group sessions and at what happens during those sessions. The chapter also includes ways in which we have been able to adapt to changes in policy and to use technology to support the building of relationships with families.

Why share knowledge with parents?

In 1990, Athey suggested, 'Legislation cannot decree that parents and professionals should work together to increase knowledge of child development or to work out ways of how an offered curriculum might more effectively become a received curriculum' (1990: 20). The notion of parents and professionals working together as equals on curriculum issues seemed a fairly radical idea when the Froebel Early Education Project was conceptualised during the early 1970s. The very idea that professionals do not have all the knowledge about the curriculum ready to pass on to children, and about which they can inform parents, was threatening to some professionals and it still can be. Unless professionals are prepared to give up some of the power they have traditionally held, then working as equals with parents can be difficult. Many professionals talk about 'empowering' parents as though it was an easy thing to do as long as one is willing. Our research indicates that, as with any relationship, what happens in the day-to-day interactions is extremely complex and that it is not just a matter of the professional handing over some power to the parent. Freire writes in the *Pedagogy of the Oppressed* about sharing power through 'dialogue':

> Because dialogue is an encounter among women and men who name the world, it must not be a situation where some name on behalf of others. It is an act of creation; it must not serve as a crafty instrument for the domination of one person by another. (1970: 70)

Freire goes on to say that we need to have 'faith in humankind', in their ability to create new knowledge. In a similar way, professional educators need to have faith in parents' ability to create new understandings of their children. So rather than 'handing over' power to parents, it is our 'belief' in them and in the process of dialogue that results in us being able to work together for the benefit of children. Athey (2007) demonstrated that the children and their siblings benefited when their parents and teachers shared information about the curriculum.

We would argue that this process of dialogue between parents and professionals also benefits the professionals. Athey (1990: 66) pointed out that when parents and professionals work together, the professionals have an opportunity to make their 'pedagogy more conscious and explicit'. Whenever we have to share knowledge with another person, we reflect and also think about how to communicate the information most effectively, which enhances our understanding too.

We have been sharing schema theory with parents since the 1980s and found this beneficial, but it was only when we came across Janet Shaw's PhD and Patrick Easen's paper on 'Parents and educators' that we really began to understand why the 'sharing' was so critical. Easen explains that the equal partnership is created when we share what we know (about child development) and the parents share what they know (about their child's deep interests). It is this process of sharing ideas about child development theories and also listening to parents' detailed information about their own children that helps us to articulate our pedagogy more clearly. As professionals, we are sharing our specialised knowledge with parents and trying not to feel threatened by the fact that the parent will often see what is happening more quickly and clearly than we do. The recognition that parents' specialised knowledge of their own child can stimulate our thinking is part of our professional development. The Froebel Early Education Project has been an inspiration to the staff at Pen Green Centre and has greatly influenced our work with parents.

Current government policy is concerned with supporting disadvantaged families by encouraging parents to work. Whilst this may benefit families financially, there is a danger that parents, once again, become marginalised and viewed as less important when it comes to their children's education. In many educational institutions parents are seen as 'helpers' and not acknowledged as holders of knowledge. Unless practitioners truly value the contribution made by parents, parents will continue to take on this less powerful role. If parents are listened to, then their children will receive the powerful message that their family, its culture and values are worth something in the wider world.

An example of a dialogue between a worker and a parent

Carly (Family Worker in the Snug) reflects:

> A parent, who hadn't attended the key concept sessions, spoke to me about how her child is moving things ... 'Everything goes into a bag or a pram ... I find everything in a big mess everywhere'. I spoke with her about schemas. She was already familiar with involvement and well-being. I explained I'd seen her child transporting at nursery and sent some video home to illustrate. This mother shared the information with her husband, who enjoyed seeing the filmed material. She began sending me photos all of the time, that confirmed her child's interest in transporting and containing. She also bought extra resources – a double buggy with basket, a shopping trolley and several baskets.

The current context and ways of being involved

Changes

For almost twenty years Pen Green staff ran the nursery for four days a week and on a Wednesday we opened the nursery to the whole community. Very few of our parents worked and those who did made other arrangements for their children on our community day. This changed with the Neighbourhood Nursery Initiative, which was launched in 2001 and aimed to 'help parents into employment, reduce child poverty and boost children's development. By 2005 45,000 new childcare places had been created in approximately 1,400 neighbourhood nurseries' (Smith et al., 2007). As part of this initiative, we had to provide day-care from 8 till 6 on five days a week so our community drop-in was no longer run in the nursery but in a smaller room on site. In 2004, after a long consultation process with parents and professionals, we opened our Baby Nest, providing early care and education for children aged from 1 to 3 years old. Since then, we have extended our provision for 2-to 5-year-olds (three spaces: the Den, Snug and Studio, each offering 40 full-time equivalent places) and also opened the Couthie, which mirrors the Baby Nest in offering early care and education to children from 9 months to 3 years. Often children move into the adjoining nursery from the Nest or Couthie but sometimes children at the age of 3 go to other nurseries in the town. We no longer have a catchment area so parents may choose to send their children to the Nest or Couthie and may move them to other nurseries nearer home or attached to the school they hope to attend after their third birthday. This creates a moving population.

There have also been changes in the demographics of Corby, as a town. We now have a significant population from Eastern Europe, as well as Portugal, Africa and other countries. This is reflected in our staff team as we now employ in the nursery two Polish-speaking Family Workers and one Portuguese-speaking Family Worker, as well as two workers from Africa. This enriches our community and, because the Polish population is fairly large, we now run study groups for parents in the Polish language.

Formula funding means that children are offered their free entitlement to nursery education, currently 15 hours a week term time or 12½ hours a week all year round, the next term after their third birthday. This means that, although we are an all-year-round provision, we have new children starting nursery every term as well as children newly arrived to the area. So our nursery population is less stable than it previously was.

Ways of being involved

A main finding from our original research on 'involving parents in their children's learning' was that we need to use many different approaches, as parents are all different and have diverse needs. Another relevant factor is that technology has moved on apace in recent years. We have, for a very long time, shared video filmed at nursery with parents, and encouraged parents to film their children at home to share with us. We have recently started using an online learning journal for each child, which makes that sharing much easier and more spontaneous. We still sometimes have to convince parents that the process is a two-way dialogue, but as most parents now have smartphones, access to cameras is much easier. We do need to know which families do not have a computer or smartphone so that we can use another method of sharing.

Parents are currently involved in their children's education at Pen Green in the following ways:

- Through daily chats with their child's family worker and other nursery staff.
- By attending 'information sharing' sessions about key child development concepts and other relevant issues (these sessions will be fully explored later in this chapter).
- By attending a nursery open evening.
- By accessing photos, video and accounts of their child's learning online.
- By contributing photos, video and comments to their child's secure online learning journal.
- By receiving some video of their child filmed at nursery on a DVD.

- By attending a weekly study group during the day or in the evening.
- By going on a trip to the Science Museum in London with their own child, members of staff, and other parents with their children.
- By attending issue-specific workshops, such as science and technology or 'Learning to be Strong' (assertiveness for young children).
- By attending individual sessions.

Sharing a language about the curriculum

In Chapter 2, we talked about the need for an honest exchange of ideas with parents in a shared language. Any field of knowledge has its own language or jargon. A specialist language may be a barrier to communicating with parents. If we want power to be shared with parents, the first step is to share any specialised language we are using. As I have mentioned, we have been exchanging information with parents about 'schemas' or 'patterns of behaviour' for almost thirty years now (Mairs and The Pen Green Team, 2013). Parents usually pick up this technical language very quickly and apply it to what their own children are doing. Below is an example from a child's online learning journal written by his mother illustrating her understanding of his 'connecting' schema.

Case study

PARENT VOICE

Angus is mad about winches, pulleys and helicopters at home too ... particularly rescue helicopters. He plays with a gears set at home and often attaches hoisting equipment to various vehicles. The belt from my dressing gown is constantly going missing for this purpose! He likes to attach grabbing hooks and magnets on the end of his hoists. The other week he was using a stethoscope as a grabbing/hoisting hook – the bits that go in your ears!

When we share this technical language with parents, we also share our knowledge about how their children learn. It gives us a clear focus. So, as workers, rather than just saying to a parent, 'William has had a lovely time playing today' (which, in fact, tells them very little about what he has actually been doing at nursery), we can say, 'William really enjoyed building a vertical tower with hollow blocks today' (a more specific statement about what he has actually been doing).

We could choose to simplify our language, but parents might find that patronising. We can hardly claim a wish to be equal partners if we arbitrarily decide that the language is too difficult for parents to understand. Of course, we might explain that it was a 'very tall tower' and that William called it 'Notre Dame'. Video or photos of what happened immediately or later that day could support the information sharing. As soon as we begin to share language about the curriculum, usually on the initial home visit, we are making our pedagogy more explicit. Each explanation we offer helps us to understand the concepts more fully.

Although the dialogue with parents begins with the initial home visit (before a child starts nursery) and continues throughout each child's time at nursery, we do not expect parents just to pick up ideas in a haphazard way. We plan and devote time to giving every parent the opportunity to learn about the key child development concepts we are using in the nursery to help us understand their children's learning. There are four concepts that we find particularly helpful:

- Involvement (Laevers, 2011).
- Well-being (Laevers, 2011).
- Adult style (Rogers, 1983; Pascal and Bertram, 1997; Whalley and Arnold, 1997a).
- Schemas (Athey, 2007; Arnold and The Pen Green Team, 2010) (these concepts will be explained later in this chapter).

Opportunities to share language about the curriculum

Home visits

With a less stable nursery population, it is important for us to grasp every opportunity to talk with parents individually about their children's learning and the concepts we use to understand their learning. Our first opportunity is on the initial home visit. A child's Family Worker (key person) visits the family at home a few days before the child starts settling in at nursery. We plan for home visits to be relaxed; to be a time when parents can feel confident to ask us anything about nursery they are concerned about. We leave a 'home visit pack' with them as we realise offering a lot of information all at once can be overwhelming. Within the pack is information on the four key child development concepts – involvement, well-being, adult style and schemas – as well as other information about our philosophy and practical issues.

Settling in to nursery

Families usually stay in the environment of the nursery for two weeks when their child starts attending nursery. This provides another opportunity to share with parents the four key child development concepts (involvement, well-being, adult style and schemas). We also set up 'information sharing sessions' each term, offering a morning, afternoon and evening session for parents to attend. These sessions will be fully described later in this chapter.

Daily chats

Informal chats about what children have been engaged in that day either at home or nursery are another opportunity for us to share with parents on a daily basis. Obviously we need to be aware of parents' various work schedules, but there is usually time for a brief chat at the beginning or end of the session or day. These chats help us to connect with what children have been doing at home as well as informing parents about their child's learning at nursery. Over time, the dialogue can become richer and deeper.

Online learning journal

The online learning journal for each child is another opportunity to articulate our understanding of children's learning using the language connected with their involvement, emotional well-being, schemas being explored, and the style and strategies we adopt to support and extend their learning. When it works well, the online journal illustrates the 'Pen Green Loop' described in Chapter 8 and is a continuous two-way dialogue with the child at the centre.

NOTE: we are not currently using the assessment tool offered as part of the online learning journal because we think that what we have developed is more rigorous and personalised and cannot be replaced by a computer program.

Weekly study groups

Following on from informally sharing ideas and running information-sharing sessions, we offer parents the opportunity to attend a weekly study group to engage in further dialogue about their children's learning. We offer a morning, afternoon and evening group. Each group meets weekly and is open to all nursery parents though membership tends to be stable.

Using a group work model to share ideas with parents

Although a great deal of our communication with parents is on a one-to-one basis, we find that a group work model is very productive when it comes to adult learning. Early childhood educators are in the unique position of coming into contact with children and their parents or carers on a daily basis. Because of this daily contact and a shared interest in the children, they are well placed to work with those adults as well as with their children. However, initial training, whether it is nursery nursing, social work, nursing or teacher training, does not usually prepare early educators for working with adults. Therefore, workers do need to undertake some group work training. This kind of training is offered to all staff at Pen Green on a regular basis.

When planning the curriculum for young children, educators use a constructivist approach to consider what each child brings to the learning situation (Athey, 1990: 43). In a similar way, we need to consider the rich experiences that adults bring to any learning situation and to adopt a 'person-centred' approach to adult education (Whitaker, 1986: 277). Whitaker says, 'Experience of small group work had led me to the belief in the power of groups to provide a particularly rich and creative learning environment for human growth' (p. 276). He goes on to describe ways in which adults can 'share and draw on the considerable knowledge, experience and expertise present in the group' (p. 278). The study groups we have set up at Pen Green, as part of the Parents' Involvement in Their Children's Learning (PICL) project, are discussion groups during which parents 'compare notes with nursery staff and watch video tapes of their children playing in nursery and at home' (Whalley, 1997a: 17). We are trying to create an environment in which 'adults reflect on their own past experiences, relate their present to their past experiences and access new information' (Whalley, 1996b: 7). Within this type of environment, there are 'tangible gains' for the leaders as well as for the group members.

Creating an environment for adult learning

Whether parents are attending a one-off 'information sharing' session or a weekly study group on a regular basis, we need to plan in order to offer a really good experience for them. Parents are most keen to know about their children's development when the children have just started nursery. Therefore, it is crucial to arrange to run our 'information-sharing' sessions during the first month or six weeks after their child has started attending nursery. These initial sessions are an important foundation on which to base our ongoing dialogue with the parents. We run these sessions at least three times a year, following our intake each term. Time of day is also important. In order to give each parent an opportunity to attend the session, we run a session three times a day, that is, morning, afternoon or evening. Comfortable armchairs arranged in a circle help parents to relax. (If armchairs are not available, adult-sized chairs will do.) We try to make the room more like a living room than a classroom. It is important to have tea and coffee available and to make drinks for parents as they arrive.

Parents are offered a crèche for their younger children but we also provide treasure baskets and other resources for younger children who come to the session with their parents. Invitations are given to all parents, with special attention being given to inviting parents who live apart.

An example from practice

Leanne (Family Worker from the Snug), reflects on a family using the Snug this year:

> I have a child in my group whose parents live apart but they want the best for their child and come to all of the meetings together. However, parents don't always want to do that so I would always invite both parents and then let them decide for themselves whether they want to attend separately, as we always provide more than one opportunity. I can always meet them separately to talk about the concepts in relation to their child.

Planning the sessions

We have found that groups run more smoothly if two workers run each session. The content delivery needs to be planned well in advance. However detailed and meticulous the planning, it is very important to be flexible and to allow plenty of time for parents to express their views. This is often the first time the parents have returned to an 'educational environment' since they left school, and strong feelings about school and their experiences of school often emerge in the group. Although parents may themselves have had a poor experience of the education system, most are clear that they want their children to succeed. If, as workers, we do not allow parents to express their views freely, they may continue to experience the system as letting them down in some way. This is particularly relevant in Corby, where very few adults have experienced further or higher education.

The group leaders can consider in advance what is likely to happen during the initial meeting of the group. Like any small group, to be effective the group has to work on at least two levels:

- group task – tackling the business of the group; and
- group process – satisfying social needs and meeting people's needs for acceptance, recognition, belonging, etc. (Whalley, 1996b: 11).

Training in group work prepares us to think about what to do if a group member completely dominates the session or seems not to participate at all. The two workers can agree beforehand to take on different roles during the session. One can lead and try to keep the group on task, while the other can support individual parents and make sure that quieter parents are heard. Rather than the two workers sitting together, it can be more enabling for group members if the two leaders sit separately and are part of the group. Sitting alongside a parent, who might be vulnerable, is a helpful strategy.

However well we have planned the content of the group in advance, each group takes on a dynamic of its own which no one can anticipate. This makes each session exciting and interesting for everyone involved.

Information sharing: a typical session

Each of the initial 'information-sharing' sessions begins with one of the group leaders introducing themself and trying to put parents at their ease. Humour might be appropriate; for example, if everything has gone wrong for the leader that day, they might share that with the group.

One of the leaders then asks each parent to introduce themself to the rest of the group and perhaps say something about their own child. Occasionally parents are reluctant to do this, and we must accept their decision. If they agree to introduce themselves, then the ice is broken and they have spoken in the group for the first time. People can get quite anxious waiting for their turn.

For these initial sessions, we try to engage as many parents as possible. The weekly study groups work best with eight to ten members, as borne out by the research. If the group is larger than the optimum number, it works better to ask each person to move around the room and introduce themself individually to other group members. This is less threatening and can be fun, but may take longer. During the 'information-sharing' session, one of the group leaders introduces the four key child development theories used by staff to interpret children's learning (involvement, well-being, adult style and schemas). This is not done in a formal or didactic way but briefly explained and then applied to children. Parents bring their own agenda so it is important to also spend time discussing, for example, the online learning journal, pupil premium, applying for schools and anything else parents want to discuss.

The four key child development concepts

We draw on language that describes these concepts in our interactions with parents.

Involvement

We would give a brief introduction to the work of Professor Ferre Laevers and the theory underpinning the concept of 'involvement'. Laevers' work is well established and rigorous, and it is particularly accessible to early years workers. We have found that parents readily take on these ideas.

The important point to convey to parents is that Laevers has been looking at the processes of learning as well as the outcomes or products. He is interested in what is happening *inside children* as they learn. He has developed a scale and signs to describe how 'involved' each child is in what they are doing at any given moment

(Laevers, 2011). Being deeply involved means that a child is developing and learning, and that fundamental changes are occurring.

The signs of involvement Laevers has identified are:

- concentration;
- energy;
- complexity and creativity;
- facial expression and composure;
- persistence;
- precision;
- reaction time;
- verbal expression;
- satisfaction (Laevers, 1997: 20–1).

Not all of the signs would necessarily be present at once, though four or five are usually apparent when a child (or adult) is deeply involved. The signs are considered alongside 'a continuum ranging from "no activity at all" (level 1) to "total implication in the activity" (level 5)' (Laevers, 1994a: 163). Further discussion with the parents would then follow. We emphasise the point that when we are rating a child's involvement, we are not judging the child but how well the provision we are offering them at nursery is meeting their interests and needs.

Figure 4.1 Ridwhan and Shakila involved with pouring

Well-being

One of the workers introduces the work that Laevers has been carrying out on children's emotional 'well-being' (Laevers, 2011). The workers at Pen Green have met Professor Laevers and have been impressed with his value base. We have found that his theory of the concept of 'well-being' is one on which we can operate. The emotional well-being of their children is always a concern of parents and carers, especially when children are starting to attend nursery or any new setting.

Alongside 'involvement' Laevers and his team consider children's 'emotional well-being'. His is a process-orientated approach. Laevers is interested in what is going on inside children while they are learning. Many factors can stop children from being able to learn. The way that Laevers describes the inability to learn is through each child's 'level of well-being'. He says that 'the level of well-being in children indicates how they are doing emotionally' (Laevers, 1997: 15). Once again, we are looking at how well we, in the nursery, are meeting the needs of individual children: 'The degree of well-being shows us how much the educational environment succeeds in helping the child to feel at home, to be her/himself, to remain in contact with her/himself and have her/his emotional needs (the need for attention, recognition, competence…) fulfilled' (Laevers, 1994b: 5). Laevers comments that 'crying is not necessarily an indication of low well-being' (Laevers, 1995). Crying may mean that children are in touch with their own feelings.

Laevers has identified 'a number of characteristics in a child's behaviour' to which we might refer in order to assess each child's well-being. Not all of the characteristics need to be present for a child to be at a high level of well-being, however, at least half of the signs being present indicate a high level of well-being. These are the signs:

- Openness and receptivity.
- Flexibility.
- Self-confidence and high self-esteem.
- Being able to defend oneself.
- Vitality.
- Relaxation and inner peace.
- Enjoyment without restraints.
- Being in close contact with one's inner self (Laevers, 1997: 18–19).

Some of the signs link closely with our own work on the programme 'Learning to be Strong: Assertiveness for Under-fives'. Whalley states:

> Our concern with children's emotional needs also led us to watch the withdrawn, vulnerable children in the nursery more carefully. We became more and more aware that these children had few strategies for coping with anger or hostility from their peers.
>
> Whalley (1994: 78)

In 1986, we began working with children in small groups, using role-play to explore ideas about friendships, bullying, boundaries, strangers and feelings. Now we routinely offer children an opportunity to express their feelings and fears, to learn some new strategies, and to practise using these strategies in a safe environment with the support of adults. (More information on the 'Learning to be Strong' (LTBS) programme can be accessed at the Pen Green Centre.)

During the 'information-sharing' session we discuss strategies for helping young children to express their feelings. We have a good selection of storybooks in the nursery that deal with a range of feelings, and we can suggest suitable stories that parents might then use. A parent mentioned that her child was scared that Santa Claus would come into her bedroom. *Worried Arthur* by Joan Stimson (1995) deals with this issue and even describes a strategy, that is, leaving Santa a note saying, 'Please if it is at all possible, as my bedroom is a little untidy … could you leave any presents just here?' This parent borrowed the book to read to her child and found it very helpful.

This session might also alert us to the fact that a parent has painful, unresolved feelings. We can acknowledge this afterwards with the parent and make sure that they know that professional help is available. We can recommend organisations or individual counsellors if the parent is ready to seek help.

Following on from the 'Involving Parents in Their Children's Learning' study, we studied for three years, and alongside parents, their children's emotional well-being and resilience.

Adult style

Our original research into Adult Style, resulting in a list of helpful 'Pedagogic Strategies', was carried out alongside parents in 1997. At that time, we were drawing on the work of Pascal and Bertram (1997). Pascal and Bertram drew on the work of Carl Rogers, who noted that therapists displaying a 'facilitative attitude' demonstrated 'genuineness, prizing and empathetic understanding' (1983: 128). Pascal and Bertram translated these qualities into styles adults could adopt when interacting with young children: 'stimulation; sensitivity and allowing autonomy' (1997).

We have continued to carry out research into 'Effective Pedagogic Strategies' across the years alongside parents and our most recent research on strategies to support 0–3 year-olds has resulted in the following framework.

The Revised Adult Pedagogic Strategies (2013)

1 Subtle Intervention – The adult watches and listens to what the child is doing before intervening.

2 Linking Experiences – The adults are aware of the child's experience with other adults at home and in the setting.

3 Acknowledging – The adult acknowledges the child's presence, emotions and capability by being physically close to them including using touch if appropriate to make contact (see also strategy 8), and tuning into the child's facial expressions and vocal intonation, including playfulness and teasing.

(Continued)

(Continued)

4 Working with the Child's Initiative and Agency – The adult considers what the child is bringing to each interaction, checks out their meaning and gives them time to respond or to question. The adult encourages the child's curiosity and ability to make choices including taking appropriate risks.

5 Adult Learning – The adult is committed to their own learning. They are open to playing and learning alongside the child, encouraging new learning for both child and adult.

6 Adult Attitudes – The adult is aware of the impact of their own attitudes and beliefs and how these might affect the child's learning.

7 Using Language – The adult knows about the child's home vocabulary, and offers new information to the child, including preparation for what is about to happen and describing what has just happened, and language to support the child's actions.

8 Using the Body – The adult affords learning experiences using the body, ranging from using slight touch to whole body experiences if appropriate. The adult knows how individual babies and children like to be held, rocked and comforted.

(Lawrence and Gallagher and The Pen Green Team, 2015)

This framework can be used by workers or parents to reflect on their interactions with children.

Schemas

We explain that schemas are 'patterns of action' and that all human beings use repeated patterns in order to learn about how their world works. On the initial home visit, one of our questions is, 'What does your child do that does your head in?' If parents do not understand this particular expression, we would ask the question in a slightly different way, for example 'What does your child do that annoys you?' We might remind them of that question, as often children's persistent behaviour is also schematic. As soon as we begin to give examples of 'lining up toys', 'carrying things about from one place to another' (transporting), and 'enclosing or enveloping' everything in sight, parents begin to chip in with their own examples of what they have observed. Our belief is that most parents of young children have noticed their children exploring through repeated patterns but may not realise the significance until we discuss it as a concept. Some parents are worried that their child may be odd when, for example, they line up their toys repeatedly, so are reassured by our conversations. We would show video clips to illustrate some of the common patterns (see Chapter 10 for examples from parents).

Working with the sceptics

Occasionally, parents will express the view that schemas are 'a load of tosh'. Even these sceptical parents can become intrigued or interested after watching or videoing their own children at home. Sometimes parents will come back when a second or third child starts attending nursery. At this point, with more time to watch their child, they sometimes begin to understand the significance of schemas.

Parents are always given *A Schema Booklet for Parents* (Mairs, 1990) on their initial home visit as well as a booklet describing the four concepts. They can use this to refer to initially, and they will often ask for more information on schemas. We would recommend various booklets and articles and we would also say:

- watch your child,
- talk to your family worker, and
- attend one of the study groups.

We invite parents both to attend and to speak at conferences held at the Pen Green Centre. By talking about their own children to a wide range of workers, the parents contribute a great deal to current knowledge about young children. Nothing is more impressive than hearing parents speak with passion and confidence about their own child. The experience of speaking to an audience of 150–200 people can have a huge impact not only on the audience, but also on the parents themselves and on other parents who use the centre.

Sustaining interest in the key concepts

The 'information-sharing' sessions are just the beginning of the dialogue. It is not simply a case of sharing the concepts with the parents, who then go away with a full understanding, able to operate on them effectively. Unless the parents become involved in discussing and making use of these concepts, they will have very little impact. We continue to use this language to dialogue with parents about their children's learning on home visits, during daily chats, during open evenings, in their online learning journal, and in their celebrations of achievement folders. We encourage parents to contribute to their child's nursery record. We ask them to look out for what their child is doing when they are deeply involved as this is the key to knowing when 'deep-level learning' is occurring (Laevers, 2011).

Professional development and ongoing support for staff

All staff at Pen Green are offered professional development opportunities in order to support their work with children and their families. Through the project on children's

'Emotional Well-being and Resilience', staff studied 'attachment theory' in greater depth as well as Winnicott's work on 'transitional phenomena' and theories on 'resilience' and 'self-regulation'. These concepts, when applied to oneself or to children and families, lead to a deeper understanding of emotions. In recent years, many staff have attended a year's course on 'The Emotional Roots of Learning' run at the Pen Green Centre by staff from the Northern School of Psychotherapy.

In addition, all staff are supervised on a monthly basis. This enables workers to have their needs met and their feelings contained. It is important that supervision is offered regularly and reliably so that staff can prepare for sessions in advance. There are three separate strands that are considered in supervision: professional development, work matters, and personal issues.

Suggestions for your own practice

- In your staff team discuss why working with parents is important and any related fears individual staff members have e.g. 'I might not know enough about the concepts' or 'The parents might take over'.
- Practise what you might say to parents with colleagues.
- Make small changes one step at a time.
- One small plan would be to ask for some information from home and then to use that information to plan something specific at nursery.
- Keep a record of who is becoming involved and how so that you can offer equal opportunities to all families and include mothers and fathers.

Key points

- Sharing knowledge with parents is about sharing power.
- Contexts are different and ever changing – you need to establish what you are trying to do and believe in and find ways to adapt to changes.
- The knowledge we share with parents: involvement; well-being; schemas; pedagogic strategies.
- The knowledge parents share with us: their intimate knowledge of their child; important people; what a child is doing when deeply involved at home; their culture.
- We take every opportunity to share children's learning through: home visits; daily chats; information-sharing sessions; study groups; a secure online learning journal; special events.

Recommended reading

Shields, P. (2009, October) '"School doesn't feel as much of a partnership": parents' perceptions of their child's transition from nursery school to Reception class', *Early Years*, 29 (3): 237–48.

Whyte, L. and Karabon, A. (2016) 'Transforming teacher-family relationships: shifting roles and perceptions of home visits through the Funds of Knowledge approach', *Early Years*, 36 (2): 207–221.

Websites

Joseph Rowntree Foundation: www.jrf.org.uk
National Children's Bureau: www.ncb.org.uk
Pen Green Centre and Research and Development Base: www.pengreen.org

5

Parents and staff as co-educators

'Parents' means fathers too

Margy Whalley and Trevor Chandler

Introduction

In this chapter we explore the importance of the adult role in supporting and extending children's learning within early years settings. Parents and early years professionals need to work closely together if we are to provide the optimum opportunities for children to learn and develop: 'Parents and teachers can help children separately or they can work together to the greater benefit of the children' (Athey, 1990: 66). We have used two pieces of action research to highlight the importance of recognising mothers' and fathers' roles as their children's first and most consistent educators.

Parents and staff as co-educators

The approach that we use in working with parents is rooted in the philosophy and ethos of our centre. Traditionally, parent education programmes have been based on a deficit model, targeting the families perceived to be most in need. For example, workers in the original Head Start programme in the USA assumed that 'parents would benefit from the intervention of professionals, organised the relationship on professionals' terms, and tended to see children as needing to be rescued from inadequate backgrounds' (Ball, 1994: 44). Pugh and colleagues critique this kind of approach, as 'programmes that rely on professionalism disempower parents' (Pugh, De'Ath and Smith, 1994: 88). In Chapter 1, we describe the community development approach to working with parents that Pen Green has adopted, and it is this way of working that underpins our approach to developing a deeper understanding of the adult's role in extending children's development and learning.

Social constructivists

The importance of the adult in supporting and extending children's learning is well documented. The way in which the adult supports the child is determined by the adult's belief in how children learn. The relationship between the professional and the parent or carer is also influenced by our beliefs, as early years educators, about what working together in partnership really means. Malaguzzi, the philosopher and pedagogue who worked in partnership with parents and educators in Reggio Emilia, describes this process:

> understanding the child as a co-constructor and active participant, wanting and responding to a wide range of relationships, in the home and outside, with other children and adults ... We can open up the possibility of a childhood of many relationships and opportunities, in which both the home and the early childhood institution have important, complementary but different parts to play.
>
> (Malaguzzi, cited in Dahlberg et al., 1999: 52)

The timing and level of intervention by the adult are crucial in helping or hindering a child's innate desire to learn (Trevarthen, 2004, personal communication). To require children to work within an adult-imposed framework is not helpful. If what is being offered to children bears no relation to their own interests, then they will not become deeply engaged. On the other hand, if children are left to 'just get on with it', they may become frustrated. It seems that the natural instinct of many adults is to do things for children, especially if they are in a hurry or if they cannot bear to see the child struggling. Alternatively, adults often focus exclusively on what they are 'teaching' the child rather than focusing on what the child is actually wanting to learn (Holt, 1967).

At Pen Green, we have always subscribed to a social-constructivist approach. Athey describes constructivists as 'child-centred teachers who are trying to become more conscious and more theoretically aware of what is involved in the process of "coming to know". Constructivists are interested in the processes by which children construct their own knowledge' (Athey, 1990: 30; Carr, 2001). It seemed to us that parents and staff needed to share their understandings about this process of engaging with children's central concerns. We needed to know more about the strategies that parents and nursery staff adopt when interacting with children in the home setting and in the nursery setting. We wanted to look more closely at the ways in which *all* the important adults in children's lives support their learning and development so that we could identify strengths and avoid inconsistencies or dissonances in our various approaches.

Adult engagement styles

In Chapter 4, we described the concept of the adult engagement style and how this concept is shared with parents. It was from the start a far more problematic concept for parents and staff than 'involvement', 'well-being' or 'schemas', which are dependent on closely observing the child. Pascal and Bertram (1997) apply three main descriptors to the adult styles of engagement:

- Autonomy.
- Sensitivity.
- Stimulation.

Nursery staff and parents struggled with these definitions and the exemplars offered when we first encountered them through the Effective Early Learning Project (Pascal and Bertram, 1997). We were well aware that the adult's ability to engage the child was a critical factor in terms of the child's ability to become deeply involved in learning. However, we found it hard to achieve any consensus as to the degree of autonomy that was optimal for children's learning or what behaviour on the part of the adult constituted 'sensitive engagement'. Memorably Katey, our Head of Nursery, a passionate advocate on behalf of children and the mother of a 2-year-old, would, like Danish early educators do, allow her own child Ellen to experience teetering on the edge of the river bank so that she could learn what being grounded felt like. Inevitably Katey ended up soaking wet so that Ellen was able to be masterful and have the 'full experience'. Early years educators often go to unreasonable lengths on behalf of the children in their care; sadly early childhood education settings and schools are becoming increasingly risk averse.

Some of the nursery team had used the EEL measures with groups of primary teachers and had found that it was often excruciatingly difficult to achieve a consensus on the basis of these classifications. Early years practitioners tend, in the first instance, to make judgements from their own value base (Drummond, 1993). During the training programmes that are a core part of the EEL project, early childhood educators are given time and training to work through these issues so that their judgements are moderated against those of others, with time given to teasing out the roots of their beliefs and how hands-on experience had impacted on their initial training. Margaret Carr describes this shift from what Olsen and Bruner call 'folk pedagogy' (Olson and Bruner, 1996). Early years educators' every day intuitive theories about learning and teaching, which often reflect ingrained cultural beliefs and assumptions, shift to a more informed pedagogy and understanding of children's learning dispositions (Carr, 2001: 1–20) through dialogue and reflection.

When we watched videos of adults providing stimulating 'activities' for children, it often seemed to us that the interventions were too adult-directed to encourage real participation. Although we used Pascal and Bertram's descriptors in the pilot phase of our research, it seemed to us that this was a critical area for development in our own study. At Pen Green we were not simply concerned with defining appropriate adult engagement styles in terms of the role of the early childhood educator. We were also concerned with the adult engagement styles in terms of how parents, as the child's first educator, could most effectively engage with their children in the home setting. Indeed we wanted to honour and learn from some of the pedagogical best practice that we saw when home visiting parents or when watching them settle their children into nursery.

Developing our own categories of effective teaching strategies

Instead of focusing, as so often seems to happen, on what parents were *not* doing well, we decided it would be salutary to build on what parents were doing really well. The parents involved in the project agreed that nursery staff could video them interacting with their children in the nursery early in the morning during the settling-in period. Subsequently, nursery staff were also videoed working with the same children and the video vignettes were matched up for comparison and contrast.

Obstacles to progress

We were aware that during the first phase of the project the nursery team were often reluctant to be filmed. In fact, we had many hours of videotape in which the nursery resembled the *Marie Celeste* with all the adults having abandoned ship. It was clear that staff consistently avoided being in front of the camera although they were always keen to make video documentation about the children's learning.

At this point we came across the work of Maggie Haggerty (1996) writing about student teachers in New Zealand; the New Zealand student teachers expressed many of the same anxieties as our nursery team. We decided to run a training day at Pen Green with an external consultant to discuss and debate all the issues nursery staff had about being filmed, and about filming other people. Maggie Haggerty subsequently joined the Pen Green team for a six-month sabbatical and helped to support us on the project. Working together with the parents, staff acknowledged their fears and anxieties, which included:

- their feelings about being judged by others;
- their issues about power, particularly the power of the person holding the camera;
- their issues about personal shyness;
- their issues about how their performance was affected by the pressure of being videoed.

A plan was drawn up for the rest of the research programme, and all the nursery staff agreed that they would be filmed working with at least one of the research project children over an eight-week period. They decided to set up a 'buddy' system so that they both filmed and were filmed by a colleague in whom they had a high degree of confidence. Each member of the nursery staff was filmed with a project child, and then they filmed the child with his or her parent at the beginning of each nursery session. At the end of this period we had made 16 video vignettes of nursery staff and parents working with individual project children. Staff then agreed to continue to use the 'buddy' system so that they could make videos of all the other project children during the spring term.

The parents did not express the same kind of reservations as the nursery staff about being videoed. Since all new parents settle their children into nursery for the obligatory two-week settling-in period they were accustomed to the nursery routine at the beginning of the day. Most parents regularly spent time at the beginning of each day settling the children in and because of the flexible start (parents can bring children in from 8 a.m. onward) this was a relatively relaxed and unpressured time in nursery. It seemed that the reservations and anxieties parents would naturally feel on interacting with their children in the public eye had already been worked through on these occasions and they had a high degree of confidence in the staff. They did not assume that the nursery team were making negative judgements about their parenting styles even when children appeared stressed or reluctant to let them leave. As a consequence the camera's presence did not seem to have the same negative impact on parents.

Video analysis session – developing a partnership approach

On the last day of the autumn term, we held an informal video analysis session for both nursery staff and project parents. On this occasion, we wanted the nursery staff and parents to view the video clips as empirical data that needed to be closely observed and then analysed. We decided to try out a new approach to watching and analysing the tapes (Jordan and Henderson, 1995). Staff and parents shared a meal together, and then sat down in front of the video screen. We set aside a 2½ hour session, with 1½ hours of video clips to view. The agreement between staff and parents was that we would watch the clips and anyone could ask for the tape to be stopped if:

- they wanted to discuss what they had observed; or
- they wanted clarification about what individual staff or parents were doing on the tape.

The only caveat was that the ensuing discussion could be sustained for only five minutes, after which time we had once again to focus on the videotaped evidence. We could either go back over a controversial clip or move on to look at a new clip. In this way, we could make sure that the dialogical process (Freire, 1970) was grounded in the evidence base of the tapes, rather than on preconceived assumptions.

The video analysis group comprised the children's parents and their family workers. We watched the videos in sequence so that we saw particular children interacting first with their parents and then with their key worker. Staff were intrigued by the fact that they sometimes appeared to unconsciously mimic parental patterns of behaviour when they were trying to engage particular children within their key worker group. Some staff expressed anxieties about this and were concerned that parents might feel they were usurping the parental role; the parents, however, reassured them and affirmed how much they valued staff developing warm, responsive relationships with their children. The parents began to comment on their own styles of interacting with their children and were keen to explain why they had behaved in certain ways at certain times.

We hoped that through this discussion we would be able to identify both consistent behaviours and differences in behaviour. We hoped to identify the strengths in both parents' and staff's interventions. We wanted to consider how, through this co-construction model, we could identify best pedagogical practice that would enhance the children's development and learning at home and in nursery.

Inevitably, even though we had allowed 2½ hours, we were only able to review approximately 20 minutes of the tape in the first session; the level of debate and discussion was extraordinarily high. Over the next two to three weeks, we completed three extended video analysis sessions and at the end of these discussions, we were able to identify some key features with regard to the behaviour parents exhibited when interacting with their children in nursery:

- Anticipation – parents seemed intuitively to know what to do next when a child needed something physically or emotionally.
- Recall – the parents could share past experiences and relate them to what the children were doing or saying now while they played.
- Mirroring experience through language – parents would verbally reflect back to the children what they were doing.
- Extending experiences and accompanying the child – parents were quick to think about and show children new ways to approach things. They were also willing to allow their children's interest and give them the time and space to explore things.
- Asking the child's view – parents seemed interested in what their children were thinking and feeling about things.
- Encouraging autonomy – parents encouraged their children to make choices and decisions.
- Boundary-setting/encouraging risk-taking – parents seemed to know when to step in and how to encourage their children to have a go.
- Judicious use of experience of failure/making mistakes – parents supported their children's right to experiment, to make mistakes and occasionally experience failure.

Developing the pedagogical strategies

A small group of nursery staff and senior staff working with our pedagogical consultant, Tina Bruce, spent many hours trying to identify underlying processes and the overt and conscious teaching strategies that both parents and nursery staff had used. Our aim was to develop a framework for effective teaching strategies to replace the 'adult styles' taxonomy in the EEL project. We wanted to develop categories that would help us to identify different pedagogical approaches and assess their effectiveness.

The categories needed to illuminate the complexity of the adult interventions. At the same time, the framework for observation needed to be a relatively simple tool, one that could be used regularly in our observations of each other, and with the parents. After a great deal of struggle with different forms of conceptual mapping, we established a set of fairly straightforward descriptors, which illustrated complex interactions between the adult and child. The eight pedagogic strategies that follow are drawn from our observations of the different kinds of behaviour demonstrated by both parents and nursery staff.

Effective pedagogical strategies

1. Subtle intervention.
2. Knowledge of the child's embedded context, and ability to recall the child's previous experience.
3. Affirmation of the child through facial expression and physical closeness.
4. Encouraging children to make choices and decisions.
5. The adult supports the child in taking appropriate risks.
6. The adult encourages the child to go beyond the adult's own knowledge base and accompany them into new experiences.
7. The adult has an awareness of the impact of their own attitudes and beliefs and how these might affect the child's learning.
8. The adult demonstrates learning as a partnership; the adult is committed to their own learning and generates a spirit of enquiry.

(Whalley and Arnold, 1997a)

Subtle intervention

Staff and parents were all very aware of the danger of a 'hands-on' approach where the adult's 'hands on' inhibits the children's learning. We had all watched video clips in which inappropriate actions on the part of adults clearly took the initiative away from the child. Sometimes children's physical space was imposed upon, and they were hurried along from activity to activity within an adult-determined timescale.

There were some subtle differences in the way that parents and staff intervened. Some parents seemed, at times, to be able to anticipate the next step that would keep their child engaged that little bit longer. Other parents knew just when to gently divert children's attention so that their emotional needs were met and at the same time they could continue to learn at a deep level.

For the nursery staff, subtle intervention was often about waiting and watching before intervening. It involved the adult maintaining a respectful distance until children were clearly signalling that they needed help. It was about supporting and encouraging children to the point at which they were excited by the struggle and the intensity of the challenge, and then moving in gently to extend the learning.

Staff at staff meetings extended their understanding of subtle intervention through discussions of Bruner's concept of 'scaffolding' learning (Bruner, 1977), Vygotsky's zone of proximal development (Vygotsky, 1978), Bruce's concept of 'match plus one' (Bruce, 1997) and Athey's work on disequilibriation, assimilation and accommodation (Athey, 1990).

We shared the view with parents that an overzealous focus on teaching could inhibit the children's learning. What worked best for children was an approach that combined observation, subtle intervention and reflection.

Knowledge of the child's embedded context and ability to recall the child's previous experience

From our observations of parents and nursery workers, it seemed that parents had a decided advantage in terms of their in-depth knowledge of their child's recent and relevant experiences. Often 2-and 3-year-olds would try hard to communicate important contextual information to staff about things they had done last night or at 'nanna's', and they were not always able to make themselves understood. Parents, however, were able to recognise what the children wanted to say and help them to articulate their experience, gently prompting them, at times, to assist them when they were trying to recall experiences over an extended period of time.

The importance of home visiting cannot be overstated. Pen Green nursery staff, who are called family workers, regularly home visit the children in their key worker groups. They have some understanding of the child's home environment, and will probably know many of the important adults in the child's life. However, understanding the impact of the child's context was something that staff had to work at, whereas for parents it came quite naturally. Staff sometimes needed to make life books with photographs of family members or home-to-nursery link books to keep in touch with the important people and events in the children's lives. Once again, this kind of information was not as subtle, or as intimate, as the knowledge held by parents, but it was knowledge that could be built on to support and extend the children's learning. For example, Chelsea, a 3½ year-old in nursery, had gone to visit relatives in Scotland and had taken a much-loved bag full of her favourite toys and her make-up box. She saw it disappear down the conveyor belt, which carried the baggage out to the plane, and had been wild with excitement when she came back to nursery to share the experience. With support from her father Warren she was able to share the formative experience of seeing her baggage disappear and then reclaiming it. She was also able to express her fascination with the conveyor belt that had carried her precious luggage away. Nursery staff and her parents were able to build on this shared information and extend her learning by visiting together a much more complex conveyor belt in the Science Museum.

Critics of the oppressive politics of 'parental involvement' such as Patrick Hughes and Glenda McNaughton (2000) and reconceptualisers such as Debbie Pushor (2007) from Canada, remind us that too often parents that seem different are 'othered' by professional staff who experience them as too challenging. Hughes and McNaughton (2000: 24) describe the 'othering' of parent knowledge by early years staff who subordinate parental knowledge of the child and elevate professional knowledge. At Pen Green we have built on the work of Athey in her powerful book *Extending Thought In Young Children: A Parent Professional Partnership* (1990, 2007) and our colleagues Patrick Easen, Pippa Kendall and Janet Shaw's seminal paper 'Parents and Educators: Dialogue and Development Through Partnership' (1992). If the parent isn't offered space and time to share knowledge with the family worker about how their child is developing and learning at home then the family worker will have less than half the picture of that child's developmental progress. In Amy's case study below it is possible to see how as a member of the travelling community she and her partner Simon engage with the nursery team as co-educators.

Case study

AMY'S STORY

Amy (pseudonym) describes herself as 'a member of the travelling community'. She lives with her partner Simon, her 9-year-old twins Bob and John, and 4 year-old Josh who was attending nursery at the time of the interview. Her oldest son Robert, 17, is now living on a different site.

Amy and her family have moved in the 20-mile radius around Corby for the last twelve years. As her family grew, her beliefs about children accessing state education changed. Amy felt her way of life offered her children many rich learning experiences alongside people she had chosen to live with but she also wanted them to have the opportunity to 'integrate with people who live in different environments'. As Robert had struggled with a late diagnosis with dyslexia she also wanted continuity for her other children.

After the twins had left nursery, Amy and her family moved sites and she lost touch with the centre. She happened to meet the Head of Nursery in a local supermarket and she told her where she was now living and they swapped current mobile phone numbers. Nursery staff had also kept in touch with other traveller families who helped staff to hold members of their community in mind. Staff went to visit Amy, Simon and Josh on the new site before he started nursery.

Amy had poor experiences of her own schooling and she felt she was never given a chance due to the reputation of her older brothers and sisters. She felt she had also experienced prejudice against her lifestyle when admitted to hospital following a car crash. Engaging with services was therefore difficult for her and engaging in learning experiences for herself at the centre was a challenge.

Amy's access

A new experience

'I had had no experience with nurseries, due to not many travellers having their children in nursery when my eldest was young, so it was a whole new experience for me.'

The initial contact

'I think it was suddenly realising that the boys were nearly ready for school and the traveller education said "oh, we'd better get you into nursery". So they sort of fast tracked it very quickly because [the twins] only had six months before they had to go to school, because I didn't realise, I thought they were going the year after but there were ten days between that year and the next year.'

'It was the [county] traveller education, yeah because they'd always worked with my eldest son as well so as soon as they came out and realised – oh – they start in six months not a year and six months it was like a panic so they got them in because they only had six months there.'

Amy feeling welcome

'I was made to feel very welcome by all of the staff and was overwhelmed by the facilities that were at the centre. I had never experienced an Education Authority that had been this welcoming. Usually, going to school with my eldest son was actually a very daunting and horrible experience, for example, standing in the playground at the end of the school with parents telling their children not to come near or even holding their noses ... very narrow-minded people who would push their views onto their children which would then mean our children (travelling community) would never fit in.'

'Sometimes it's a bit daunting [now] because I haven't been for ages so I don't but when I was going all the time I knew everyone so it was alright.'

Amy's motivation

'Well it just gets them to socialise, if you are living on site you are just socialising with that sort of society – it's good to integrate with other people and it gives them other views that other people do live differently ... they have got to be able to communicate through their life.'

(Continued)

(Continued)

> 'The facilities – you can do courses, that's a good one; you don't get that often much, not while your kids are going to nursery. It's just enjoyable, just getting out to do something.'

The two-week settling-in period

> 'I loved it, I had to stay there for weeks, the twins wouldn't let me leave. It wasn't just a two-day thing it was weeks and I was in the sandpit building dragons and everything ... they just wouldn't let go of my leg ... they just didn't want me to leave them. They were alright after about two to three weeks ... whereas Josh was the opposite. Josh, he didn't even want us there for the first day but we had to stay.'

The children's documentation in nursery – the celebration of my achievements file

> 'Oh they are lovely, they are (the children's files). It's just something to keep isn't it – it's a keepsake. They are always going to look back at and I think that is brilliant just to do that and to give them something like that to keep after is amazing. Even just some of my friends who have looked at those files, they just say that they have never seen a nursery do that, what they really just go and do that for every kid? They are gobsmacked.'
>
> 'Well they are just really good with the kids I think, they listen to what they are saying, they take everything in. I have never known anywhere else to write everything down daily.'

(Hayward et al., 2013)

Affirmation of the child through facial expression and physical closeness

There were striking differences in the way that key workers and parents physically related to the children. Kristen, Naomi's mother, settled 3-year-old Naomi into nursery by encouraging her to play with the blocks, a favourite occupation. Naomi became absorbed quite quickly, and Kristen sat very close by but to one side of Naomi. Kristen gave Naomi all her attention and quietly played alongside until it was time for her to leave. A taped sequence of Naomi with her family worker illustrated a parallel scenario but with some key differences. Karen, Naomi's key worker, sits, physically, very close to Naomi while she is playing in a sandpit with other children moving in and out. Naomi repeatedly goes up to Karen to make sure that she has her full attention. At one point, Naomi touches Karen's chin to redirect her gaze.

It seemed that in many of the video clips family workers had to work physically closer to the children to reassure them and affirm that contact between adult and child. The children seemed to be fairly confident that their parents were there for them and at times were rather less confident that they had the undivided attention of the nursery worker. Perhaps reasonably so, in that, at least for the duration of the settling-in period, the parents were very much focusing on one child, whereas nursery workers had to constantly respond to other children in their family group. Parents often demonstrated a physical closeness to the children, but, to be most effective, staff almost always had to engage intimately and exclusively with the children if the play was to develop and be sustained.

Encouraging children to make choices and decisions

Both parents and staff avoided over-directing the children. At the start of the day, the children were gently introduced to different areas within the nursery by their parents; adults were willing to follow the children's lead and accommodate their interests. It was obvious that for some children a side-by-side approach, with the key worker gradually taking over the support role as the child's parents withdrew, was the best way to accomplish a smooth transition into nursery. With other children, it was important to immediately establish peer support and assist them in finding their best friend before they could accept their parent's departure.

Some children came to nursery knowing exactly how they wanted to spend their time, and the adults would encourage them in that decision-making process. For example, Harry sometimes hid a favourite piece of Brio underneath a cupboard; while accepting that he could not take toys out of nursery, he was determined not to be thwarted in his extended play with the track and trains. Alice *needed* to sit on the rocking horse where she could watch her mother leave. From this secure vantage point, she could, with the support of her family worker, identify in which workshop area of the nursery she wanted to start her day. Zaki, knowing that the minibus would go out most days, would take responsibility for the clipboard and identify whose turn it was to go out and negotiate the destination.

Encouraging decision-making is a key feature of the Pen Green nursery philosophy, and it became obvious, from this shared piece of work, that parents were prepared to give the children time to learn how to make good choices.

The adult supports the child in taking appropriate risks

In our analysis of the parents' interactions that we had on video, we noticed a huge strength in their ability to encourage and support the children in experimentation. The parents were able to support their children's right to experiment, make mistakes and occasionally experience failure. We needed to be equally aware, in the nursery, of the value of a 'judicious' measure of risk-taking and mistake-making. Parents seemed accustomed to diverting children when the experience of failure was overwhelming. They were very committed to allowing children several 'shots' at a task before they gave up. Sometimes nursery staff were overanxious and overprotective. Perhaps this was because they lacked confidence in their ability to comfort the child and they did not want things to go wrong during this critical settling-in period. On some occasions, however, the parents were more anxious than the nursery staff – for example, over the use of scissors in the nursery or when children were pouring drinks. Children who are overwatched and assumed to be incompetent will inevitably spill their juice and drop the tray of cups they are carrying. When we were involved in an exchange programme with the Reggio nurseries, staff and parents who visited the Italian centres often commented on the children's assurance with fetching and carrying glasses and real food. Paradoxically our confident and competent nursery children who are trusted to do so many things in nursery often find their confidence undermined at primary school when the dinner lady takes control.

Risk-taking at a deep level, such as encouraging nursery-age children to stay away overnight at a well-organised farm holiday, an event that we have encouraged children to participate in for twenty-five years, was something that daunted both parents and staff at first, but all the 3-and 4-year-olds who participated made huge gains in confidence and self-esteem despite all our shared anxieties.

The adult encourages the child to go beyond the adult's own knowledge base and accompany them into new experiences

At times, both staff and parents struggled to understand the children's persistent concerns. On many video clips, the adults watched the children deeply engaged in activities that were hard to define, for instance, when children were intent on Sellotaping around the door handles and then connecting doors up and down the corridor with Sellotape, and then with string. However, parents and staff were able to watch respectfully and follow up the observations with dialogue and adult-level investigation. Both staff and parents drew on their knowledge about Leuven involvement levels (Laevers, 1997). Watching children who were clearly deeply involved, all the adults were prepared to suspend 'disbelief' and encourage the children to develop their cognitive concerns, even when what they were doing was extremely challenging. Children with beetle brows and tongues sticking out between their teeth, intent on making some new discovery, were always supported in their endeavours. The adults engaging with them often had to dialogue at length with colleagues, study key texts, and go with hunches to accompany the children into their new experiences.

On one memorable occasion, Alice became deeply involved in conveyor belts (see Chapter 8 for Alice's portfolio). She had been taken to see a conveyor belt at the Science Museum and was keen to understand how it worked. Staff improvised a conveyor belt in the nursery by securing paper around a tabletop, and she spent hours intently learning how to manoeuvre the belt and watching objects move along it and drop into the metal container. Having experimented with many solid objects, she finally experimented with a ball, and both Alice and the nursery staff stood by perplexed when, unlike all the other solid objects, the ball failed to drop off the conveyor belt. At 3½ years of age, Alice had a 'false hypothesis' (Harlen, 1982) that all objects would follow the same laws and move forward and drop off the end of the conveyor belt. Most of the staff shared her view. Other staff had a vague awareness of the laws of motion and the force of gravity that were in operation. Much discussion was needed before we could successfully extend Alice's learning opportunities appropriately.

The adult has an awareness of the impact of their own attitudes and beliefs and how these might affect the child's learning

Staff and parents had to work hard to develop a shared understanding as to how their own values, beliefs and attitudes were impacting on, and sometimes inhibiting, the child's intent to learn. We all became aware that overanxiety was a common feature of staff and parent behaviour. The over-watched child who was always offered assistance when climbing the trees in the nursery garden or when experimenting on the climbing frame could not develop a sense of competence and confidence as a climber. Girls dressed in skirts and dresses were almost always at a disadvantage and were often offered assistance by our largely female staff group. In Loris Malaguzzi's words, 'every child has the right to be away from the ever watchful eye of the adult' (Malaguzzi, 1992, personal communication). Our intrepid New Zealand colleagues have enlivened our lives and enriched our nursery curriculum with their commitment to encouraging children under 4 to be risk-takers within *the* most challenging and stimulating outdoor spaces.

(With thanks to Lorraine Sands and her nursery team in Tauranga)

Sometimes our debates and struggle over values and beliefs went even deeper. One parent experiencing an overwhelmingly painful separation from a partner had chosen to tell her nursery child that his daddy was 'dead'. In fact, his father was well known in the community, passed the nursery every day, but had no contact with the child. Another pregnant mother was not permitted, because of her religion and culture, to share with her son information about how the baby was developing – information which nursery staff would have considered to be appropriate and essential. Ironically, her son's family worker was also pregnant, and all the other children in his family worker group would pat their nursery worker's tummy and eagerly ask questions about what was going on. Faced with these value-based dilemmas, staff and parents shared their views and feelings respectfully. While, in many cases, there was no easy reconciliation of different perspectives, the issue of a child's right to understand was at least aired, and the best possible practice was ensured.

The adult demonstrates learning as a partnership; the adult is committed to their own learning and generates a spirit of enquiry

Despite the fact that many of the parents were juggling bringing up a family, part-time or full-time work, and coping on a low income, it was clear that, without exception, they had aspirations for their children and were anxious to support them in any way that they could. They responded to the challenge of videoing their children and thinking about their learning with as much enthusiasm as the nursery staff. Many of them were stimulated by their involvement in the project to go back to study or to pick up half-completed training.

Staff became aware of huge gaps in their own learning, particularly in the area of science and mathematics. Much of our in-service training over the last three years has focused on these areas of the curriculum. In Chapter 2, we described how nursery staff had been deeply concerned about a disengaged group of four-year-old boys in February or March each year. It cannot be coincidental that when staff became more highly attuned to the children's need to explore and develop their understanding of scientific and mathematical concepts, that these kinds of challenging behaviours diminished. Almost all Pen Green staff undertake further- or higher-education courses, and the requests for continuous professional development are respected. Wherever possible, staff who have undertaken training in their own time have been financially supported, given some time back, and offered 'time out' to complete assignments.

Involving fathers and male carers is critical

'Fathers interest in involvement in their children's learning is statistically associated with better educational outcomes. There is a strong relationship between the different aspects of parenting and parent's health and well-being and their children's outcomes' (Field, 2010; 44).

At Pen Green, we have worked hard for a number of years to tackle issues of gender stereotyping (Ghedini et al., 1995: 36). In a review of our work with fathers in 1990, we found that local fathers often failed to get involved in services and were either excluded by other parents or they excluded themselves. For example, during the research study (1997–2000) when the staff at the centre decided to positively encourage fathers to settle their children in nursery and worked hard to engage the fathers during the two-week settling-in period, 87 per cent of fathers turned up. In our discussions with parents, mothers initially assumed that their partners did not want to be involved, and fathers often assumed that their partners did not want them to be involved. In the vast majority of cases, these assumptions were not well founded.

By 2016 gender issues and developing work with fathers had become an integral and ongoing part of the work and culture of the centre. From 1985 to 1990 we developed a clear strategy to promote the participation of fathers and male carers in the life of the centre. We initially identified two main reasons for the low level of involvement of fathers in the integrated centre for children and families. In the early days the centre was seen as a service primarily for women and children. Despite the high levels of unemployment and the availability of dads, prevailing attitudes within families' and society's expectations meant that dropping children off and settling-in periods were seen as primarily the woman's responsibility. We set up an action plan to raise awareness with parents and staff about how the largely female workforce and the dominant user group might be colluding, consciously or unconsciously, in keeping men out. We also explored the positive reasons why women culturally and socially might want a safe place of their own. We provided training for all staff on gender issues and the role of men in nursery, and we set up practitioner-based action research to help us to develop direct work with fathers and make the centre's environment more men friendly. A video project on how we met and greeted fathers and mothers challenged us all to recognise our gendered approaches and shift our behaviour. We wanted Pen Green's strong model of community involvement to include not only mothers but also fathers and male carers.

An invitation to present at a European seminar on men as carers in 1994, organised by the EU Childcare Network, acted as a catalyst to re-energise and progress the next stage of this work. We examined our group work programme, considered group leadership issues, made contact with fathers by home visiting and set up a group for fathers on parenting issues. This led to a two-year (1992 to 1994) transnational project with the Reggio nursery which was of huge benefit to teams in both the UK and Italy. It resulted in a conference in Bologna in 1994 and the publication of 'Fathers, Nurseries and Childcare' produced by the European Commission Network On Children. Both the Reggio nurseries and Pen Green were absolutely committed to community engagement but Pen Green's particular strength was involving parents in the daily life management and governance of the centre. Both teams were concerned with long-term social change and wanted to encourage mothers and fathers to share family responsibilities. By the late 1990s the majority of male parents in Corby were employed and many of the women were now in part-time or full-time work. Although Corby continues to have complex shift and work patterns, many fathers stated that participation on weekdays was problematic. With Sure Start funding we were able to staff the centre on Saturday and Sunday from 9.30 a.m. to 1.00 p.m. for drop-in activities. Saturday proved to be the preferred time for weekday working fathers. Sunday was used primarily by fathers who did not live in the family home and wanted to have access to their children and a chance to meet and play with them in a familiar environment; the alternative being McDonald's or a hot, steamy and expensive soft play environment (for more information on Pen Green's weekend services see our publication on *Working with Families in Children's Centres and Early Years Settings* (Whalley, Arnold and Orr, 2013, ch. 12)).

Extending the research to explore fathers' and male carers' engagement styles

Pen Green Centre's focused work to include fathers has met with some success. Fathers particularly enjoyed attending meetings that focused on science and technology. One father spent 40 minutes exploring our key concepts CD-ROM at a parents' evening and said, the next day, that the information he had acquired had revolutionised the way he saw his son's play.

The establishment of the research base in the centre has led to a further increase in the involvement of fathers. It was clear from the beginning that if the research to study parents' involvement in their children's learning was to be successful, it was vital to involve fathers and other primary male carers in the work.

Although there were two fathers involved in the original Pen Green pilot project involving parents in their children's learning and a significant number of fathers involved in the second year, the video observations that informed our framework for pedagogical strategies included only one father. We had not, at that time, considered the particular qualities that fathers might bring to their role. It seemed to us important to replicate our research project with a group of fathers.

Using the framework we had already developed on effective pedagogical strategies, we looked at the interactions between fathers and children in the nursery. The fathers who were invited to be part of this project had already demonstrated an interest in knowing more about their children's play in nursery and were happy to let us video them settling their children into nursery.

Six fathers got involved. It was interesting to note that all these fathers had been present at their children's birth and felt that this experience had had a strong emotional impact on their lives. Two of the fathers had two sons and found interesting parallels between their children. Both had older sons whom they described as 'typical boys', that is, loud and noisy and needing to run about a lot and play rough and tumble games. Their younger sons were quieter, and enjoyed drawing and stories. Those fathers who had more than one child often struggled with sharing their time between their two children.

The fathers who became involved (Figure 5.1) were:

- Alex, who is married with one daughter, Chloe. Alex and his partner are both in full-time employment;
- Rory, who is married with a daughter, Lindsey. Rory and his partner both work;
- Lewis, who is separated, has two sons, is unemployed and shares the care of the children;
- Dave, who is married with one son and one daughter, is in full-time employment, and his partner also works away from home;
- Marcus, who has three children, lives with his partner and is employed in the nursery full-time; and
- Nick, who is married with two children, and both parents are employed.

Three of the fathers, Alex, Rory and Lewis, were video recorded as they settled their children into the nursery before going to work. Alex stayed with his daughter Chloe for 30 minutes while she was deeply engaged in block play, Rory chatted to his daughter Lindsey, and Lewis helped his son Aaron on the nursery computer whilst encouraging another boy to join him. Dave was video-filmed with two children as he read them a story while sitting on a sofa. Dave already works in the nursery on a voluntary and sessional basis to gain experience of working in an early years setting. He was planning to make a career change and study for an NVQ in education and childcare. His own child also attended the nursery. Marcus, a family worker in the nursery, sat with two nursery children playing with dough, cooking utensils and cones. Marcus is a full-time member of the nursery staff and his own child attended the nursery. Nick was filmed as he helped the children empty and clean out the fish tank.

Analysing the videotapes

Two of the centre staff met with four out of the six fathers to analyse the video recordings that we made (two of the fathers were unable to meet because of work commitments). The purpose of the meeting with the fathers was to look at the nature of their interactions with their children. We also wanted to see if our framework of pedagogical strategies was as relevant to men working with children as it was to women working with children. In other words, were the pedagogical strategies gender neutral or were there gender-specific differences?

Figure 5.1 Fathers who were involved in the project

David (1994) reflects on this issue when she notes that research on mothers and fathers concentrates too much on what fathers do in comparison with mothers, rather than on the quality of their time with children: 'What may be more important is their sensitivity (or not) to their child during such interactions' (David, 1994: 6).

From our shared analysis session, we made the following observations and identified some key issues.

Subtle intervention – fathers interacting with children gently and respectfully

All six fathers demonstrated this quality, and it was particularly strong in four of the six observations that were made. The first two examples illustrate what is meant by subtle intervention when fathers are interacting with their children or, indeed, with other children in the nursery.

Example

Dave, who was sitting on the sofa in the nursery, is reading a story to Jessica. She is sitting on his lap in a very relaxed way. They are both involved in the story when Christopher walks up to them and sits beside Dave on the sofa. Dave invites Christopher to join them in the story and notices that Christopher has a plastic apron on, which is uncomfortable now that he is sitting down. He offers to help Christopher take off the apron and with his agreement does so. Christopher now chooses to sit by Dave and involve himself in the story. During this important interaction with Christopher, Dave maintains eye contact with Jessica and talks to her. He shows awareness of both children's needs and is able to engage and maintain their interest in the story.

Example

Alex is with his daughter in the block-play area. Chloe is very involved in building with the blocks. Alex maintains a discreet distance from her when she is using the blocks in a competent way. He is very quick to intervene when she gets stuck and she asks for help. Her request for help is both verbal and through eye contact. They are very much in tune with each other's signals. She asks for help when she could not get a block out of the shelf because they were too tightly packed, and Alex intervenes when he sees that the task is too difficult for her. When she tries to stand on a round block and she finds it difficult to keep her balance, Alex very quickly moves in to hold her hand and allow her to experiment safely.

Fathers demonstrate knowledge of their children's previous experiences and interests and/or current concerns

This strategy was demonstrated in all the observations, whether it was with the father's own children or other children in the nursery.

Example

When we are looking at the video together, Alex picks out the way that his daughter Chloe is walking with a long block in the block area. She is banging it up and down and walking with a stoop. He remarks that both Chloe's grandmothers use walking sticks, and she seems to be incorporating this into her block play.

Example

Rory fixes the button on Lindsey's dungarees. In doing so, he celebrates with Lindsey the fact that she dresses herself in the morning and does it very well. He plays a counting game with her by asking her how many names she, her mum and her dad have. She then goes through everyone's names.

What follows is a case study from Banbury demonstrating a father's deep understanding of his son's interest, much of which was based on his own previous experiences.

Case study

EAST STREET CHILDREN'S CENTRE BANBURY USING THE PICL APPROACH

Whilst studying with Pen Green, Claire Bell at East Street Children's Centre developed a PICL case study on Casey, who was 3-years old at the time and attended nursery at the East Street Centre. Claire took a video of Casey when he was deeply involved at the water tray (Laevers, 1997). She could tell that he was interested in catching the fish and he was having fun throwing himself at the water with two nets in his hands. However, it was only when she watched the video with Casey's dad, Kevin, that the true depth and understanding of his actions were revealed as the following conversation shows.

(Continued)

(Continued)

Claire and Kevin dialogue whilst watching Casey's video;

K: Watching the videos made me realise he was actually re-enacting when we go out fishing. We go out fishing a lot. He's been sea fishing, coarse fishing, down the canal, down the lakes, and he really enjoys it ... he has a big involvement in fishing ... all my sons have ... all my foster children [have] as well. We do a lot of off-roading and camping, just generally out and about having a good old-fashioned time away from the Wi and the Gameboys.

Where he's using what he calls 'two nets', one is the fishing rod and one is the 'landing net'.

And when he puts it into the fireman's helmet that's the 'keep net'. He seems to be picking out the bigger fish with his fishing rod.

C: Does that reflect something that his dad does when he's fishing? Is it very important to have big fish?

K: Yeah! The bigger the fish ... because your arms only stretch so wide ...

fish back at the end of the day. He puts the 'keep net' in and rinses it off. That's what he is doing with the helmet there.

K: When he's actually doing that business with the net, he's actually casting the rod and the float in.

(Continued)

(Continued)

C: So what would you say Casey is interested in at the moment?

K: He seems to be walking round a lot at the moment with an off-road defender ... and a tow truck. The last time we went out we got towed back.

C: Oh right, how long ago was that?

K: About a month ago.

C: Ok that was after this (the video).

K: That was after this ...

C: Yeah because he showed an interest in towing with the truck in the nursery garden on that day ... but he's probably seen it or experienced it before hasn't he?

K: Yeah ... I've broken it quite a few times ... I'm on the RAC's Christmas list!

K: There you see him ... catching the fish and putting them into the keep net there ... rinsing the net out ... yeah ... he's put them back, rinsed the net out and I think that's the end of a day's fishing.

Casey's father then provided information and technical language to support Claire, the early years practitioner, in planning for Casey's future learning.

Fathers show that they appreciate children's efforts and want to support them by getting physically close, working physically alongside, and through positive, reassuring facial expressions

Fathers in many of the video sequences clearly enjoyed being physically close to their children and were physically responsive and sensitive to their children's need for truth and reassurance.

Example

Nick moved in and out of being physically close. This may have been due to the activity that he was involved in, emptying the fish tank. It is interesting to note that when Nick was standing at the sink and was briefly involved in a conversation with another adult, the children's level of involvement dropped quite noticeably. Nick was, however, quick to pick this up and squatted down to talk to the children. The children's level of involvement in the activity increased when he was actively focusing on them.

Example

Rory remained physically distant from his daughter. He remained standing throughout their time together, often with his arms folded. He did, however, engage his daughter in conversation even at a distance and sustained good eye contact with her with a lot of smiles and laughter exchanged between them. As he was about to leave Lindsey, he touched her face and they kissed goodbye.

Example

Lewis was with his son Aaron and another boy, Samuel, on the computer. Both Lewis and Aaron are sitting in chairs of their own while Samuel stands beside Lewis. They are all three very focused on the computer screen, and Lewis is sharing the mouse with the children. There is little eye contact between them while they are focused on the computer. However, there is one point where Lewis takes over the mouse from Aaron to achieve a task that they are sharing. At this point Aaron appears to lose interest in the activity, and he makes a move to walk away. Lewis disengages himself from the computer and gently touches Aaron on the arm to gain his attention. His father then invites Aaron to return to the computer task. Lewis also invites Samuel to sit on his knee so that he can reach the mouse and see the computer screen more easily.

Fathers respect their children's right to make choices and decisions

The video recordings showed many instances of the fathers showing sensitivity to the children in terms of when to intervene and when to leave the children to carry on independently.

The fathers discussed this particular strategy at length. All the fathers believed it was appropriate to respect children's desire to make their own choices and decisions. They did, however, say that this was hard to achieve. When they were under pressure to get to work, they would do tasks for their children in order to get them to nursery on time. They felt that the times spent playing alongside their children and not under pressure to be anywhere else were very precious.

Example

Nick moves in and out of supporting the children to siphon the water out of the water tray. He explains the importance of keeping the tube submerged in the water. The children experiment with taking the tube out to see what happens. The children were experimenting through direct experience and were in control of what they were doing in this complex task.

Example

Marcus always checks with the children when he intervenes to help them and never takes any intervention for granted. He offers the children different materials to use in their play, which they accept or reject. They usually accept what he offers, and his interventions are always in keeping with what the children are doing. His interventions extend the children's play and do not disrupt the flow of their play.

Example

When reading the story to Christopher and Jessica, Dave responds to their questions and requests. When Christopher first joins in the story he wants to turn the pages very quickly before hearing the story in detail. Dave allows him to do this rather than telling him to wait and listen to the story. Dave remains child focused rather than task focused.

Fathers encourage and support their children to take risks appropriately

There were very few obvious examples of risk-taking in the video observations. As a staff group and with the fathers, we discussed the concept of 'risk-taking'. What may seem like an ordinary, safe, day-to-day activity to the casual observer, can, for an individual, be a huge personal risk. For Christopher, aged 3, to interrupt the storytelling between Dave and Jessica may have been a big risk.

Chloe took risks in building a tower with the blocks until they collapsed. She looked over to her dad when this happened and was reassured by his response that it was okay.

Some fathers felt that they were at times overprotective of their children. It was not always easy in practice to know when intervention was helpful and when it was either controlling or disempowering for the child. Fathers said that they felt as protective of their sons as their daughters, and they were also aware of their children's different emotional needs.

Interestingly, the observations of these fathers were very different from project work with men and male carers that we had undertaken previously. From 1985–1990 we had focused hard on developing a more gender-balanced workforce. We had taken positive action in recruitment and through offering on-the-job training to encourage men in the local community to start the journey to becoming early childhood educators through the NVQs in childcare that we offered on site. In many of the video vignettes we observed fathers and male educators working with boys and girls in a highly differentiated way: supporting and encouraging play fighting and superhero play very effectively. Our longest-serving male member of the nursery team, and our male deputy head, were very determined that whilst men working in the integrated centre could provide positive representations of nurturing and supportive masculinity they didn't want to be stereotyped or boxed into certain ways of being and behaving. Marcus who worked for many years both in the nursery and the research base was a dance and movement expert and led on these aspects of the curriculum. It seemed to be the case that fathers in this research project were also determined to be led by the children, and the pedagogical approach that they adopted did not conform to stereotypes.

Fathers encourage the children to get involved in deep-level learning that goes beyond what the adult already knows; fathers support/accompany them in their play/learning

This strategy was the one that gave rise to most discussion. Most of the fathers said they had not experienced their children raising any questions that they did not know the answers to! They had a range of strategies for explaining things to their children. One father said that he would make up stories to answer his children's questions. These stories were used to explain what the child wanted to know in terms that the father thought he would understand. Another father said that he responded by giving the facts in as straightforward a way as possible; if he felt that the explanation would be problematic, he would change the subject.

The fathers in the group who attended the key concept training days on the curriculum had found them very useful, as they felt that these helped them understand more clearly how their children were involved in learning through their play.

Fathers appear to be aware that what they say and how they behave reflects their own attitudes and beliefs, and that this has an effect on what the child is able to learn from them and share with them

Through their interactions with the children, all the fathers showed a high degree of sensitivity. This was reflected in the degree of non-verbal communication that was put into practice; for example, getting down physically to the child's level, maintaining good eye contact and using a tone of voice that was soft and animated.

The language they used was clearly pitched at a level the children could understand and was related to the children's interests. Alex was very concerned that his daughter Chloe had the right to take the lead in her play, although, in fact, what she wanted was a reciprocal relationship. Sometimes she took the lead, sometimes she watched her dad, and sometimes they both played together.

Example

Alex allowed himself to be observed during the video recording sessions because he understood that his daughter Chloe was deeply involved in block play when he brought her into nursery. Throughout her play, he maintains a distance and is respectful of his daughter's personal space so that she can develop her play.

Chloe is confident and playful in her block play. She pushes her building to the limit and celebrates her achievements with her dad and members of staff. She is not discouraged when her building collapses. She works and plays with confidence knowing that her dad is there to support her and that she has his undivided attention. When he gently tells her that he has to leave and go to work, she protests at first and then accepts that he needs to go. After he has gone, Chloe returns to her block play and continues to build with continued energy and commitment.

Fathers work alongside children as resourceful friends and partners in their learning; adults enjoy learning in their own right and are curious and want to know more

Many of the mothers and female staff had commented on how quickly the average 3-and 4-year-olds' thinking moved into the realms of physics, science, maths and engineering and how they enjoyed discussing the qualities of whoopie cushions, mattress springs, hosepipes with holes in them and the like. The fathers involved in this research were very much in agreement with the idea of the adult as a resourceful friend; however, they struggled with the idea that they needed to develop their own knowledge and understanding. Unlike the mothers, these fathers did not feel that their children challenged them intellectually in terms of their understanding of the world around them.

Fathers communicating with their children

An analysis of the fathers' use of language showed that the amount of language used varied considerably. Two fathers talked with their children much of the time in their interactions, one of them using very little physical contact. Another father used very little language but was physically very close to the children and involved in the activity alongside them. All the fathers used language to explain things and extend the children's learning. One father very effectively used language to reflect back to the child what the child was doing. Two of the fathers were fairly task-centred in the activity they were involved in and used language to encourage the children to complete the task.

There was also a lot of eye contact between all of the fathers and the children they were working with. The children showed themselves to be very comfortable with physical contact with the fathers. The fathers responded sensitively to the children, who set their own boundaries in terms of proximity and touch.

Issues that arose

The range of adult pedagogical strategies the fathers used were generally very similar to those we had noted in mothers at an earlier stage in the project. Differences often seemed to be more closely linked to personality than to gender. However, there *was* a difference in the fathers' perceptions of how far their own knowledge and understanding might be challenged by the child. It seemed that these fathers accepted their roles and responsibilities as teachers and advocates but did not see themselves as 'learners'.

The process of involving fathers in their children's learning is one that has to be constantly reviewed and renegotiated. The fathers' responses to this project and their general engagement in the nursery and with their children's key worker has been very positive and demonstrates that fathers, as well as mothers, clearly care passionately about meeting their children's emotional and cognitive needs.

Almost all the parents using Pen Green nursery over the last thirty-three years have wanted to work in a genuine professional relationship with the early years educators who spend a great deal of time and energy engaging with their children. There are enormous benefits to all early childhood settings in developing a close working partnership between parents and early years workers because:

- parents benefit from increasing their knowledge and understanding of their children through group discussion with other parents and staff;
- staff benefit through increasing their knowledge and understanding of the children's learning opportunities at home; their ability to provide continuity and new experiences for the child within the nursery is then extended;
- children benefit because the significant adults in their lives – parents, carers and early years professionals – are able to provide richer learning opportunities;
- children also experience their parents and carers working closely together; this gives them a sense of continuity and of being cared for, and creates a trusting and secure environment in which they can learn and grow.

Our research on effective pedagogical strategies is a work in progress. We constantly review the evidence from our observations of interactions between workers and children and parents and children. We revised our framework in 2005 and included some additional strategies, as set out in Table 5.1 below.

Table 5.1

	Adult pedagogical strategies (Checklist for observations)
1	The adult watches and listens to what children are doing before intervening.
2	The adult knows about children's family experiences and links what they have done previously to what they are doing now.
3	Adults show children they are interested by their facial expression, by being physically close to them, by mirroring children's facial expressions and verbal intonation, and therefore by empathising with children's expression of emotions.
4	The adult encourages the child to make choices and decisions and to take appropriate risks.
5	The adult encourages the child to go beyond what the adult knows about and is open to learning new things alongside the child.
6	The adult is aware of the impact of their own attitudes and beliefs and how these might affect the child's learning.
7	The adult plays and learns alongside the child. The adult is committed to their own learning and encourages the child's curiosity.
8	The adult checks the child's meaning and gives the child time to respond or to question.
9	The adult offers language to support the child's actions and offers new information to the child.
10	The adult acknowledges both the child's feelings and the child's competence and capability.

(Chandler, 2005; Pen Green, 2005)

With the expansion of our nursery provision we have revisited the project twice more with new staff teams (see Chapter 4 for the 2013 version). On one occasion we specifically focused on work with children under three (Lawrence, Gallagher and the Pen Green Team, 2015). Subsequently, because there was a huge demand for professional development and learning materials in this area we developed video materials and an adult pedagogical strategies training pack. This material was essentially to help other nursery teams build their capacity to undertake peer-to-peer observations and develop reflexive practice discussion groups within their own settings.

As we now run courses and training from Diploma to Foundation Degree, BA, Early Years ITT, QTS and Master's degrees, many hundreds of mature students have engaged in this PICL work encouraging colleagues and parents in their own settings to discover, in their own time and in their own way, how sharing knowledge and information from the home and from the early childhood setting can improve outcomes for all children.

Suggestions for your own practice

- As a team, think about your engagement with all the important adults in the life of a particular child in your setting – in what ways do these adults engage with nursery staff?
- Monitor your engagement with the fathers/male carers of the children in your care.
- Discuss how you could increase your engagement with fathers.
- Try out some small action steps and review.

Key points

- It is important to engage with fathers and male carers as well as mothers, and parents may experience real barriers when they are trying to participate.
- We need to make our services more flexible and responsive to the needs of fathers and male carers as well as mothers.
- Notice how a small group of parents and staff undertook rigorous practitioner research and developed a set of pedagogic strategies that have been used to inform practice in many UK settings.

Recommended reading

del Carmen Huerta, M. et al. (2013) *Fathers' leave, fathers' involvement and child development: Are they related? Evidence from four OECD countries*. No. 140. OECD Publishing.

Goldman, R. (2005) *Fathers' Involvement in their Children's Education*. London: National Family and Parenting Institute.

Trowell, J. and Etchegoyen, A. (2002) *The Importance of Fathers: A Psychoanalytic Re-evaluation*. East Sussex: Brunner-Routledge.

Websites

Fatherhood Institute: www.fatherhoodinstitute.org

6

Working with parents who traditionally find our services 'hard to reach'

Cath Arnold

Introduction

This chapter looks at why we want to engage all parents of nursery children and how we adapt our methods to ensure that we are giving all the parents equal opportunities to be involved in their children's learning. The chapter draws on two parents' stories: the first is a parent who was involved in the original research study (1997–2000), whose own educational experiences, as a child, left her feeling that the education system had let her down; the second parent is multilingual and from a minority group, in that her family live on a traveller site in a double decker bus. She and her family are using services in 2016.

The background

As part of the Parents' Involvement in Their Children's Learning (PICL) project, we carried out semi-structured interviews with each of our nursery parents each year of the three-year project (1997–2000). We are aware that Corby has among its total population very few adults who go on to further or higher education. We feel that this is likely to have a significant effect on the parents' aspirations for their children. Therefore, we asked the parents about their own experiences of education during the interviews. Often parents expanded on this by telling us more about their educational experiences during the interview or, informally, afterwards. A substantial number of parents interviewed (30 per cent) expressed their dissatisfaction, particularly with the secondary phase of their schooling. A small number (6 per cent) were frequently excluded, were suspended from school, or were habitual truants.

Either way, this small group of parents missed a substantial amount of schooling and, consequently, had very little experience of achievement as children.

Narrowing the gap

Since around the year 2000 it has become apparent and frequently reported in the media and in government reports that in this country, there is a significant gap in achievement between children from poorer or what are considered disadvantaged backgrounds and children from more advantaged or more affluent backgrounds.

In the past, the anti-social acts that led to exclusions have sometimes been viewed as the fault of the children or their families. The educational underachievement of children from working-class families was seen by sociologists in the 1960s as 'their inability to defer gratification' or as 'a lower priority placed upon educational success' by families (Abbott, 1998: 65). Abbott, however, argues, 'It might be the case that working-class parents were unconfident in their ability to deal adequately with the norms and values of schools and teachers' (ibid.). There was a feeling that schools and teachers knew best and only by conforming to their rules and values would pupils succeed.

What was not always acknowledged was that the expectations that teachers and schools have of their pupils and their families affect how those pupils feel and act. The judgements of parents made by staff affect how the family feels about school and, possibly, create a barrier to becoming more involved with school or education in general. So our thinking was that *some barriers to the success of disadvantaged pupils are located in the teachers, rather than in the pupils and in the interactions between teachers and pupils.*

The UK government has responded to recent research by introducing several measures: the offer of a free nursery place to less advantaged '2-year-olds' designed to give children an enriched experience in the early years; extra money for schools (pupil premium), which can be used to enhance the school experiences of children; and 'raising the bar', which in effect means having higher expectations of the test results and particularly the progress of less advantaged children. I would argue that involving families amplifies the effects of these measures.

Why we want to engage all parents

Having an Equal Opportunities Policy does not necessarily mean that we offer equal opportunities to all families. We realise that we are working towards offering each child and family an equal opportunity to education and care. Parents are all different, and, therefore, to make the provision accessible to all families means that we are constantly questioning our ways of engaging parents (Whalley, 1997a). Each child is entitled to have their parents involved in their education, and we have a duty to provide the means by which parents are able to be involved. We have found that offering different ways to become involved, at different times of day and with a crèche, helps (see Chapter 4).

Longitudinal research studies give strong evidence that involving parents in their children's education benefits the children, their families and society (Athey, 1990; Rutter and Rutter, 1992; Easen, Kendall and Shaw, 1992; Fuerst and Fuerst, 1993; Weinberger, 1996). From a purely financial viewpoint, in the US it is claimed that for every $1 spent on early education, $7 is saved because students are well-adjusted citizens and have a better quality of life (Sylva, 1999). A similar claim was made (*TES*, 2000: 11) about Early Excellence Centres in the UK: 'Preliminary research by University College Worcester shows for every £1 invested in Early Excellence Centres, £8 is saved on alternative services such as foster care and counselling'.

Sylva was concerned with assessing the 'quality' of early education on offer to the child. The Early Excellence evaluation programme was concerned with the quality of services to the whole family. Projects which involve parents and local communities in decision-making seem to have the most long-term impact on children and their families.

The EPPE Project has shown that 'what parents do, rather than who they are' is what makes a difference to children. What happens in the home is even more important than what happens in settings, as far as children's long-term development and learning are concerned. Parents who are involved and know how to support their children have higher aspirations, and their children do better within the education system (Sylva et al., 2004).

Athey (1990: 20) makes the point, 'Most research in the 1960s and 70s was designed to assist the inadequate parent'. Parents were taught 'parenting skills' by experts. It was believed that child-rearing skills could be transmitted to parents by telling them what to do and encouraging them to practise it. The rich experience of bringing up their own children from birth, which parents brought to the learning situation, was not acknowledged as important. In the Froebel Early Education Project (Athey, 1990), the agenda was still set by the educators. However, the parents' contribution to professional knowledge about each child was acknowledged. Since the 1970s, there has been some shift in thinking in the sense that parents are recognised, at least in government rhetoric, as 'experts on their own children' (Athey, 1990: 61). Many parenting programmes still work from the premise that there are a lot of parenting skills that can and should be taught to 'less effective' parents. At Pen Green we begin with a different attitude, that is, that *parents truly are their children's first and most consistent educators and that we have a great deal to learn from them about their children*.

Shaw (1991), working in the tradition of Athey and Bruce, set up a home visiting project in the north-east of England. The six families that Shaw worked with were described as 'vulnerable'. They all lived in the 'inner city', were 'unemployed and had limited resources available to them, materially and in terms of their own previous education' (Shaw, 1991: 105). In addition, all of the families were living in 'highly stressful circumstances' (ibid.). Despite their individual needs, 'The agenda for discussion was negotiated between the parents and researcher' (Easen et al., 1992: 282–96).

Shaw offered the parents a schematic interpretation of their children's actions, which enabled the parents to have an alternative way of understanding those actions. This led to the parents reflecting on their own education and upbringing. Shaw discovered that:

> Unremarkably, the parents' learning process appears to be similar to the child's learning process as described by Athey; that is, both children and parents have developed cognitive structures which have built up from experience and which underpin behaviour. First-hand experience is therefore central to the learning process for children and parents.
> (Easen et al., 1992: 287)

As a result of watching their own children and discussing what might be happening with the researcher, the parents and the researcher gained knowledge and saw things 'in new ways' (Easen et al., 1992: 288). Mezirow (1977) calls this process 'perspective transformation'. Because perspectives have 'dimensions of thought, feelings and will', people begin to see things differently and to behave differently (Mezirow, 1977: 158).

In a similar way, our evidence shows that parents who become involved in the PICL project see their children's development and learning in a new 'light'. Our aim is to give all our nursery parents opportunities to become involved in the ways that suit them best.

Early in the project, it became apparent that *all* of our parents are potential participants. The respect we show for the parents' prior knowledge and experience can make a difference to how they feel about themselves and about their children. Easen et al. (1992: 294) comment, 'Through the validation of their experience, parents' self-esteem and confidence in their role as a parent and as an individual is enhanced.' Whalley (1997a: 92) makes a similar point: 'Parents need to know that staff care about them as well as their children'.

We were aware of parents using the centre facilities who had had poor experiences of education and schooling during their own childhoods, and we very much wanted to improve opportunities for them and their children.

The small group of parents attending the Pen Green Centre who, as children, were excluded from school or were habitual truants can give us an insight into what happened from their perspective. The first case study in this chapter is from a mother, who I will refer to as Julie (a pseudonym), who was a regular user of the centre over a number of years. She agreed to tell the story of her own education, and also agreed to share her views about what she wanted from the education system for her children. Julie checked the full transcript of her story and this new version has been updated in 2016.

This parent had been involved in the PICL project, but only in a peripheral way. She attended a study group for six months and came to various other meetings and events.

Her story is an individual representation of the experiences of one parent and may help us to gain further insights about how we, as educators, can adapt our organisations and behaviour to accommodate the needs of a wider range of children and parents. Julie represents one minority group. Laevers (1995) refers to children who 'fall out of the boat', and this description seems to fit her childhood experiences.

Case study

JULIE'S STORY

What is different or special about this parent?

Julie attended the youth club in the centre as a teenager and then has had three children attend the nursery over a number of years. They are now aged 21, 16 and 9 years and Julie is about to become a grandparent. We feel that we know Julie quite well. She was not afraid to ask us for what she wanted for her children. Julie has engaged in adult community education and is therefore in a position to compare this model of education with her own earlier experience of schooling. Miller (2000: 140) says, 'the respondent will slant their account to fit with what they see as being the interviewer's area of interest and tell their story in a way that they believe will be sensible for the interviewer'. My role as interviewer was to listen to her story (initially in 2001 and revisited in 2016) and to try to discover whether, in her opinion, the PICL project had had an impact on her or on her children.

It became obvious during the interview that Julie had a huge personal agenda about her own schooling. The interview process itself gave her an opportunity to reflect on these experiences. Anderson (1987: 100) says, 'If we want to know how women feel about their lives, then we have to allow them to talk about their feelings as well as their activities'. The feelings about school that Julie expressed during the interview indicated the kinds of feelings that entering school buildings might still evoke for her today. Until she has some fresh and more positive 'first-hand experience' of school or education, that earlier experience continues to be the basis of thoughts, feelings and actions (Easen et al., 1992).

Julie's story about her education (a brief summary)

Julie enjoyed junior school but was repeatedly excluded from senior school for disruptive behaviour. She was not allowed to sit any GCSEs, although she says she was 'good at Maths and English'. Julie feels she has done well, compared with many of her peers, who are 'junkies, alcys [alcoholics] and shoplifters'. She mentions 'a guy who was in my class all the time up the town. It used to be him I used to mess about with – he's an alcy, a junkie – he's a shoplifter'.

When Julie's first child, David, came to nursery, she was invited to record what David was doing at home, and she began to keep a diary. She says that is what 'made me want to go back to learning'. She appreciated understanding what and how David was learning, 'whereas before I wouldn't probably think of ... well, he's throwing things, now I think "scattering"'. She recognised his schema.

As an adult, Julie began studying GCSE maths and English, but found it difficult along with housework and a part-time job. She got a distinction on a computer course but says she 'is not really interested in computers'.

In 2001 with one child, Julie decided that she really wanted to work with 'problem children'. She began a college course in the next town, but was told she had missed too much time after the first three weeks (both she and David had been ill). She still felt that things were stacked against her – she was juggling housework, money and caring for David. Subsequently Julie had two more children. She became involved in the study of 'Resilience and Well-being' at Pen Green when her daughter was in nursery (2001–2004). Her youngest child (born seven years later) has additional needs and needed several operations as a young child. Julie has been involved in his learning journey with nursery and now with his primary school.

Strauss and Corbin (1990: 63) say, 'One can count "raw" data, but one can't relate or talk about them easily'. The full transcript of Julie's story can be analysed by 'conceptualising the data', that is, 'taking apart' each sentence and coding 'each discrete incident, idea or event'. When each incident has been coded in this way, we can compare phenomena with each other and examine any emerging themes.

After the initial 'open coding' of Julie's story, a pattern began to emerge. Central to that pattern were Julie's feelings (Table 6.1).

Julie's story analysed – childhood, lived experience

Table 6.1 Julie's childhood experience

What was said or done	Feeling invoked	Consequences
Being blamed by teacher for brother's bad behaviour	Anger	Wanting revenge/disrupt lessons
'They knew where I came from.'		'I start messing about.'
Being treated as less important than other children 'I wanted to take exams. I wasn't allowed.'	Feeling like an'outcast'	Disrupting lessons and exclusion
A couple of teachers 'all right'	Not specified	
Getting caught or being blamed 'I was either kicked out or on the report card.'	Numbness	Accepting exclusion as norm
Fighting with teacher over jacket 'She's pulling it and I'm pulling it.'	Loss of control – going crazy/anger 'I started kicking – I don't know what I done.'	Being kicked out
Exaggerating and lying about school events at home'I'm going to get done if I go home with this little rip.'	Fear of getting into trouble	Excluded/'bored at home' 'It's a loser's game.'
Community placement 'You could get privileges.'	Excitement/enthusiasm	Enjoyment

There seems to have been a chain of events (Table 6.1) that was repeated during Julie's secondary education:

1. (conditions) being treated unfairly
2. (phenomenon) feeling angry
3. (context) teachers don't help
4. (action) being disruptive
5. (consequences) being excluded (Strauss and Corbin, 1990: 124).

This happened over and over again. Repressed anger, which spilled out when Julie lost control, seemed justified when we consider what happened from her perspective. Goleman (1996: 60) says:

> Given the roots of anger in the fight wing of the fight-or-flight response, it is no surprise that Zillman finds that a universal trigger for anger is the sense of being endangered. Endangerment can be signaled not just by an outright physical threat but also, as is more often the case, by a symbolic threat to self-esteem or dignity: being treated unjustly or rudely, being insulted or demeaned, being frustrated in pursuing an important goal.

Julie's mum would always go down to the school 'with the pram' and 'argue' with the teachers. Julie and her mum are alike. When her dad became involved, he would only say one word, 'Bed!' Mostly, Julie was 'grounded' by her parents for her behaviour.

Once, she remembers, she and her mum had to go in front of the governors: 'Me and my mum on two seats in front of about 15 governors'. On this occasion, Julie felt that her mum was 'made to feel small', and Julie 'felt bad' about that. Julie was asked to leave the room so that her mum could defend her behaviour.

Deep down, Julie knew that she was capable of studying and passing exams. Sadly, she became resigned to not fulfilling her potential. In the context of the classroom, where she felt 'an outcast', the only way in which she could feel powerful was by disrupting lessons.

According to Robin Hobbs, a psychotherapist running a Pen Green staff training session, one of our basic psychological needs is for excitement or drama (Hobbs, 1998), and school, to Julie, was generally boring. Children and young people who primarily learn kinaesthetically need first-hand experiences and to experiment in a practical way with various resources in order to sustain interest and to learn (Gardner, 1991). Julie opted for the '14–16 Curriculum Project' so that she did not have to sit still and listen in school all day and every day, and could participate in some practical and vocational experiences. This indicates that she recognised that her own learning style required variety.

Research on how our brains work shows that, broadly speaking, men are 'less likely to endure routine patiently', that 'boys are harder to teach', and that 'disruptive behaviour is not voluntary' (Moir and Moir, 1999: 134). The type of behaviour Julie displayed is more typical of the 'macho culture' of boys (Epstein et al., 1998: 82).

Often there is a 'class dynamic' to this type of challenging behaviour. The stereotype is that middle-class, neat children work hard and prize academic achievement (Epstein et al., 1998: 100). In contrast, working-class children are sporty and can do well but only without appearing to do any work (ibid.).

What follows is Julie's experience of education, as an adult.

Julie's story analysed – adulthood, lived experience

Table 6.2 Julie's adulthood experience

What was said or done	Feeling invoked	Consequences
Having to grow up/pregnant 'Shock! I didn't speak to anyone for six months.'	Fear/uncertainty	Isolation 'I'd walk to the shop for something to do.'
Finding out what was available 'I didn't know all this was here.'	Hope/enthusiasm	Start keeping diary '.... back into writing and understanding what he's doing.'
Start studying mathematics and English	Hopeful	Confidence
Took on too much 'I couldn't keep the two going.'	Had a 'downfall'/ despondent	Gave up English
Became too hard 'I started getting stuck on it.'	Despondent	Gave up mathematics 'I know it's there.'
Went on computer course 'Looked through Tresham leaflet – I was stuck in limbo.'	Able	Achieved distinction
Began college course 'I wanted to work with kids in children's homes.'	Hopeful	Setting long-term goal
Being treated like a child 'They forget all them young girls have got no family. We're changing it to this day, that time.'	Powerless/disheartened	Gave up
Being capable/looking after house 'I'll cook the dinners, clean the house.'	Proud	Self-respect
Caring what son thinks 'I hope I'm not a down and out.'	Pride	Dignity/responsibility

As an adult learner, Julie has had varied experiences (Table 6.2). Clearly, she is keen to learn, but when things become too difficult to sustain, she does not have earlier positive experiences to remind her that she can succeed.

Julie has experienced the system and people within it as 'unfair'. Several times she has begun studying and has not gone as far as she hoped. It seems that her expectation of herself is that she will not succeed. Each time she has to give something up or the obstacles become too great, she says that she is 'disheartened', that she 'knew it would come'. She says, 'school dis-heartened me'.

This is an analysis of a chain of events that has occurred more than once for Julie, as an adult:

1. (conditions) being treated unfairly
2. (phenomenon) feeling despondent
3. (context) being treated like a child/feeling powerless
4. (action) giving up
5. (consequences) not achieving goal.

This chain of events does not mean that Julie has not made progress. It means that she has *not yet* achieved all the goals she has set herself. Dweck talks about the 'Power of Yet' in that we can change our mindset by thinking about 'learning goals' rather than 'performance goals' and be told by our teachers and tell ourselves we have 'not yet' reached a goal (Dweck, 2014).

Ironically, Julie did well on a computer course, which, she says, 'is not really what I want to do'. She described herself as 'being in limbo' after giving up mathematics and English, and looking for something else to do. She sees using computers as a useful skill, but she would not want to make a career of it.

As time went on and Julie gained experience in various courses, she became much clearer about what she wanted to do and why she wanted to do it. She sees herself working with disadvantaged children in this area of the town, mainly because she has a social conscience and cares about facilities for young people like herself. She feels that there is even less provision for teenagers now than when she was a teenager. She has some good memories of attending a youth club at Pen Green Centre when the building was much larger. She says that the youth workers 'treated us like adults'.

Julie says that using the centre has been significant for her, that she 'started to learn from' when she discovered what was on offer for adults in the centre.

In 2001, Julie's belief in her own ability was still tenuous. With a few more small successes, she might gain confidence and be prepared to fight for her right to an education, which suits her pocket and family commitments.

In 2016 Julie says that she is ready to take on some voluntary work now that her youngest child is 9 years old. He still needs her support but she now feels that she has some experience to offer to other parents.

Case study

RENATE'S STORY

What is different or special about this parent?

I got to know Renate (real name) when I was using Pen Green services with my granddaughter and she was attending with her youngest child. We would often chat over the water or sand tray or in the soft play area while the children were playing. We both seemed interested in encouraging the children's explorations and would discuss how sometimes in the more formal environment of school, those explorations were sometimes curtailed. So, I immediately picked up that Renate was deeply interested in her children's education in the broadest sense.

I also realised that Renate was German and I was interested in hearing about her trips back home as I lived in Germany for a few years when my children were young. The most interesting fact about Renate and her partner and five children was that they are currently living in a double decker bus on a traveller site in Corby.

As time went on, I noticed that Renate had begun volunteering in one of the groups I attended, which showed a deep commitment to contributing to the experiences of other families using the centre. This also meant that Renate had engaged in some adult learning experiences within the centre. Two of her children had attended the nursery and her youngest was just settling in.

So I asked Renate if I could interview her to discover more about what had attracted her to the centre and how she had become engaged, particularly in her children's learning.

Renate's involvement at the Pen Green Centre

Renate was born and brought up in Germany. She had an average school experience but had an older sibling who was quite academic. She trained to be a hairdresser when she left school but has never used that skill.

She met her husband when travelling in India 21 years ago and they now have five children aged 20, 16, 11, 9 and 3 years. Their eldest child is a daughter and the other four are sons. She says '... from then on we've travelled quite a lot trying to find a place to settle really ... from Germany, England, India, other places in Europe'. In 2004:

> just before Ashanti was born, we came back to this country and lived in Wales for four years ... we were very unsettled there and moved six or seven times. It was nice being in Wales. There's a nice, big alternative scene and everything. We just didn't find a proper place to settle. We were living in a truck. We tried to find a place and at one point we were made homeless ... it was really difficult and Ashanti was ill quite a lot. He had a weak chest and the climate in Wales wasn't very good for him. Then a place came up here to live ... we were about to move anyway ... we didn't know where to go ... we thought 'Give it a try'. It's more the way we wanted to live anyway ... being in a vehicle. So now we live in a double decker bus. That was 2008. Ashanti then came to nursery when he was just over three.

I asked what attracted Renate to Pen Green: 'It was basically because where we moved to (the site), the people there, they'd all been through nursery. I think

(Continued)

(Continued)

a couple worked here as well. They said "You'll have to have a look at Pen Green, definitely."' Renate went on to say that:

> Some of our older children had been in and out of nursery ... they'd been to a Steiner nursery ... I was really (unsure) ... I'm not a town person. I was a bit dubious about going to a town nursery.

I asked whether Renate remembered the first time she came to Pen Green: she recalled meeting Diane (one of the Family Workers) at Messy Play (a drop-in group for parents and children):

> It was just the fact that straight away we had somebody to talk to. Diane's really open and said 'Yes I know all of these people (from the site). Some of them have been in my group. There's a boy the same age as Ashanti'.

Renate recalled that 'They were all quite interested in our lifestyle. It's great that you don't feel left out. There's so much acceptance, especially in Corby. It helps that there are so many different nationalities'.

Following on from this first meeting, Renate described how Diane arranged for Ashanti to start nursery and to be part of her family group. It took a long time for him to settle:

> It seemed to go on for weeks and weeks and weeks. Once he settled, he was just so happy here ... it was so lovely seeing him develop self-confidence, being happy and being able to talk to other people.

Renate's next son was two years younger so for a short time both boys attended the nursery and Renate attended the PICL study group and put together a portfolio about both children's learning:

> It was just so lovely seeing the little films every time and what they'd done and also seeing the other kids ... Because I do feel conscious of my lifestyle and sometimes you see people's reaction. Some people, they just 'Oh my God!! Help! Oh no!!' and they never talk to you again. It's really nice breaking down those barriers and realising that you're just another person.

The documentation of the children's learning is important to Renate:

> I've seen so many nurseries in so many different countries and I know a lot of my friends in Germany work in nurseries. I very proudly bring my Pen Green folder and they're like 'Ahh!! We would never be able to do that!' None of the other workers would even think of doing something like that. It does make you feel really good.

She also showed off the portfolio she had put together from attending the study group. Her friends were 'amazed to think people do involve parents'. Renate went on to describe her view that:

> Most of the time you pass on the responsibility and for me, that is so strange ... It's such a lovely part before they actually have to go to school. If you miss that ... if you just let that go so easily ... I'm sure you'll regret it some day.

I asked about the key child development concepts and whether they were helpful to Renate when thinking about her children's learning:

> Yes especially with well-being because like I said Ashanti was so shy and inside himself ... the longer he stayed, the more you could see he did relax ... it's such a long process when they've been ill, they want to be part of something but something seems to be holding them back 'cos the whole constitution has been so shaken.

Renate could also recognise the boys exploring trajectories and lines:

> They used to have this piece of foam and they used that as a car ferry 'cos we'd just been to Germany. All the cars had to be parked in exactly the right way and a lot of transporting – they always loaded the cars up and moved the cars around.

Renate also reflected on her daughter's play when she was younger, saying that 'She did a lot more role-play and dressing up ... she would dress up the boys. She was a lot more into boxes and enveloping and bags – she had loads of bags'.

Renate finished by reflecting on the great relationship Ashanti and JJ have now at 11 and 9.

Analysing Renate's Story: The important factors

It has to be acknowledged that staff at Pen Green spend a great deal of their time investing in relationships. So it was no coincidence that Renate and her family, when they moved to Corby, the community they became part of, knew of and were known to Pen Green staff already. The initial factor seemed to be the *recommendation* from this minoritised group that Pen Green had something to offer to all families. As we have seen, Renate was already interested in her children's education so it was not a huge step for her to visit and try out some of the services on offer. The next factor seemed to be the *acceptance and interest* Diane showed in the family's lifestyle. As a nursery Family Worker, Diane also acted very quickly in *offering a nursery place* to Ashanti. All barriers were removed. Diane seemed to act autonomously. Only a great deal of discussion and professional development could result in a worker feeling confident enough to act so spontaneously. Next was the *settling-in*, which took much longer than the usual two weeks and meant that Renate got to know other staff and they got to know her. Eventually when two of her children were attending the nursery, Renate attended a study group and appreciated getting to know and being accepted by other parents, as well as discussing the four theories.

Renate has gone on to become a volunteer in a weekly group and is currently training to be a yoga teacher.

Summary

- Recommendation – other site families knew of and recommended the Pen Green Centre.
- Immediate acceptance by the first worker Renate came into contact with.
- The offer of a nursery place for her son.
- The settling-in period could last as long as it needed to for Ashanti's well-being.
- Renate joined a study group when she was ready to and made a portfolio about her two sons' learning.

The adults' learning processes

Julie has learnt to control her anger but still feels that the system is unfair. She seems resigned to not yet achieving her personal goals. Renate has found a place where she and her family feel accepted although she still hopes to continue travelling in the future.

We hope that by engaging parents in the PICL project, and encouraging them to discuss their children's emotional and intellectual development, many of them will feel confident enough to discuss their children's all-round development with other professionals.

We want parents to be involved in discussing their children's education. Listening to Julie's and Renate's stories can help us to be more aware of some of the barriers to coming into nursery or school for a minority of parents.

The barriers to becoming involved from the parents' perspectives

Personal and interpersonal barriers

Julie expressed personal feelings that might be evoked whenever she enters a school environment and might therefore prevent her from feeling at ease in such environment:

- anger, fear and anxiety
- not fitting in
- feeling undervalued
- feeling numb
- isolation
- tendency to run away/avoid authority
- inadequacy.

Some of these feelings were evoked originally because of the way Julie was treated by other people in the school environment, usually teachers. Her feelings about teachers and other authority figures might also be reinforced by family attitudes. These attitudes to other people are described as interpersonal.

Slighted pupils can react by telling lies, exaggerating, dramatising, running away from school and disrupting lessons. They feel justified in behaving in this way.

The role of Julie's parents was crucial. They were unable to convince her that attending school and working hard would have long-term benefits. Her parents felt uncomfortable in the school environment. They did not view teachers as being like them and therefore they were 'unconfident' in dealing with them assertively.

Renate's experience, as she described it, was very different. However, she did allude to having adopted a different lifestyle and to being shunned by some people, when they heard that she and her family chose to live in a double decker bus. So she did face some similar challenges and possibly felt that she did not 'fit in'. Renate was fortunate in meeting Diane, who was interested in getting to know Renate and her family, and Renate had the confidence, over time, to get to know some of the other parents.

Organisations are usually run by powerful people or people who have succeeded in attaining a position of authority. Often they are run to suit the majority, and this may exclude minorities. We are aware of 'institutional racism'; that is, organisations may have rules or structures that prevent minority ethnic groups from joining. Schools sometimes have rules that prevent some children from having an equal opportunity to attend; for example, obliging pupils to buy an expensive uniform. These sorts of barriers are structural.

Structural barriers

The over-structuring of the curriculum seemed to be a barrier to Julie becoming engaged at school. There seemed to be a lack of information for pupils and their parents about courses. Julie did not seem to realise that if she chose the 14–16 Curriculum Project, she could not sit her GCSEs. Julie's parents were not knowledgeable about curriculum issues. Were any efforts made by the schools to communicate with them about curriculum matters? Did they attend open evenings? If not, how would they know what was available for their children? Were open evenings easily accessible?

When Julie's jacket was torn in a tussle with a teacher, that was a huge issue for her. She felt she had to exaggerate what had happened so that she was not blamed for spoiling her new jacket. In this instance, her mum went straight down to the school to complain. Replacing the jacket was a serious concern in Julie's household. Money is often tight and prevents some children from taking part in extra-curricular activities that might engage them more than the regular curriculum.

Often transport to nursery or school can be an issue. In Renate's case, she drives and has transport but if that was not the case, Pen Green have a minibus and volunteer driver, so children can be collected from home to come to nursery. Timings are fairly flexible at Pen Green and there is no uniform, so families are encouraged to dress their children in old clothes that will not be spoilt by messy play.

Strategies we have used to engage Julie and Renate and other parents at Pen Green

Bearing in mind the sorts of barriers that may have prevented parents from participating in education in the past, we have developed strategies, set out as follows.

To overcome barriers connected to personal feelings

Often parents are anxious and lack confidence. If we accept them and their children and genuinely like them, parents will begin to loosen up. We must always be scrupulously fair, and sometimes this involves explaining our decisions and policies to parents. They have a right to know how decisions are made. Whenever possible, we can involve them in the decision-making process. We always try to listen to complaints and apologise if we are in the wrong.

It is important to acknowledge feelings, the parents' and their child's. Often something quite small makes parents angry. If their child goes home in wet socks, they are entitled to feel cross with us for not noticing. We can apologise and make sure we check socks in future.

We offer one-to-one support if parents are shy or lack confidence in a group situation. Sometimes they might want to express an anxiety, or we can spend time discussing the key concepts and how they relate to their child's progress.

Sometimes parents need convincing that they and their child have potential. We closely observe children, and our observations are invaluable information to pass on to parents on a daily basis if possible. This can alert the parent to specific things to watch out for at home and to share with us.

We often reflect back to parents the major role we see them playing in their child's development and learning. For example, when Julie began keeping a diary about David's play, he was seeing her writing each day and that increased his knowledge of communication. Soon after, he became interested in numbers and letters. When Renate attended the study group and focused on her two boys' learning, she was making their learning visible to the boys and their Family Worker, as well as to other people.

To overcome barriers connected to attitudes to other people

We want parents to get to know us as individuals and we want to get to know each of them as an individual. The only way to do this is to spend time together. During the two weeks that parents spend settling their children into nursery, we have a golden opportunity to chat informally with them and to get to know a bit about them. It is only fair to tell them about ourselves and our families, if they are interested.

Once we know something about their life, we can try to engage them in coming to a group. Some parents might be ready to study or meet with other parents to discuss their children. Others just want to get a job or have some time to themselves. We have high expectations of parents and we know that the majority want more information about how children learn and how they can help them.

As time goes on, there are many other ways that we can build our relationships with parents. We can invite them on a trip with their child or to a social event in the centre, or ask them to show visitors around the centre. This acknowledges that they are our equals, that we enjoy and value time spent together, and that they have gained knowledge as a user of the services, which they can share with visitors. Renate recently spoke to a group of trainee teachers about her experiences as a parent and shared some of her beliefs about education, which was illuminating for the group.

Although we are working hard to build relationships, we try not to patronise parents. Being honest with them is important. Parents who are not confident about writing often like using a video camera. Often fathers are interested in technology for themselves and for their children. Julie's partner became very engaged in observing David when they borrowed the nursery video camera.

To overcome barriers to do with the rules and structure of the organisation

When the organisation is inflexible and unresponsive, it is not helpful. We find it is a good rule of thumb to think through the reasons for having rules.

Coming out of the organisation and making visits to children's homes on a routine basis is something that staff and parents seem to appreciate. Julie says, 'When

Lorna (family worker) came, David was taking her up to his bedroom. He thought everyone lived at nursery. I said, "Lorna's got a house. Lorna's got children."'

When we evaluate our work, it is important to ask parents how things have been for them. New ideas stimulate our thinking, and often these come from parents. We are constantly listening out for what parents want and trying to offer it.

How Julie got involved in the research and development project

Julie

- Became involved in attending a session on schemas.
- Kept a diary of what David became involved in at home and attended a weekly study group for six months.
- Borrowed the nursery video camera and Tommy got interested in filming David.
- Each year we run an assertiveness programme for the children who are due to start school. We call it 'Learning to be Strong'. We begin by having a parents' meeting to discuss the programme with parents. Julie and Tommy attended this meeting. In 2016 Julie said that she still uses those ideas with her 9-year-old.
- Julie went on a day trip to the Science Museum in London with other parents and staff and also attended a family group meeting at nursery.

Both parents came to a meeting about reports for school. During the interview, Julie said that the following ways of being involved were significant for her. Keeping a diary was a turning point for Julie. She said that that was 'when she started to learn'. She was 'back into writing and understanding what he's doing'. She also enjoyed attending the study group. Sometimes she would say outrageous things, but we all knew and liked her, and there was a spirit of fun in the group. Julie remembers borrowing the video camera, although it was Tommy who did most of the filming: 'David would carry on with what he was doing when Tommy filmed him'. The 'Learning to be Strong' parents' meeting was important and helpful to both parents. The discussion about bullying helped Julie and Tommy to make a difficult decision about which school to choose for David. The 'Learning to be Strong' sessions for David were 'well worth doing'. When David first started nursery, the family had just moved back to the area, and he was quite insecure. His family worker and parents put together a book containing photographs of people who were important to him. This 'family' book was significant for David. It helped him to settle at nursery. Julie says, 'He used to walk about carrying his book'.

How Renate got involved many years after the research and development project

Renate

- is currently settling her fifth child into nursery;
- joined a study group and produced a portfolio about her two sons' learning;
- is volunteering in a drop-in group for parents and children;
- has engaged in adult learning in the centre (e.g. breastfeeding support and a computer course).

Professional development for staff

All staff need to engage in continuous professional development. This may be through: visits to other centres, particularly where the practice is considered to be outstanding; a variety of experiences of working with parents within the centre, in groups for parents with their children and groups where parents are studying or engaging in activities without their children; in-service training either within the centre alongside colleagues or outside of the centre and feeding back to colleagues; and conferences or other events that enrich learning. As an organisation, we want to encourage staff to be reflective thinkers and reflexive practitioners. As mentioned in Chapter 4, an important process for all staff is monthly supervision during which workers can discuss and reflect on their experiences. The supervisor is there to reflect alongside, as well as to support and challenge, workers. These processes enable us to build a resilient workforce.

Suggestions for your own practice

- Monitor your involvement with each family – this can be done quite easily and visually by having a chart with family names down the left and ways of involvement across the top and either ticks or dates to denote actions.
- Share your fears, as a team, about what might happen if parents you are less drawn to become involved.
- Think of ways parents might feel more comfortable and valued, e.g. in a 1:1 situation or in a small group with a friend.

(Continued)

(Continued)

- Ask the parents themselves what they would like to discuss (rather than leaping in with your own agenda).
- Value and document what you observe their children doing.
- Be fair and be seen to be fair.

Key points

- All parents have a right to spend time with their child's family worker and discuss their children's learning.
- All parents have knowledge about their children's interests that they can share with us.
- Sometimes as staff, we are drawn towards parents who seem to be more like ourselves.
- It may be harder to convince some parents that we really value the information they can offer.
- Persistence does pay off and so does flexibility.

Recommended reading

Hayward, K., Fletcher, C., Whalley, M., McKinnon, E., Gallagher, T., Prodger, A., Donoyou, H., Potts, J. and Young, E. (2013) 'The architecture of access: a grounded theory on the nature of access to early childhood services within a children's centre, derived from nine parent voices', *European Early Childhood Education Research Journal*, 21 (1).

Websites

Joseph Rowntree Foundation: www.jrf.org.uk

7

Parents as researchers

Penny Lawrence, Hannah Howe,
Darren Howe and Sarah Marley

Introduction

This chapter describes a single participatory case study with:

- Oscar,
- Hannah and Darren, the parents of Oscar,
- Sarah, Oscar's Family Worker (key person), and
- Penny a doctoral researcher (see Figure 7.1 and 7.2).

The research was characterised by extensive dialogue between all participants and the chapter includes extracts from this process. Each of us had a different research emphasis:

- Hannah, Oscar's mother, was interested in seeing ways in which Oscar communicated with other children of his age. She wanted to understand how children communicate other than verbally.
- Darren, Oscar's father, was interested in seeing how Oscar deals with sharing with children his age. At home Oscar only shared his parents' attention with his brother Max, whereas at nursery there were many more children. Darren was interested in how Oscar managed with sharing in that context.

(Continued)

(Continued)

- Sarah, Oscar's Family Worker, focused on interactions where the children have very different intentions from each other. She was curious to observe the relationships Oscar developed with others and the strategies he used to engage others.
- Penny, the researcher, focused on moments where the child seemed to make decisions while interacting with other children. Penny is currently writing her doctoral thesis, 'Observing and Understanding Decision-Making in Two Year Olds', which includes the case study in this chapter.
- As the first author I will write in the first person and identify the other voices as they appear.

Figure 7.1 Penny (the researcher), Darren (Oscar's father), Hannah (Oscar's mother) and Sarah (Oscar's Family Worker)

Oscar was 14 months old when we first worked as a research team with parents on the Pedagogic Strategies project (Lawrence and Gallagher and The Pen Green Team, 2015; Lawrence and Gallagher, 2017). Our relationship was already established when we followed Oscar in a new case study, 'Being in Relation', until he was 34 months old and started the transition into a setting for over 3-year-olds. It was fundamentally important to us that we constructed the research relationship together at the outset and as we went along. We had regard for the differences in each other's roles and this helped us negotiate a power balance. Our understandings were generated as a process, travelling together in a participatory way (Haw and Hadfield, 2011; Kvale, 1996). As Hannah, Darren and Sarah reflected:

Sarah: Every step along the way you always said this is about all of us.

Hannah: You've sent information beforehand making sure that everybody had a chance to look through it, to have input, to take it away again and think about it. Like you really have valued it rather than it just being done because you feel you have to.

Sarah: We've felt like you wanted it [the input].

Darren: I feel like we have got closer to Penny and Sarah as we worked together on the project. I felt like I could be open and honest without feeling silly.

Penny: I wanted to acknowledge that you know Oscar much better that I do, and so I always felt like I was throwing some ideas out and seeing what resonated with you.

Another consideration was that involving parents in research could not be separate, it always involved the children. There was also Oscar's brother to bear in mind in observations at home. The children in any recording reviewed the videos and we sought the assent of the children and consent of all the families at all stages (see the later section on relational ethics).

In our experience the parents were actively constructing knowledge about their children before the project and this was validated by their participation:

Sarah: Parents reflect all the time, they are always trying to understand their children better, 'how can I understand what you're thinking, what you're trying to do?'. They are so curious about their children.

Hannah: It builds on your knowledge. I didn't know a lot of the words, I didn't understand until we were doing it so I learned the phrases and what they mean.

Sarah: Having the language to have the discussion about it.

Penny: I'm wondering if calling it a research project is making more obvious what it already is, but also ring-fencing it so some time does get set aside for it to go deeper, and introducing methods to research with.

Hannah: I definitely think having the title makes you think this is what I'm involved in rather than this is what I do everyday.

(Continued)

(Continued)

Hannah's comment, 'I learned the phrases and what they mean', is significant because we were aware of not only increasing knowledge, but also how that applies. We were building our understanding (Schwandt, 1999). We named the case study 'Being in Relation' during research discussions at the Pen Green Centre for Children and Families in England with Professor Vasudevi Reddy and Dr Ellie Singer about a relational approach to see the child both learning to be themselves with their own intentions, and learning to be with each other in learning relationships.

Preparing for the case study

Theoretical perspectives

Theories referred to in the case study include:

Inter-subjectivity and dialogic theory: Buber (1970); Duranti (2010); Gergen (2009); Linell (2009); Reddy (2008); Schütz (1966); Singer and de Haan (2007); and Trevarthen and Schögler (2007).

Intersubjectivity can be seen as the openness, the understanding of the other person to exist (Duranti, 2010).

Dialogic theory encompasses the approaches underpinning this study, it is an umbrella (Linell, 2009) for the theories of relationships we draw on to understand how children interact, and how we adults understand each other when we are interpreting the children. The 'I-You' relationship in Buber (1970) identifies an attitude of reciprocity between people, as distinct from regarding the other as an instrument for one's own purposes – an 'I-It' attitude. Mutuality was extended in Reddy's (2008) second-person approach through which the researcher acknowledges their relation with the participants.

Social-Constructivist Understanding: Schwandt (1999, 2000)

Competent children: Malaguzzi (1998a)

Adopting a social-constructivist stance[1] helps us answer the fundamental question, 'How should I *be* toward these people I am studying?' (Schwandt, 2000: 203).

---

[1]*Constructivism* 'preferred when the focus is on the active sense-making processes in the individuals when these individuals "construct" that which they think or talk about there-and-then, in the specific situations' (Linell, 2009: 105). *Constructionism* 'is used when the topic is those concepts, words, assumptons or theories that have already been "constructed", perhaps by our predecessors in sociohistory' (Linell, 2009: 105), i.e. the world is already populated with social constructions, assigned meanings.

The distinction of this stance is that it involves the observers (Schwandt, 2000), in this case our research team, in the shared construction, or construing of knowledge beyond an individual experience. As in the Reggio Approach, the children in this case study were viewed as competent protagonists (Hoyuelos, 2013; Malaguzzi, 1998a).

Multimodality: Goffman (1963); Kendon (1990, 2004); Kress and Van Leeuwen (2001); McNeil (1992); Norris (2004, 2011); and Streeck, Goodwin and LeBaron (2011).

We have been able to apply the theory of multimodality to explore how the children communicate, significantly for this age group, including combinations of non-verbal communication, e.g. gesture, gaze, etc. (MODE, 2012; Streeck et al., 2011). Multimodality aligns with the hundred languages of children celebrated in Reggio Emilia. Although we included speech, Kress and Van Leeuwen (2001) argue that in certain contexts spoken language cannot be thought of as the primary mode of communication. This project draws further on the dialogic theory of inter-subjectivity to study embodied making meaning with and relating to others, the 'we' quality of togetherness (Schütz, 1966; Singer and de Haan, 2007). Both Gergen (2009) with co-action and relational flow, and Trevarthen and Schögler (2007) conceptualised inter-subjectivity as a dance of interaction. In summary, we worked with relational dialogic theory in our research dialogue, and in our study of Oscar's dialogue.

Methodological approach

We worked together in a participatory approach using video observations. The relationship of the parents with the researcher and practitioner was integral to the approach.

Ethics

To be clear, the main and overriding responsibility for the conduct of the project was mine as the researcher, however, it was a dialogical methodology integrating all our values (Linell, 2009). As a research group we were developing judgement not only of the children's experiences, but also of how we conducted ethical relationships in our setting. Rather than expecting parents to develop expert researcher or practitioner knowledge, our research demonstrated 'a particular attitude that leaves open the possibility for ethical reflection' (Ramaekers and Suissa, 2011: 198). Leading the research we were mindful of our diverse roles and

(Continued)

(Continued)

knowledge bases, not assuming nor intending that parents, practitioners and researcher were, or ought to become, the same.

We sought the assent of the children and consent of the families. We were mindful of what the children would think about the research in future years (Harcourt and Keen, 2005). We also had a responsibility for thinking about the participation of the parents of the other children. When were they going to see the video clips? What were they going to know about who was seeing the clips? I was never just working with one set of parents because as soon as there is another child involved in interactions, there is also another set of parents.

Participation throughout the process

As parents, practitioners and researcher, we shared the responsibility for revising the initial transcripts to arrive at the final text representing the experience:

Sarah: None of it was edited so we could say 'I didn't mean to word it like that, thinking about it that's not what I meant' and we could always go back and change it.

The parents and staff were not expected to write the transcripts. According to the British Educational Research Association (BERA) guidelines (2011) we need to balance a manageable amount of involvement and allow for participation without having predetermined most of the interpretation:

Sarah: You facilitated it and made it happen in terms of us meeting and having the video prepared. In terms of the discussions I don't think you even spoke at the beginning of it. You'd play the video and wait for us ...

Hannah: Wait for us to see what we'd pick up from it.

Darren: I felt it was good that Penny let us watch the footage and pick out bits to focus on first before sharing what she noticed or thought.

The expectations of participation were realistic and they exceeded a box-ticking exercise of grabbing a few sentences from a parent (Kvale's 1996 mining) and made the relationship effective rather than tokenistic.

Multimodal interaction analysis

Multimodal interaction analysis gave us the visual method and language to read the potential non-verbal meaning in Oscar's interactions. Our approach was inspired by the work of Sigrid Norris (2004, 2011). For example Darren interpreted how Oscar interacted with another child Henry while both of them were drawing. Oscar manipulated the paper, used gaze towards Henry and gesture pointing to direct Henry's attention. Frequently observed modes were:

Vocalisation – any sound with which the children may express themselves and through which they may interpret in others.

Gestures – indications such as dietic gestures (pointing) and iconic gestures (hand back to indicate 'all done' or 'over now').

Manipulation of objects – through which children relate to their environment as well as each other.

Gaze – we noted when each child was looking at another child and when they were looking at other people and objects and so on.

Posture – we noted the shape of the body in any position.

Proxemics – we noted if the children got closer, increased their proximity to each other or increased the distance.

We selected which modes seemed to be important in each episode for our detailed analysis. According to Norris it would help us see how the children were paying attention to each other, first through what individuals expressed, and second through the other child's awareness and reaction (Norris, 2004: 4–5). The children we observed interacted by expressing their perceptions, thoughts and feelings, intentionally or not (Norris, 2004: 82). The challenge that multimodal interaction analysis does not address is what people are *actually* perceiving, thinking and feeling. We acknowledged that the children's experiences may sometimes have been different and more complicated than that which they expressed.

Data analysis

Observations were made in the setting for children under the age of 3 attended by Oscar at The Pen Green Centre in Corby, UK, and at home in recordings made by his parents. During the course of the study we had over 50 hours of recordings

(Continued)

(Continued)

with Oscar interacting. From these recordings each month we selected an episode of typically three minutes duration of sustained interaction. The episode was determined by the children having a high level of involvement (Laevers, 1996) and their working consensus to maintain the interaction (Goffman, 1963; Kendon, 1990). The episodes included a decision[2] (for example Oscar either continued to persevere with a first option, or changed track to pursue a second), and ended when there was no further interaction between the children.

Figure 7.2 The process of open and structured analysis of video clips

We needed sufficient time to develop our thinking and to balance this with requiring only a manageable amount of time for participants to analyse together as a group. We started from an uninterrupted open viewing of the whole video episode together, after which we discussed our first interpretations of the experience in 'flow' and identified critical sequences that triggered questions to analyse further. These critical sequences were the focus for the second cycle, the detailed analysis with a shorter unit of analysis, at times 15 seconds. I transcribed this and we then viewed the detailed transcript as a group, before returning to

[2]In this study decisions are understood to be moments when the child, while relating with another child, seems to have paid attention to more than one possible course of action and selected one *after consideration* (*Concise Oxford English Dictionary*, 2011).

the complete video clip for the last cycle, an open viewing. This re-encounter placed the detailed analysis back within context, within the flow of the child's experience, and our evaluation drew upon this renewed whole open view.

We used ELAN, a professional tool for the creation of complex annotaion on video and audio.

Findings

This chapter selects one interaction in the setting for children under the age of 3. In this interaction Oscar was 30 months and Camille 29 months-old (Figure 7.3).

Figure 7.3 Oscar with Camille and the rings

Description of the episode from initial notes

I observed the children highly involved while taking turns to slot seriated rings on a ring holder pole. They were both animated and employing a broad range of modes: maintaining close proximity to each other; manipulating objects; gaze; facial expression; vocalisation; and sequences of changed posture in exaggerated upper body movements. These exaggerated movements were synchronised with vocal exclamations after the completion of an action when a ring had been slotted on or removed. At a certain point Oscar moved over to the side to look at some larger rings and put one over his own head. Camille stayed with the smaller rings. Oscar returned and continued the turn-taking interaction with Camille and the small rings, slotting them on all the way up the pole and then taking off

(Continued)

(Continued)

several at a time. When the pole was empty they made louder vocalisations and Oscar took the pole and walked a few paces away, to put it around a corner. He then returned to the larger rings. He was orientated towards Camille and called for her attention. After a short while he brought a large ring closer to her, and in this close proximity she paid attention to Oscar as he put the large ring over his own head. She then stood up and walked over to another large ring and placed it over her head, orientated towards Oscar (Figure 7.4).

Figure 7.4 Camille and the large ring

Findings from the open analysis

The open analysis identified the overall tone of the interaction, evident in the smiling, humorous facial expressions and the playful manner in which the rings were handled. We also appreciated the effort to which Oscar went to engage Camille:

Sarah: He's playing with them really playfully, isn't he? He's really trying to get her attention.

Hannah: Look at his face. I think he's so expressive with his face, especially when he wants somebody else to interact with him. He seems to be quite the comedian doesn't he? Trying to make her laugh.

We acknowledged inter-subjectivity in the 'we' quality of togetherness expressed in their synchronised movements as well as vocally:

Hannah: They worked quite well together without really needing to talk to each other about what they're doing. They just knew, 'I'm going to do this, you're going to help me do this and we're going to do this together'.
Darren: and they both jump about every time they put the ring on.

We zoomed out to consider the backdrop, the broader context of Oscar's learning in terms of schema, a theoretical framework embedded in observations at Pen Green (see Chapter 4). Schema are 'patterns of repeatable actions [or thought] that can lead to early categories and then to logical classifications' (Athey, 2007: 49). We interpreted his actions with the rings, as a repeated interest in 'going through' a boundary schema:

Penny: Does he have a hoola hoop at home?
Darren: We used to.
Hannah: No, but we've got one of those pop-up tunnels that he loves putting over his head.
Darren: When we've been to 'Growing Together'[3] there's a tambourine down there and he likes putting that over his head.
Sarah: He's going through a boundary. There is a book box [shelf] where he can put his feet through.

We found that a focal point for detailed analysis was the moment when Oscar removed the small ring holder pole:

Darren: This interests me because he was sharing the rings with Camille for so long, and then he's taken the ring holder away to get Camille's attention.
Hannah: he did the 'Well I'm taking this away now 'cos I want us to both do the [large] ring'.

(Continued)

[3]A parent and child group at Pen Green.

(Continued)

Sarah: I found that bit quite interesting where he did take it away. What was his intention with that? I think he thought 'Right I have to get this out of the way so you can focus on these [large rings] now'.

Penny: So there was something maybe about changing the focus.

Sarah: and I don't think it was enough for him that he just explored those on his own. I think he really wanted to explore them with her.

Penny: Being in Relation – doing that kind of thing but with somebody.

Hannah: He's in a very sociable mood. He seems to be doing things for Camille's amusement as well as his own. I wonder whether the interaction with Camille is more important than the actual activity?

What did the detailed analysis tell us?

In the episode with the sequencing rings both Oscar and Camille seemed to make conversation and meaning through their handling of the rings, and this became more apparent in the detailed analysis. The children used their readings of each other to make their own co-ordinated responses and decisions in the context of how the other was relating to them. This was true of both decisions made before any action such as moving one of the rings, and decisions made in the midst of an action, say holding a ring and performing the exchange of head and body movements and vocalisations:

Penny: How much is there an expectation that 'I'll do it and then you'll do it'? Like in a conversation, I'll speak and then you'll speak. There is a lot of interaction in many many ways combined.

Darren: and they both jump about.

Penny: I thought when I started that she'd started the reactions, that 'dance', but actually it was Oscar, but how do I know that if yesterday or the day before that they hadn't been doing it … so all we have is what we have in front of us. There does seem to be a well-matched watching of each other.

Sarah: Mirroring there of the arm. That's actually like a mirror image isn't it?

Penny: I hadn't seen that.

Sarah: Oscar's reaching out and she's reaching out. Both of them have got their hands up. He does that a lot doesn't he? He holds his hand like with *energy* I think you know like …

Penny: poised.

Sarah: Yes.

Penny: There are quite a few things they do because the other one does. He looks through the ring. She looks through the ring. But when he puts a ring over his head, she's got her back to him.

Using the detailed analysis we considered what Oscar could read in Camille's reactions, and she in his. We noted what each expressed and the other child's awareness and reaction (Norris, 2004: 4–5). In the details (Figures 7.5 to 7.10) we noticed that Oscar had not always been aware when Camille had been paying attention to what he was doing with the large rings. We had not seen this in the first uninterrupted viewing of the video clip. However he acted according to the awareness of where her attention was (see Figures 7.5, 7.6, 7.7, 7.8, 7.9 and 7.10).

Table 7.1 Penny (the researcher), Darren (Oscar's father), Hannah (Oscar's mother) and Sarah (Oscar's Family Worker)

Figure 5.	Figure 6.
Camille's attention may be not on what Oscar is doing when he first explores the larger rings	Then Camille's attention may be on what Oscar is doing but he did not see her looking
Figure 7.	Figure 8.
Camille's attention does not seem to be on what Oscar is doing when he puts the large ring over his head	Camille's attention may be on what Oscar is doing but he did not see her looking
Figure 9.	Figure 10.
Camille's attention may be not on what Oscar is doing when he brings the large ring over	Camille's attention may be on what Oscar is doing with the large ring

We noticed that Oscar had not tried to move Camille over to the large rings straight away after his first engagement with them, Oscar had returned to continue moving the small rings with her (Figure 7.11):

Penny: He's prepared to come back to her. She's stayed with that.
Hannah: I didn't remember him going back to that. In fact when Camille didn't follow him Oscar seemed happy to go back to the tower of rings (Figure 7.11.) before taking the pole away to possibly encourage Camille to change activity.

We also realised as the ring holder was emptied it had been Camille who had picked up the holder itself (Figure 7.12):

Hannah: So she picks it up first.
Darren: That's when he takes it away.

(Continued)

(Continued)

Figures 7.5–7.10 Where Camille's attention may be

The emptiness of the pole possibly afforded the moment to remove the pole and take the play on. Our co-constructed detailed reading also helped interpret the action and what the speech[4] had been when Oscar left the pole (Figure 7.13):

Hannah: He's saying 'All done' and now he's saying, 'That one'. So I wonder if he's saying, 'No we're all done with that, that one's next, we're playing with this one'.

[4]For example Oscar's speech was corrected on the detailed analysis from 'there you go' to 'All done'.

Figure 7.11 Oscar with large ring and Oscar returning to Camille

Figure 7.12 Camille lifting up the ring holder

(Continued)

(Continued)

Penny: and he does this kind of [gesture] one of these [iconic sweeping arm behind him] gestures.

Even after removing the ring holder Oscar continues to work with where he perceives Camille's attention to be,

Hannah: Even when he took that away she still didn't go to the hoops [big rings] like he was wanting.

Penny: Where was her attention? You wouldn't necessarily know that on your first viewing that she had her back to him. (Figure 7.9)

Hannah: And then Oscar tries to get her attention again to possibly say 'look at these, these are fun, join me'? (Figures 7.9 and 7.10)

Sarah: I think Oscar wanted to engage Camille in a game putting his whole body through the rings, and for him the only way to draw her attention from the seriated rings to the larger ones was to physically move the pole away. He places it at the bottom of the corridor and he says, 'All done'. By his body language there, that frame particularly (see Figure 7.13) he's saying 'All done' and we're going to leave that there now, a full-stop. Then he goes straight over to the larger rings so I think this is him saying 'Look Camille, come and engage with this with me'. He keeps looking to Camille as if for her to engage with him with the larger rings.

Although I made the transcription on ELAN we all engaged with interpreting the detailed analysis:

Hannah: This links particularly with my research question about seeing the ways in which Oscar communicates with other children. Vocalisation including speech is of course important, and we can see here so are the other modes of manipulating objects and gaze. We've seen Oscar and his peers using these modes repeatedly. I think you definitely see more of him and you think, 'Oh yes, he did do that', and then you slow it down and go, 'Wow, look he did that as well!' I think it's just seeing that detail of what may be going on.

As Hannah points out, the children do vocalise but the use of other modes, in this section the use of object manipulation and gaze, is comparatively denser in both complexity and intensity when it is perceived in the detailed view.

Figure 7.13 Oscar's gesture as he says 'All done'

Darren and Sarah also appreciated the insights gained from this level of analysis:

Darren: It's helped a lot because to watch it on the video it seems to me a lot quicker. When you're looking at the pictures you can see a lot more what's going on.

Sarah: Seeing the images frame-by-frame gave me the opportunity to closely observe subtle changes in Oscar's gaze, body language and proximity. There were moments when I noticed mirroring of gestures for the first time once looking at the transcripts. We had selected to focus on the moment when Oscar takes the ring holder away. Detailed analysis revealed subtleties in Oscar's interaction that we had not discussed in the open flow analysis. The co-ordination of the movements between them seemed very clear.

Camille and her family

In other circumstances we would have involved Camille's family in the interpretation at the same time as Oscar's family. They did consent to the research and the

(Continued)

(Continued)

interpretations of the research and staff team; however, they then moved to a different area and had a new baby. I met with Camille and her mother Susana at a later date when it was more convenient for them to participate. Camille noticed her own head shaking movements in particular, and Susana confirmed the range of ways that Camille moved the rings was typical of a dancing kind of creativity she sees at home, taking the initiative with her older brother:

Camille: I shaked my head.
Penny: Why do you shake?
Camille: So they will follow me.
Susana: Her brother, who's five, he follows Camille. Camille's very creative and when she's at Pen Green she got very comfortable and now she's very good. The way she tries to move the rings.

Camille's initiative changing from taking the small rings off the ring pole, to pick the holder up was significant for her, as it had been in Hannah's interpretation, noticing that she did it first (Figure 7.12):

Camille: Me!
Penny: Who decided?
Camille: It was *me*. I did it.

Susana interpreted Camille's reaction and decision after Oscar moved the ring holder:

Susana: at first her expression is [perplexed face].
Penny: Is Oscar taking away?
Camille: He took it away because I wanted to play with it.
Penny: ... and then?
Camille: so I not play with it.
Susana: She could still play [with small rings and holder] if she wanted. She would go there, pick it up and bring it back, but she changed her mind. I think so because she saw Oscar playing with the rings and she thought 'Oh I'm going to decide to play too'.
Penny: So she was fully aware that, she knew what she could do.
Susana: Yes, yes. I think so. Yes, because if she wants something, she tries to get it.

It seems that Camille understood that Oscar wanted to end the interaction with the ring holder. She had expressed uncertainty and then she had continued to handle the small rings. According to Susana, Camille was aware and capable of two immediate options open to her, playing with the small rings, or going to get the ring holder and continue playing with that. When he brought the large ring to her (Figure 7.9) she was paying attention to her foot. Susana translated Camille's comment 'meu pé' from their home language, Portuguese, which was perhaps about a sock or about not being trodden on. When she saw that Oscar returned with the large ring she did make the decision to join him with them.

Oscar's own reading

Hannah watched the rings clip with Oscar at home and he talked about what he had wanted to happen with the pole:

Hannah: Where are you going with that?
Oscar: What?
Hannah: Where are you taking it?
Oscar: 'way.
Hannah: Out of the way?
Oscar: Yeah.

I also explored Oscar's perceptions of his intentions by showing him the video episode:

Penny: What did you want to do?
Oscar: [makes arms moving upwards gesture] (Figure 7.14.)
Penny: Did you want to put it on your arm? (Figure 7.15.)
Oscar: Mmm [nods].

Figures 7.14 and 7.15 Oscar reviewing the video gesturing what he wanted to do, and a still from the interaction showing where he began to put the larger rings

(Continued)

(Continued)

Oscar's account is that he intended to remove the pole to a distance and wanted to go through the large ring. We could see thought in action (McNeil, 1992) in Oscar's explanatory gesture of his arms as if they had rings on them, and within the original interaction with Camille when he is thinking about and deciding on what he wants to do with the rings.

Discussion

We saw the details in the context of the whole uninterrupted episode in another open viewing. Our evaluation in the third cycle forms the basis for our discussion of the findings. Oscar made a choice, a decision about what to pay attention to, moving from the small to the large rings. Oscar's communication about the shift in focus took the form of speech, 'All done', and an iconic gesture (Figure 7.13), waving his hand back down at the pole left behind him. Oscar was signalling to Camille the shift in focus to the larger rings that was about to happen. In addition to the communicative function we could interpret this gesture as serving to punctuate and help Oscar restructure his own interaction – it was a reorientation for himself, a thought (McNeil, 1992). So this pronounced 'All done' gesture was functioning in two ways. The detailed analysis helped explain how Oscar structured the interaction and what he was focusing his attention on, including remaining aware of Camille; this is an example of secondary inter-subjectivity (Trevarthen and Hubley, 1978). What the movements and expressions communicated was a humorous mood (Bakhtin, 1986: 92), and perhaps expectations of inventiveness. Trevarthen read the rings episode in this study as being 'like a spontaneous piece of theatre' (2015), indicating the improvised-in-action quality of the interaction. Oscar's overarching decision was to interact with Camille, and within that he made decisions to interact with her using different modes, and with different objects, small and large rings. They both demonstrated dialogic agency in taking initiatives and maintaining the interaction (Goffman, 1963; Kendon, 1990). All these ways of being together are part of a 'relational flow' (Gergen, 2009), relating to each other while embedded in the flow of a number of intermingling activities.

Reviewing our research questions

Darren reviewed his research question in relation to Camille and the rings. Through the analysis he had seen how extensive Oscar's sharing was:

Darren: I think the rings clip fits with my interest in Oscar's sharing quite well. He seems to be really enjoying sharing his experience with Camille and taking it in turns with the rings. I had wondered if he was struggling with sharing when he took the pole away. He is just trying to encourage Camille to swap activities.

Hannah evaluated her original focus on Oscar's communication with other children:

Hannah: This clip makes it clear that Oscar is using so many more ways of communicating as well as verbal communication. I've learned more about the gestures he uses and can interpret them more easily to understand his needs. I've been able to see how he uses comedy and sensitivity when communicating with other children and I feel more secure knowing that he is enjoying his time at nursery with his peers when I'm not there.

Both parents had found answers to their questions and had seen more deeply into the processes within Oscar's interactions. The research process has implications for practice as when Sarah evaluated her likely responses in the future when children appear to have different intentions:

Penny: What difference has it made?

Sarah: I think initially I might have actually stepped in to defend her play a little bit. I'm still building a relationship with Camille so I don't know how much she might have asserted herself and said, 'No, I'm not finished, Oscar'. I might have said, 'Oh Oscar, I think Camille's still busy with the rings'. But after watching the video together, having the time to reflect on it, and really analysing the facial expressions and body language I don't think Oscar was taking it [the ring holder] away to be unkind. I think it was about changing the direction of the play and wanting Camille to be part of that with him.

Penny: So where does our process leave you? What would you do as a practitioner?

Sarah: I think we quite often talk about 'Watching and Wondering'. I think that's what I would have done, stepped back and let the children decide for themselves where this game is going to go next rather than jumping in. I was not too sure how she felt. She looked really unsure about what he was intending to do, and then she smiled. I think if Camille had looked at me I might have offered some reassuring body language or facial expressions, and maybe some words, 'Where's Oscar taking it?'

(Continued)

(Continued)

Oscar's humour softened the control he exerted to change the focus of their play. Without the humour his action may have been unacceptable in the setting, or to Camille, but she had been willing to read his signals. His social skills made it more acceptable to move their mutual play on. The timing was also a factor because Oscar's intervention occurred when the pole was empty, at an interval that Camille herself had marked with her own initiative lifting the pole. They had reached a moment when they had finished taking off all the small rings. The way in which Oscar made his decisions demonstrated subtle and complex dialogic agency.

Limitations of the study

This is one episode in the experience of two children. However it was selected and interpreted with the parents' lifetime knowledge of their child, and the practitioner's knowledge of him in the setting during a research period of 20 months. The quality of this study is enhanced by the rich information (Flyvbjerg, 2006) contributed by the participants and the thick description (Geertz, 1973; Ryle, 1949). Not all parents can or wish to participate in this detail of research, however we found a balance to make it a manageable and comfortable process. Although too time-consuming to be a routine part of practitioners' observation, assessment and planning making multimodal readings could be part of teacher training and CPD. We accept that our reading of one 2-year-old or even ten 2-year-olds cannot be generalisable to all. We will still need responsiveness to the actual children who are with us on an ongoing basis:

Implications for researching with parents

The practitioner and parent perspectives both appreciated the sustained dialogue and deeper thought process that they could sustain as part of a research partnership:

Sarah: Research really did strengthen our relationship, it did. The conversations were very different. They were much more focused on Oscar's interactions with others.

Hannah: There were small parts in a long conversation. So instead of 'look at Oscar, he was doing this', actually breaking it down side by side, you're having those deeper conversations. Having the time to go deeper, it opens up conversation that we wouldn't have had if the research project wasn't going on.

There were also benefits for the focus child, Oscar:

Sarah: I think it helped me to become a lot more in tune with Oscar. I could watch it really closely with you and see how you were with him at home and how adults and children were with him in the setting. Before we may have touched on things like relationships he was developing with other children.

Hannah: or interests.

Sarah: ... yeah, but not necessarily the cues for how he interacts with others, I don't think we'd have spoken about that.

Hannah: and the interpersonal skills that he's using.

We valued bringing together different interpretations, and linking to our existing knowledge of Oscar in the Pen Green Loop (see Chapter 8):

Sarah: When we were doing the open views, when we were watching the video for the first time, you [Hannah] would maybe say, 'Oh I think he was trying to do that' and I'd say, 'Do you know I really think he was trying to do *that*'. Although quite often it was the same thing that we thought.

Hannah: The video with the water and he was saying about fire, we were all trying to interpret it differently as to what he was saying and what he was meaning in the water. You wouldn't have thought about it quite so much without having everybody else's interpretation. It's not I'm right and you're wrong, it's 'Oh well he could be doing this and he could be doing that'.

Sarah: ... and we'd all see him do different things so I knew about his experiences in the Couthie [setting for children under the age of 3], you knew about his experiences at home, and may say, 'He was doing that last week with me at home too!'

Both Hannah and Sarah can make links from the research to their own study:

Hannah: I did my diploma after we started doing this so I think that it's helped me with my diploma no end. There's a whole section on working with parents so I did that from both sides, as a practitioner and then obviously I'm a parent when we're meeting, so I saw it from two sides.

Sarah: I'm thinking about my child study. I think I learned a lot from that about going deeper. This was different because it was about interactions with others, which is something I'd never done before. I found it really interesting how he interacts, I found it quite hard to take that step back.

(Continued)

(Continued)

Concluding remarks

We have not made identical interpretations, nor have we synthesised them into one version. The research questions of each have complemented and defined the other. Our participation was full and beneficial for ourselves and, since we were meeting to understand the children, it was beneficial for them. As parent participants, Hannah and Darren accomplished a working ethical relationship using theory and methods in a balanced three-way partnership with Sarah and me. Although there was no requirement to become research experts, the increased understanding of each was clear and confident. Significantly all of this is situated within a maintained dialogue and relationship with each other. The parents' voices were integral throughout the process right through to dissemination. This was demonstrated when we presented the research at symposia of the European Early Childhood Education Research Association Conferences in 2013 and 2014, and by our joint authorship of this chapter.

Suggestions for your own practice

- Think about your approach. What will your working relationship with parents be like? How can you make that happen in practice? Can you keep expectations open for their engagement with the theory and methods you are working with?
- Start small with a discussion group with the parents from your key group, so the research commitment is manageable (consider involving other parents at a later date). Arrange to meet a couple of families at a time to make the meetings straightforward to organise. Choose a video recording in your area of research interest such as outdoor play with natural materials. Select an experience the children are highly involved in, that matters to them, which will reward analysis, and the thought processes can be integrated into their learning. Make notes and share the notes and video for home viewing with absent family members after the meeting. Remember to view with the children and note their responses also.
- In addition to personal research interests you have identified for your own CPD, consider national agendas such as BERA and TACTYC calling for research to access parents' perspectives.

Key points

- Children are always integral to research with parents. Process assent of the children needs to be in place at all stages. View material with the children so that they can be informed about what is being observed and contribute also their responses to the interpretation.
- Access to the data – make material available. Send notes beforehand so everybody has a chance to look through the content, think about it and have input into the next discussion.
- Consider all the stakeholders. How will parents outside the research project have access to material and give informed consent?
- Consider meeting at the families' homes. This could facilitate children's participation in particular. This decision will be made according to convenience and personal preference, but is worth considering.
- Keep it manageable for everyone. Currency is more important than quantity. Being on the pulse of the children's interests will be more relevant than masses of material you cannot process together.

Recommended reading

Reddy, V. (2008) *How Infants Know Minds*. Cambridge, MA: Harvard University Press.
Singer, E. and de Haan, D. (2007) *The Social Lives of Children: Play, Conflict and Moral Learning in Day-care Groups*. Amsterdam: SWP.

Websites

British Education Research Association (BERA): www.bera.ac.uk/wp-content/uploads/2014/02/BERA-Ethical-Guidelines-2011.pdf
The Research Ethics Blog: http://researchethicsblog.com/2009/01/25/the-ethics-of-parents-as-researchers-and-of-researchers-as-parents

8

Dialogue and documentation

Sharing information, developing a rich curriculum and a responsive pedagogy

Margy Whalley and Marcus Dennison

Introduction

In this chapter, we describe:

- the conditions under which a *dialogue* can develop between parents and nursery staff, and nursery staff and other early childhood professionals;
- the way in which information about children's learning at home and at nursery can be shared, and common understandings negotiated through the *Pen Green Loop*;
- the development of a range of *documentation* and its use as a critical tool for communication with parents, and for staff development.

Reflective practice

> Practice needs theory and theory needs practice, just like a fish needs clean water. Practice apart from critical reflection, which illuminates the theory embedded in practice, cannot help our understanding. Revealing the theory embedded in practice undoubtedly helps the subject of practice to understand practice by reflecting and improving on it.
>
> (Freire, 1996: 108)

Staff at Pen Green are deeply concerned with *praxis* (Freire, 1970). Praxis means reflexive practice; that is engaging in a focused way, then spending time thinking about what you have done and making the links between theory and practice.

Colin Fletcher, formally a research professor at Cranfield and Wolverhampton universities and a long-term advisor to Pen Green, describes praxis in this way: 'praxis is about revising and refuting action on the basis of reflection' (Fletcher, 1999: 159). What this means for those of us working at Pen Green is that we begin the process of converting our best practice as early years practitioners into theory that can be understood and then discussed with parents and other early childhood educators.

Charles Handy, the management guru, describes those of us in the field of education as 'conceptually impoverished', without the conceptual skills to resolve the dilemmas we now face (Handy, quoted in Scott, 1996: 4). He argues, 'It is no good doing things right – using technical and human skills – if they are not the right things to do'. It seemed to us that his views were apt, but that they did not reflect practice in the early years phase of education. The early years education and care phase is conceptually rich; child development concepts underpin all our day-to-day practice. What has been lacking in the past for those working with children from 0–5 years is a *shared* language with which to articulate our *shared* understandings (Drummond, 1989; Whalley, 1994). We have made reference to this shared language in several chapters because it seems to us to be a central issue for early years educators.

Relatively few settings have appropriate levels of non-contact time for staff to reflect on their practice and learn to dialogue with each other, the children, the parents and the wider community. Staff at Pen Green have always had some non-contact time, although never enough of it, and we use it well. Our practice is underpinned by a strong theoretical framework. Many of the Pen Green staff team, like early years educators in other settings, first became interested in working with young children because of a passion for social justice and a commitment to children's rights. Staff were aware that critical reflection was the key to improving practice and that we had to constantly improve our own understanding if we were to honour the needs of the children. Janus Korczak, a paediatrician who dedicated his life to supporting vulnerable children in war-torn Poland, identifies the all-important emotional dimension to this learning process: 'Thanks to theory I know, thanks to practice, I feel. Theory enriches intellect, practice deepens feelings, trains the will' (Korczak, cited in Bettelheim, 1990).

Developing a dialogue

Paulo Freire (1970: 71), the radical Brazilian educator, tells us that there is a series of steps which have to be taken before participants, in this case early educators and parents, can engage in critical thinking. What we need to do is to:

- perceive our own ignorance and give up the idea that we are the exclusive owners of truth and knowledge;
- identify with others and recognise the fact that 'naming the world' is not the task of an elite;

- value the contribution of others and listen to them with humility, respecting the particular view of the world held by different people;
- get in touch with how much we need other people and have no fear of being displaced;
- be humble – have faith in others and believe in their strengths.

Over the last thirty-three years, Pen Green nursery staff and Pen Green Research Base colleagues have worked hard to develop this way of engaging in critical thinking in collaboration with parents and other professional colleagues.

Recognising our own ignorance

In 1997 when we first embarked on this research project some of the staff were parents themselves but not all; most lived locally but others travelled in. None of us knew enough about the context in which the children lived. Often the assumptions we made about children and families were wildly out of line with reality. Through regular home visiting on the parents' terms and at times that suited their family lifestyle, staff became more knowledgeable about the children and their families. With this information, we could celebrate the richness and diversity of the children's experiences and at the same time become more aware of the pressures children and families were experiencing in the late twentieth and early twenty-first century.

Identifying with parents

Early years educators quickly learnt to 'start from where people were'; parents who were desperately trying to hold down two jobs and struggling with childcare did not want to be perceived or defined as 'uncooperative' if they could not turn up for daytime or evening meetings at the nursery. However, without exception, they valued the time staff spent in visiting them at home. When staff sent videotapes home of the children playing and learning in nursery, parents were willing to reciprocate in kind. Often the nursery video tapes would contain just a short video vignette of a child deeply involved in an interesting learning experience; sometimes the child would be engaged in schematic behaviour which the family worker could not fully understand. The family worker would sometimes add to the vignette of the child's activity, a small video clip of themself asking the parents whether they had seen the child involved in this kind of play at home. Parents would almost always offer a response. Whilst they accepted our desire to understand more about the children's cognitive concerns, they also reminded us that significant social events were also important and gave us information about the relevant life events that were currently taking place. When staff asked parents if they were willing to be interviewed about their own educational experiences, they shared their memories of struggling to make themselves heard in the school system. They made it clear to us that they wanted something more and something better for their children.

Valuing parents' contribution

Many parents did attend meetings or get involved in study groups, and these were always run in a way that respected the different needs of families. Parents arriving at 7.00 p.m., having just come off a shift at work, needed a relaxed atmosphere and refreshments, but they also wanted a well-prepared and focused discussion. In these groups, we had to establish a dialectic where contradictions could be tolerated, important problems could be posed, and important questions answered (Allman, 1983: 111). Parents were given opportunities to explore their own uncertainties; they were not force-fed content and knowledge.

Mutual need

Nursery staff were very clear that they needed the information that parents held about the children's learning at home. Without this information, we could not provide the kind of supportive, stimulating and challenging curriculum that the nursery children deserved:

> The roles of professional experience and parents' everyday experience are seen as complementary but equally important. The former constitutes a 'public' (and generalised) form of theory about child development, whilst the latter represents a 'personal theory' about the development of a particular child. An interaction between the two 'theories' or ways of explaining a child's actions may produce an enriched understanding as a basis for both to act in relation to the child. *Only through the combination of both types of information could a broad and accurate picture be built up of a child's developmental process.*
>
> (Easen, Kendall and Shaw, 1992: 287–296; our emphasis)

Recognising parents' key role as the child's first and most consistent educators did not leave staff feeling deskilled or supplanted. Parents and staff began to see themselves as *co-educators*, co-constructing an appropriate curriculum to meet the cognitive and affective needs of every child. With hindsight it is important to see how Easen's diktat makes it a requirement for all educators to recognise the knowledge and powerful theoretical understanding that parents hold and that educators need, if they are to improve outcomes for children. If every teacher in every classroom was concerned to know and understand what each child has been doing, playing and concentrating intently on at the weekend, and if each teacher was willing to build on the insights and understanding that parents could share, then primary classrooms would be richer places of learning.

Recognising parents' strengths

We were constantly having to revisit the theory and review our own practice in light of the information proffered by the parents and our detailed observations of the children. At times, we struggled to understand what a child was doing and were unable to support a child's deep interest in a particular learning experience. Then we were very dependent on parents for additional insights. Chris Athey describes the same process in the Froebel project: 'because the search was for fundamental patterns of thought, parents became increasingly involved, to the point of fascination in educational issues that, in the past, might have been thought to be the sole province of professionals' (Athey, 1990: 207).

The Pen Green Loop

In describing the Pen Green Loop (see Figure 8.1), we are trying to address what Chris Athey calls the three Ps of early childhood educators: 'parents, participating with professionals within an articulated pedagogical approach' (Athey, 1990: 56). The learning loop is a dynamic process whereby all the important adults in a child's life give each other feedback on what seems to be centrally important to the child, and how and what children are learning in the home and in the nursery. Using Patrick Easen's terminology, the early years staff have expert knowledge of the 'public' and generalised theories of child development, whilst the parents have 'personal' theories about the development of their particular child. It is the interaction between the two sets of theories or explanations about the child's actions that produces a far deeper understanding of a particular child's development and learning. All the important adults in any child's life need to use this shared knowledge as a basis for engagement in a relationship with the child. It is worth re-stating with real emphasis – it is only through the combination of both types of information that a broad and accurate picture can be built of a child's developmental process.

Parent-led observations and feedback to staff (see Figure 8.1, sequence 1–4)

Parents generally attend at least two training sessions on the key child development concepts that inform our practice in the nursery.

In the past, parents were also offered a training session on how to use the camcorder and how to make effective video vignettes of their children playing and learning at a deep level; the use of cameras has largely been superseded by the use of mobile phones. Many parents were willing to make detailed observations of their children at home and shared these observations with the nursery staff either verbally or in written form at the start of the nursery session, or during one of the study groups. In these very informal study groups, parents were given time to reflect on

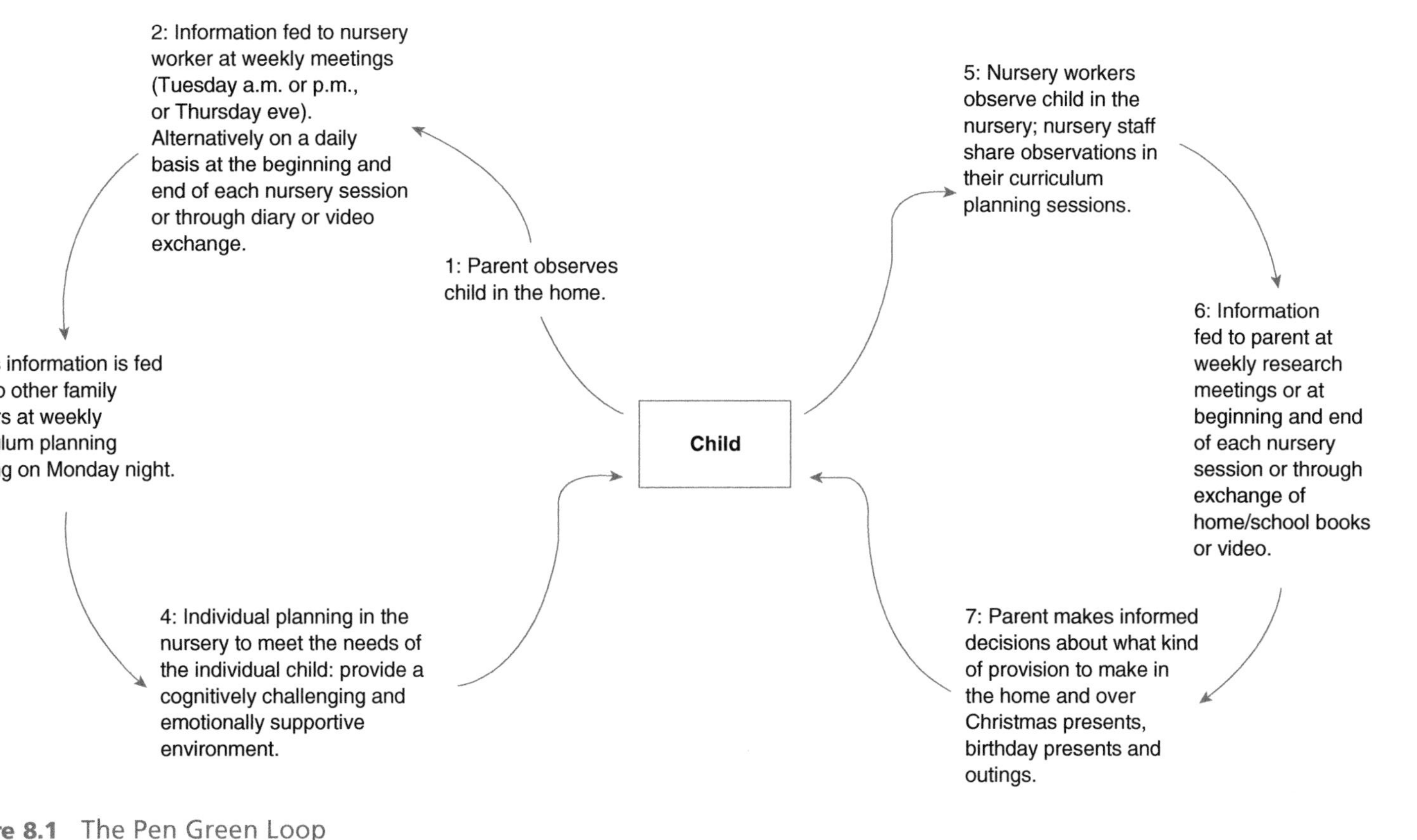

Figure 8.1 The Pen Green Loop

what their children had been doing at home over coffee and a chat. They shared ideas with other parents and received information from their family workers about what was interesting their children in the nursery. Like Louise in Chapter 10, parents often relished the opportunity to share their anxiety about challenging behaviour (Athey, 1990: 207). They were often reassured when their children's behaviour was reframed as consistent, predictable and learning-focused. Staff were able to relate the children's play to the child development concepts that parents had studied, and parents were also able to attribute new significance to what their children were doing (Athey, 1990).

Some of these parents borrowed the nursery camcorder or used their own, and made video vignettes of their children playing in the home setting; today most parents have a video application on their mobile phone. Nursery staff or admin staff were given some additional time out of nursery to copy these diary entries so that the diaries could be retained by parents. Staff also jotted down verbal information offered by the parents directly on the nursery planning sheet, or recorded it in each child's 'celebration of achievement' file. The research staff and nursery staff who ran the study groups made it a priority to watch videos brought from home and to make notes on a special data sheet, which they subsequently entered into the child's file. Alternatively, they might share the information brought from home with the child's family worker at a weekly curriculum-planning session, which all the nursery staff attend. In these staff planning sessions, individual staff would present their observations of particular children; other staff would share any other observational evidence gathered from home or from nursery. The whole staff group would then begin to familiarise themselves with the children's interests and identify their cognitive constants and any emerging patterns in their play. Staff would also share their knowledge about the children's emotional well-being and developing social relationships within the nursery.

On the basis of informed observations in the nursery (Bruce, 1997: 67), which were fleshed out by observations in the home setting, staff could then begin to plan to meet the needs of individual children or groups of children.

Staff-led observations and feedback to parents (see Figure 8.1, sequence 5–7)

In the same way that parents observe their own particular children at home, early years educators at Pen Green have a system for observing the children in the nursery. Every day, specific children are flagged up as 'focus children' (systematically, over a four to six-week period, every child in the nursery is targeted), and all staff, students and parent helpers make sure that they fill in observational records on these children if they come into 'their areas' in the nursery. These rich narrative observations provide the evidence base for planning for each child. It is the child's family worker's responsibility at the end of each session to collect all the observations that have been made that day. If staff are on leave, colleagues will put their observations in the children's files or wait and swap observations at the Monday evening nursery planning session, which lasts from 4.30 to 6.00 p.m. At this planning session, nursery staff are encouraged to challenge each other's thinking and once again make links between theory and practice.

Nursery staff all receive regular supervision from a senior member of staff. They can use these professional supervision sessions to discuss issues about particular children in more depth. All the observations that staff make and the decisions they take about planning for the children in nursery are shared with the parents. Information is passed on to parents in the following ways:

- through daily chats at the beginning or end of a session;
- through home-nursery diaries, children's celebration of achievement files and videos that nursery staff have made;
- through the study groups that run in the morning, afternoon and evening each week.

Parents use the information that staff share with them to make informed decisions about how to extend the provision that is available at home to support their children's learning, what sort of outings they might go on, and what kinds of Christmas or birthday presents they might select. Staff use the information parents share with them to plan, in a more focused and effective way, activities and interventions that will support specific children or groups of children and generate richer curriculum content based on real knowledge about children's central intellectual concerns.

Freire reflects on how knowledge emerges through just this kind of dialogue. In this way, we can 'reconsider through the considerations of others, our own considerations' (Freire, 1970: 61).

To demonstrate how effective this sort of exchange of information can be, we next consider a worked example of the 'Pen Green learning loop'.

Parents and staff as co-educators: the learning loop

Alice's portfolio: Alice and the conveyor belt

Every week, we plan to support and extend children's learning in our nursery, and we often start with their critical questions. Alice's questions were all about how conveyor belts work. However, we need to put her questions in some kind of context.

Chelsea, Alice's friend, had travelled up to Scotland in December and saw her luggage 'disappear' down a conveyor belt. She wanted to know where her luggage had gone. She came back to nursery and shared her experience with her friends and the nursery staff. In January, the nursery staff made a number of experimental conveyor belts to explain the concept to Chelsea, although it was Alice, not Chelsea, who became deeply involved. At the end of January, Alice and her mother went with a small group of parents and children from the nursery to visit the Launch Pad at the Science Museum. She found the complex conveyor belt particularly exciting. Chris Athey (1990) comments on the importance of widening children's experience beyond the school walls, to feed their schemas and to generate new learning. Susan Greenfield also reflects the same viewpoint: 'Experience is a key factor in shaping the micro-circuiting of the brain' (Greenfield, 1997: 122).

Home/nursery dialogue

Lesley, Alice's mother, is aware that, at 3 years and 10 months, Alice has a cluster of schemas. The schemas that have been particularly important to Alice for several weeks are enclosure, envelopment and rotation:

> Enclosure is concerned with enclosing oneself, an object or space.
>
> Envelopment is concerned with covering or surrounding oneself, an object or a space.
>
> Rotation is concerned with turning, twisting, or rolling oneself or objects in the environment around.
>
> (Arnold, 1997a)

Lesley regularly keeps a diary of what Alice does at home and brings it into the research study group every Tuesday afternoon. These particular diary entries show some interesting examples of envelopment:

> 16 Oct: Alice found a balloon in the drawer. After I had blown it up for her, she spent a little while chasing it. I then caught her spreading William's nappy cream all over the balloon! Aarrgh!
>
> 17 Oct: Alice was drawing on a little note pad. As she finished with each page, she ripped it off the pad and wrapped up a fridge magnet in each piece of paper.
>
> 20 Jan: I bought her a Sellotape dispenser for Christmas, and she now uses up rolls and rolls of Sellotape ... She wrapped Sellotape around her little brother in his baby walker.

Lesley's family worker also runs the study group, so he makes copies of these diary entries, shares the information with other staff, and puts her comments into Alice's file.

Problem-solving in nursery

Over several months, Alice spent time experimenting with the conveyor belt. She was actively engaged in problem-solving. It took her some time to understand that, by pulling the belt underneath, from right to left, she could make objects move from left to right, so that they fell with a satisfying clunk into a metal container.

Alice had a hypothesis that all the objects she put on the belt would move along the belt in the same way, and then drop off the end. When she put a ball on the conveyor belt, she was initially intrigued. However, after trying two or three times to make the ball behave in the same way as the flat objects, she rejected it. She chose to discard the ball because it presented her with contradictory evidence. She was excited by her own theory and she continued to experiment with other objects, which behaved in a way that confirmed her hypothesis. Wynne Harlen (1982) writes of children's need to develop a 'false hypothesis'. Alice's false hypothesis was that all the objects she placed on the conveyor belt would behave in the same way. As she becomes more experienced, she will modify her hypothesis.

In the research study group, Alice's key worker, Marcus, showed Lesley what Alice had been doing in nursery. Both Lesley and her partner were fascinated by the conveyor belt experiment and impressed by Alice's concentration and disposition to learn. In both the study group and the staff meeting, we shared ideas about just what Alice is learning.

What is Alice learning?

It seemed to nursery staff that Alice was developing an understanding of some important mathematical and physical concepts: 'Learning mathematics or science is not so much learning facts as learning ways of thinking' (Lee and Das Gupta, 1995: 219). The concepts she was investigating are concerned with:

- forces and motion;
- friction and gravity;
- surface area.

Figure 8.2 Alice and the conveyor belt learning sequence

At the research study group

Research Feedback Form
Name of Child: Alice
Name of Parent: Lesley
Group Attending: am / pm / evening 28th October

Issues Raised
Lesley has noticed that Alice is wrapping up the door handles with Sellotape. She is also wrapping up (enveloping) the television tuner in tea towels or tissues. Lesley says she will let her wrap up all the family xmas presents. Alice woke at 6am and tried to envelop her whole face with lipstick and blusher (she doesn't enjoy face paints). She also wrapped plasters round all her fingers.

Research Feedback Form
Name of Child: Alice
Name of Parent: Lesley
Group Attending: am / pm / evening 28th October

Issues Raised:
Lesley noticed that Alice was winding her lipstick out until it was fully distended and then put the top on it – squelching the lipstick inside. At this point Lesley banned further use of the lipstick. Alice also tried to cover her whole face with eye shadow but it didn't work (envelopment). Alice gave her mother a pretend 'feather' which was a straw enveloped with paper and Sellotape.

Figure 8.3 Examples of Alice's research feedback form

Lesley continues to attend the research study group, which is held on a Tuesday afternoon. Each week, she shares her diary entries with the staff who run the group and with other parents. The members of staff running the group keep a record of the group discussion that relates to Alice on a 'research feedback' form (Figure 8.3), which is then put into Alice's 'celebration of achievement' file for her family worker to read.

This particular study group spent some time discussing how parents could best support children's envelopment schema and when it was necessary to set some boundaries to inappropriate behaviour. Lesley's comment was that 'my relationship with Alice has become much more engaged – I feel I am on her level and much more in tune with her play. Finding out about schemas has helped to put me one step ahead!' Chris Athey (1990) does make the point that to 'identify a schema is not necessarily to love it'. Lesley was very clear that she had set an appropriate boundary in relation to Alice's use of her make-up bag, and David, Alice's father, was happy to offer Alice an alternative, as we can see from the extracts from the research feedback in Figure 8.4.

Research Feedback Form
Name of Child: Alice
Name of Parent: Lesley
Group Attending: am / pm / evening 18th November

Issues Raised:
Alice had enveloped an egg box in paper and wound it round with **Sellotape**. and some raffle tickets all in one big parcel. She used up the rest of the roll of **Sellotape**.Lesley asked her to go to the loo before she went out and Alice came downstairs and commented, 'the loo roll looks just like the **Sellotape**.' Alice enveloped her dolls' faces with chalk like she had her own in nursery.

David, her dad, brought her two children's lipsticks and she put the purple one on top of the pink one and said she had made a new colour. Lesley let her use some tiny paint pallets at home and she mixed colours. Sometimes she envelops her little brother, William, in the beanbag!

Research Feedback Form
Name of Child: Alice
Name of Parent: Lesley
Group Attending: am / pm / evening 25th November

Issues Raised:
Lesley reported that Alice had run into nursery saying 'my daddy's really ustaful'. She wasn't sure if she meant beautiful or useless!

Alice had made a dog lead with links and attached it to William (18 months) and encouraged him to 'walk' like a dog. She sometimes says 'the dog done it' if she spills her drink. This morning Alice was cutting out a boat and a house and colouring them in and she had to stick them in Lesley's research diary.

Figure 8.4 Extracts from research feedback

Planning to support and extend Alice's learning

Nursery staff made plans to support and extend Alice's learning with a PLOD (possible lines of direction) chart. Central to the nursery planning were the narrative and video observations parents and staff had made of Alice's cognitive constants at home and at nursery.

Alice is learning at a deep level; at nursery, we want to build on what she *can* do and encourage her to develop an interest in what excites her. The PLOD chart we have developed (Bartholomew and Bruce, 1993: 45) helps us to integrate our observations of the children's interests and schemas, and at the same time make links with the early learning goals. At the centre of the PLOD (Figure 8.5) are the names of several children who all share Alice's interests. Chris Athey (1990: 30) makes the point that 'unreflective child centredness has led to the false belief that every child needs a unique educational programme. Constructivist teachers know that many children share similar cognitive concerns.' Indeed we know that children's drive to develop social relationships often means that they will spend hours exploring and playing at a deep level precisely with these children who have similar schematic or developmental concerns (Arnold and The Pen Green Team, 2010; Carr and Lee, 2012; Hayward et al., 2013).

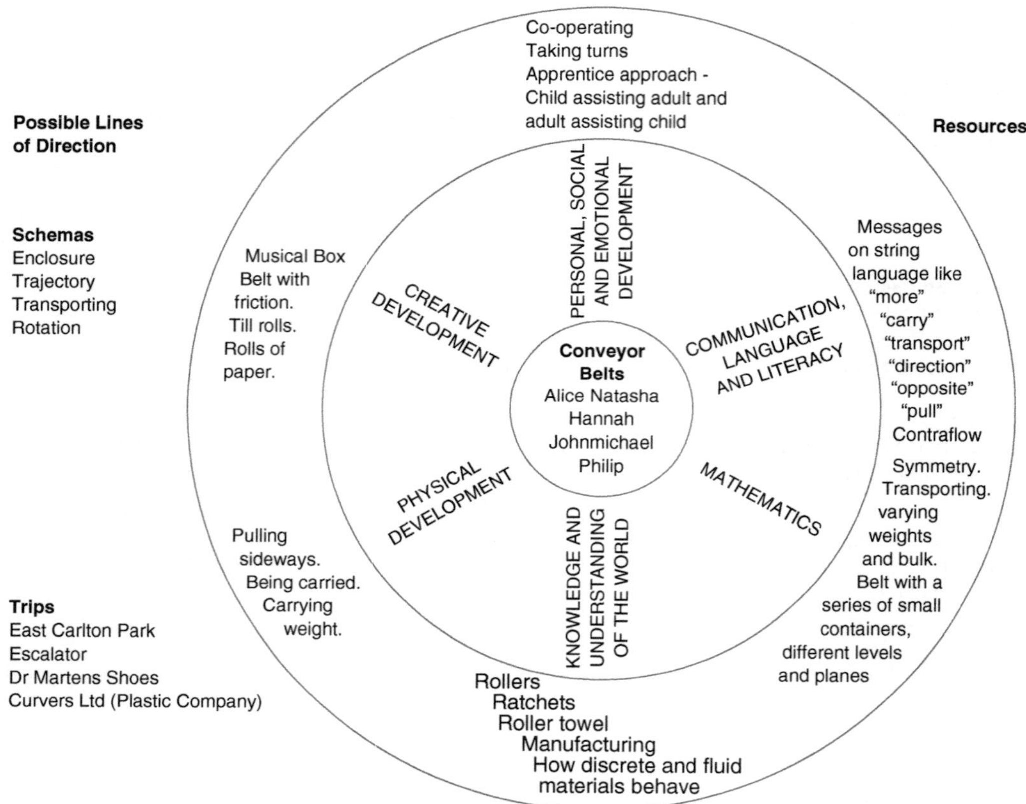

Figure 8.5 Extracts from research feedback

By four years of age, Alice was still experimenting with the conveyor belt, but by now the nursery provision not only included the improvised 'belts' that staff had made out of paper, but also a manufactured conveyor belt. This conveyor belt, when placed in the sandpit, offered Alice and other nursery children a new range of possible lines of direction. Alice's parents' deep commitment to her learning and their partnership with the nursery staff have made it possible for us to offer Alice a stimulating and challenging nursery environment.

Documentation

Pedagogical documentation as defined by Gunilla Dahlberg (Dahlberg, Moss and Pence, 1999) makes it possible for:

- the child to revisit and reflect on what they have done, and in this way to make their learning an active process;
- nursery staff to enter into a dialogue, and communicate in action with the child and their parents;
- the nursery staff group to open up the nursery, so that it becomes a public space, an arena for discussing critical questions and for reflection;
- the nursery staff to develop materials as a basis for reconstructing pedagogical practice; for reflective dialogue, negotiation and challenge; and to connect theory and practice;
- nursery staff to problematise their practice and planning and open it up to critical analysis.

Dahlberg reflects on the long tradition of pedagogical documentation in Sweden and Italy. She differentiates between the reflexive problematising approach of Kohier in Sweden and Rinaldi in Reggio Emilia in northern Italy, and the approach of traditionalists who see observing children 'as being about mapping some universal and objective social reality' (Dahlberg et al., 1999: 145). Dahlberg, writing from a Swedish perspective, defines pedagogical documentation as critically different from 'child observation'; 'as we understand it, the purpose of child observation is to assess children's psychological development in relation to already predetermined categories produced from developmental psychology and which define what the normal child should be doing at a particular age' (ibid.: 146).

Susan Isaacs, one of our UK 'giants' who set up the Malting House School in the 1920s, pioneered the use of narrative observations. She has influenced many generations of early years practitioners in the UK and she did not confine her powerful observations to predetermined categories. Whilst she was concerned with building and substantiating generalisable theories about children's learning and development, she was also concerned with *differences* in the behaviour between children and in finding out more about the particular interests of individual children and groups of children (Drummond, 1993: 49). Susan Isaacs was deeply interested in knowing more about children's rich emotional lives and showed a remarkable acceptance and understanding of children's angry feelings and challenging behaviour: 'she was concerned with explorations of both their inner and outer world' (Drummond, 1993: 4). There is nothing sanitised about Isaacs' descriptions of experimentation inside and outside the classroom (Isaacs, 1936). The children in her school were interested in life, death and bringing things back to life. Compare her notes in 1930 with those of the Pen Green nursery team in 2000.

Susan Isaacs' observations in 1930

13.7.25: Some of the children called out that the rabbit was dying. They found it in the summerhouse, hardly able to move. They were very sorry and talked much about it. They shut it up in the hutch and gave it warm milk.

14.7.25: The rabbit had died in the night. Dan found it and said, 'It's dead – its tummy does not move up and down now.' Paul said, 'My daddy says that if we put it into water it will get alive again.' Mrs I said, 'Shall we do so and see?' They put it into a bath of water. Some of them said, 'It's alive, because it's moving.' This was a circular movement, due to the currents in the water: Mrs I therefore put in a small stick which also moved round and round, and they agreed that the stick was not alive. They then suggested that they should bury the rabbit, and all helped to dig a hole and bury it.

15.7.25: Frank and Duncan talked of digging the rabbit up – but Frank said, 'It's not there – it's gone up to the sky.' They began to dig but tired of it and ran off to something else. Later they came back and dug again. Duncan, however, said, 'Don't bother – it's gone – it's up in the sky' and gave up digging. Mrs I therefore said, 'Shall we see if it's there?' and also dug. They found the rabbit, and were very interested to see it still there.

(Isaacs, 1936: 182–3)

Pen Green nursery team observations in 2000

5.2.2000: We are reading *The Dog that Dug*. On one page, there is a picture of the skeleton of a dinosaur: James asks if the dinosaur has been eaten. I explain that it died a long time ago and that the skin and flesh have rotted away. James asks, 'When we are dead, why are we always dead?' I explain how things stop working inside us and don't start again. He says, 'My grandpa Alex is dead.' I ask him if he is sad. 'No,' he says, and then 'A little bit,' and then 'My Grandma is sad.' I say that she is probably missing his Grandpa's company. James asks, 'Who is going to sleep with her now?' I say that I don't know. He asks, 'When you get old you die', and 'Am I getting older?' He continues, 'When I'm big, I'll be old. Are you old?' he asks me. I say that we get older every day. James asks, 'Am I getting older?'

Drummond (1993: 50) makes the point that Isaacs' work, celebrating, as it does, children's individual emotional and intellectual lives, also provides a salutary warning for early childhood educators: 'If we choose to see only those aspects of learning of which we approve, we will lose the opportunity to see more of the picture, to learn more about learning ... there is always more to learn, and more to see' (ibid.). It would be very easy as adults to focus our observations on what interests us, on the aesthetically pleasing, for example, rather than on those things which are of deep concern to young children.

Penny Lawrence, in our video-training sessions for parents and staff, reminded us that while the camera provides a window into the child's world, we see that world through the lens of our values and beliefs, and we focus the camera on what we consider to be worth observing (Whalley et al., 2012).

While there are some significant differences between the documentation that takes place in Sweden and in Reggio Emilia (Italy) and that which takes place at Pen Green, there are also some similarities. The time-honoured tradition of observation which underpins the work at Pen Green derives from the studies undertaken by such baby biographers as Darwin, Piaget and Navarra (Bruce, 1997: 10) and the observational approach pioneered by Susan Isaacs in the 1930s. At Pen Green, we focus on the children's learning process. We observe what children are doing and saying, and we then interpret and analyse what we see, using contemporary theory (Bruce, 1997: 67) and new theories that practitioners and parents generate. Subsequently, we share ideas with colleagues and the children's parents, and develop plans to support and extend the children's learning. We document this whole process, working in collaboration with the children's primary carers.

James's interest in death, dying, beheading and whether executioners were 'bad men' was supported and extended by the nursery staff. He was offered storybooks that enhanced his understanding, such as *Grandfather Cherry Blossom* and *Kintaro, the Nature Boy*. His strong trajectory schema, which we had observed since he was 2 and 3 years old, had led to an interest and developing competence in using the saws on the workbench and in making swords. James was supported and extended by the introduction of a special kitchen saw so that he could behead a dead fish and examine its bone structure. He was fascinated by the concept of transformation of state and tried to make the decapitated fish come alive again in a bowl of water. He also reflected to his key worker that if we left the fish in water for a long time, it would come alive, and if that did not work, we could put the fish in the lake and it would come alive. Much of James's learning about cause and effect was through hypothesising, and verbal discussion, practical investigation and reflection. James showed little interest in representing his experience, although at one point he briefly wallowed in red paint. The formal record of the experience was through the documentation of the staff and his mother, that is, video clips and notes in James's file. However, the learning process was deep and sustained over several weeks, and we have included both home video of James and his mother Louise and nursery video of James in our new PICL training pack.

Like Gunilla Dahlberg in Sweden and Carlina Rinaldi in Italy, staff at Pen Green have begun to see how making our observations, dialogue, analysis and planning more explicit can be useful for staff, parents, children and the wider community:

> Documentation offers the teacher a unique opportunity to listen again, see again, and therefore revisit indirectly and with others, the events and processes in which he or she was co-protagonist, directly or indirectly. This revisiting with colleagues helps create common meaning and values.
>
> (Edwards, Gandini and Forman, 1998: 121–2)

Portfolios of children's learning, celebration of achievement files

At Pen Green, we also produce portfolios of the children's learning and celebration of achievement files. These documents are critical if we are to develop and improve our practice for the following reasons:

- They are useful for children because they can revisit and reflect on what they have done; we describe this as a metacognitive process where children are thinking at the deepest level.
- They are useful for nursery staff because they form the basis for discussion between children and their parents; they also encourage reflection and make it possible for staff to reconstruct their pedagogical practice. Staff can dialogue with colleagues, problematise their practice, and make links between theory and practice.
- Documentation is also important for parents because when their children's work is opened up for discussion in this way, parents can ask critical questions and reflect on what their child is doing at nursery.
- These various foci of documentation also honour the contribution that parents are making as their child's first educators. The dialogue we enter into with parents, children and the wider community is not cosy. We often need to share strong views and challenge each other's ways of thinking. Parents are passionately committed to supporting their children's learning; nursery staff work with parents as equal, active and responsible partners.

All documentation at Pen Green is developed through a dialogue with the children's parents. Becky's portfolio shows how the information is collected, how observations are shared, and how parents and staff work together to support and extend Becky's learning. The final document is a *Celebration* of Becky's *Achievements* file, which she takes home and which she can share with her teacher when she moves on to primary school. If children have been at Pen Green from the age of 9 months these files can become three volumes from their early baby biographies and time spent in baby nest through to their two years spent in nursery.

Becky's portfolio

Becky starts nursery

When Becky came into nursery in September 1997, her mum reported, 'Becky can spend hours hanging clothes outdoors, moving and folding them – then repeating the process all over again'.

After being in nursery for a couple of weeks, she is enveloping herself and others in stickers. Her mum reports, 'Plain white stickers are not good enough;

they must be coloured ones ... she draws circles, cuts them out and puts them on top of each other'.

Becky seems to have an envelopment schema.

Definition of schema

'Schemas are patterns of linked behaviours which the child can generalise and use in a whole variety of different situations. It is best to think of schemas as being a cluster of pieces which fit together' (Bruce, 1997).

Becky's cluster of schemas

Envelopment – covering or surrounding oneself, an object or a space.

Enclosure – enclosing oneself, an object or a space.

Going through – causing oneself or some material to go through a boundary and emerge at the other side.

Layering – placing materials in a layer combining envelopment and on top schemas.

Supporting her schema at nursery

When we plan for children's learning, we use a chart called a PLOD (possible lines of direction).

The purpose of the PLOD chart is to ensure that staff provide children with a broad, wide and deep curriculum. Other children benefit from this type of planning. Chris Athey (1990: 30) points out:

> Unreflective child centredness has led to the false belief that every child requires a unique educational programme. Constructivist teachers know that many children share similar cognitive concerns.

Becky's PLOD (Figure 8.6) relates to her interest in making parcels and envelopes. When we have planned effectively for the children's learning in this way, they are able to play and learn at a deep level. Becky is almost always engrossed when making parcels and presents. The planning matches her educational needs.

(Continued)

(Continued)

Supporting her schema at home

At home it is nearly Christmas time. Becky's envelopment schema has led her to make up lots of parcels. She enjoys cooking with mum, but is only interested in covering the cake with butter icing and chocolate buttons.

Becky received a pram for Christmas, but rather than use it in the traditional manner, she was more interested in filling it up and covering it with a blanket.

Her mum's diary 4.1.98

'Becky's Christmas present from nursery was very successful. Four rolls of Sellotape and a big roll of paper. She then proceeded to cut out all her Xmas cards and wrap each one into a parcel. 27 in total!'

13.3.98

'No nursery today – I gave her a roll of brown paper and some Sellotape and left her to it – by bedtime, there was a huge pile of parcels for Alice, William and Sheree.'

Becky engages with the whole curriculum

Physical development – Becky is using her senses and physical actions. When Becky began wrapping parcels, it was all on a sensory motor level. She enjoyed the experience of playing with paper and Sellotape while learning and developing new skills.

Communication, language and literacy – Becky's parcel making became more intricate. She began to work at a symbolic representation level. Her parcels and presents became gifts and messages for different people. She wrote the names of her family and friends on each parcel, using upper and lower case letters appropriately. Becky is developing her emergent writing.

Knowledge and understanding of the world – Initially, Becky was making simple transformations by screwing up paper to make a parcel. She is now able to make complex transformations – she plans angles, makes corners, estimates size and fit, and positions and co-ordinates different surfaces.

Mathematics – Bending the paper when wrapping parcels involves spatial concepts and estimating how much paper is needed.

Possible Lines of Direction
Schemas

Envelopment
(Becky, Paige, Alice)

Going Through
(Drew, Ramsay, Becky)

Transporting
(Chelsea)

Layering – like a pop-up book
(Chelsea, Becky)

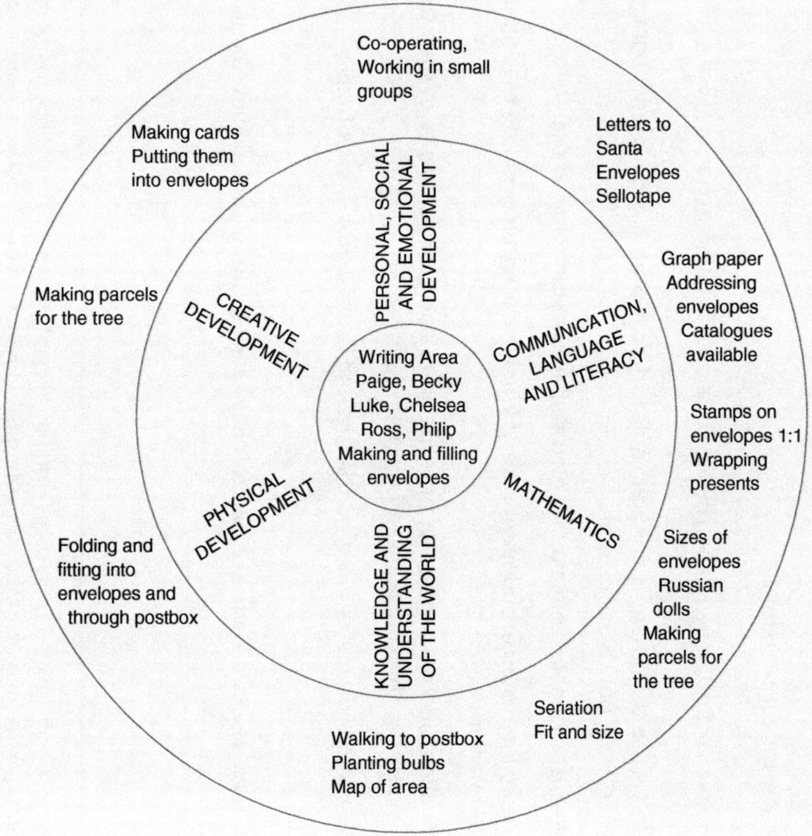

Co-operating, Working in small groups

Making cards
Putting them into envelopes

Letters to Santa
Envelopes
Sellotape

PERSONAL, SOCIAL AND EMOTIONAL DEVELOPMENT

CREATIVE DEVELOPMENT

COMMUNICATION, LANGUAGE AND LITERACY

Writing Area
Paige, Becky
Luke, Chelsea
Ross, Philip
Making and filling envelopes

Making parcels for the tree

Graph paper
Addressing envelopes
Catalogues available

Stamps on envelopes 1:1
Wrapping presents

PHYSICAL DEVELOPMENT

MATHEMATICS

KNOWLEDGE AND UNDERSTANDING OF THE WORLD

Folding and fitting into envelopes and through postbox

Sizes of envelopes
Russian dolls
Making parcels for the tree

Seriation
Fit and size

Walking to postbox
Planting bulbs
Map of area

Resources

Books
Worried Arthur
Little Red Hen & Sly Old Fox
What's Inside?
(non-fiction)

Figure 8.6

(Continued)

(Continued)

Personal social and emotional development – Becky is thinking of others, and communicating with them.

Creative development – She is making something of her own for each of her special friends.

Provision for an enveloper

How do we support, extend and challenge Becky's thinking in nursery?

- We ensure that there is enough choice of provision, e.g. Sellotape, paper, string, hole punch, stickers, etc.
- We encourage her to make her own decisions about what to use.
- We are interested in and supportive of what Becky is doing and try to extend her interests.
- We allow Becky to wallow in the experience and give her plenty of time to organise her thinking and carry out her ideas.
- We try to protect her space, so that she can use the provision optimally.

You can read Becky's own account of her later learning and achievements in Chapter 10.

Next steps

> The school is not isolated from society but an integral part of it. The school has both the right and the duty to make this culture of childhood visible to the society as a whole, in order to provoke exchange and discussion. Sharing documentation is a true act of democratic participation.
>
> (Rinaldi, 1998: 122)

Much of this chapter reflects the approach that we adopted in the second decade at Pen Green 1995 and 2005. The nursery team has engaged in many debates about the best way to develop a rich curriculum and a responsive pedagogy. We have had the chance to deepen our understanding of transnational approaches to assessment and documentation through working with Portuguese colleagues, Danish colleagues and New Zealand colleagues over the last decade.

We feel very drawn to the New Zealand curriculum Te Whariki with its strong bicultural and family and community focus. The simplicity and profundity of the key assessment questions that New Zealand practitioners ask themselves has hugely impressed us:

> Do you know me?
>
> Can I trust you?
>
> Do you hear me?
>
> Will you let me fly?
>
> Is this a fair place for me?
>
> (Podmore, May and Carr, 2001)

These inspiring engagements with overseas colleagues have supported and sustained us. With this kind of global solidarity across the early years field we can really thrash out what makes the greatest difference to children's learning and development.

We have built practitioner research action learning projects into our annual planning cycle. Most of the nursery staff at some point in their Pen Green careers will be engaged in studies at an undergraduate or postgraduate level and all staff involved in such studies have to undertake small-scale research projects. Through these projects staff have developed their understanding of best practice approaches to curriculum development, assessment and documentation, and our understanding of the importance of shared learning between home and nursery constantly deepens. We have made an absolute commitment to staff that they will at some point in their Pen Green career get the opportunity to present their research at the European Conference On Early Childhood Research (www.eecera.org) or other relevant conferences such as the AIMH conference (www.aimh.org.uk). On these occasions nursery parents who have been involved in joint projects attend and present whenever possible. Although the nursery staff will always prioritise meeting the needs of the children in their family groups they are beginning to see themselves as scholars and theorisers and as part of a global learning community.

Like our New Zealand colleagues we can sometimes feel 'besieged by school curricula and school entry assessments' (Carr, 2001), but the increased privatisation of services in the UK has led to attempts to abandon frameworks and standards and this could be dangerous. We need to participate in all these policy debates and participation involves both responsibility and resistance (Litowitz, 1997).

At Pen Green we still believe the 'Silver Bullet' is 'working with parents' in an intelligent and responsive manner around their children's learning and development and sharing our knowledge and understanding. Increasingly we are seeing how important the emotional aspects of documentation can be for parents and nursery staff who are settling children into the nest or nursery at Pen Green or supporting children to transfer from Pen Green to primary school settings. The following two case studies exemplify both how documentation can satisfy parental anxiety about separating from their child and at the same time ensure a smooth transition with powerful opportunities for children to learn at a deep level.

Case study

FLISS (PARENT), LUCY AND TRACY (EARLY YEARS EDUCATORS) AND HENRY'S LEARNING STORY

(told from the parent's perspective)

Henry has been attending Pen Green nursery since September 2014, from the age of 14 months when I returned to work. He began his nursery journey in the Couthie, a nursery provision for children aged from 9 months until they are 3 years old. He was very content in the Couthie environment having formed close relationships with the practitioners and children, in particular his family worker Lucy, made more special because of her frequent visits to our home. The practitioners supported not only him but also me with his transition from home to the nursery. Henry being the last child of five is very precious, made more so because the other four are adults and teenagers, making it very clear how quickly childhood is lost and how precious are the moments you have together.

In January 2016 one of Henry's very special friends 'Bobby' transitioned from the Couthie to the Studio. The Studio is a provision for children from 2½ to 4 years, located next to the Couthie. The two environments are separated by a gate that the children can pass through independently. With the move of his friend to the Studio space, Henry spent more time in the Studio and began to develop a relationship with Bobby's family worker Tracy. Tracy began to use a secure online learning journal, to share with me how their relationship was developing and how Henry was exploring the new environment (Figures 8.7–11 Making lunch).

In these early observations I was able to see how Tracy's understanding of Henry's learning and development was emerging. She was sharing what he was involved in at nursery (Figures 8.12–8.21 Car Tracks). I was able to share with Tracy what Henry was doing at home (Figures 8.22 – 8.26), which was very similar to the experiences he was engaging in at nursery.

Notes

Henry it was so lovely to spend some time with you today getting to know you. You have previously been very shy around me but now your friend has already transitioned into nursery you are spending more time in there too. You were chatting away very confidently, informing me that you were making lunch. You were very involved and clearly had a plan in mind. You looked like you were going through the routine of making dinner, washing dishes and tidying them away. In fact you tidied the whole kitchen away everything went into a cupboard.

I wondered if containing was something you liked to do in the Couthie and at home.

I look forward to getting to know you more.

Like

Leuven Scale

Well-being > High

The child shows obvious signs of satisfaction (as listed under level 5). However, these signals are not constantly present with the same intensity.

Involvement > High

Continuous activity with intense moments. The child' activity has intense moments and at all times they seem involved. They are not easily distracted.

Figures 8.7–8.11 Making lunch

(Continued)

(Continued)

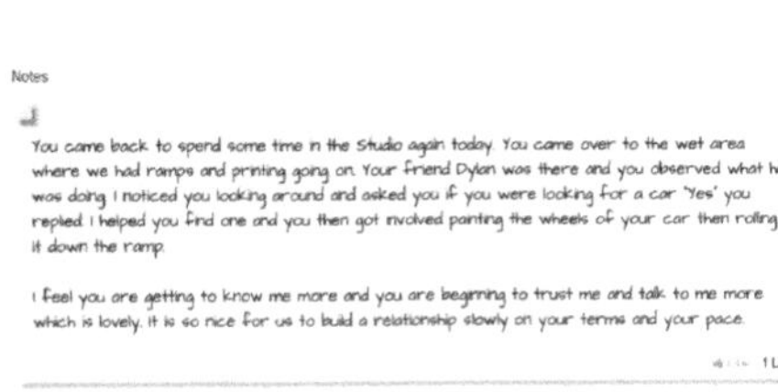

Notes

You came back to spend some time in the Studio again today. You came over to the wet area where we had ramps and printing going on. Your friend Dylan was there and you observed what he was doing. I noticed you looking around and asked you if you were looking for a car 'Yes' you replied. I helped you find one and you then got involved painting the wheels of your car then rolling it down the ramp.

I feel you are getting to know me more and you are beginning to trust me and talk to me more which is lovely. It is so nice for us to build a relationship slowly on your terms and your pace.

1 Like

Felicity Norton
- 31 Jan 2016 12:32 PM
Tracy, another beautiful observation and one of Henrys favourite things to do at home... Pictures to follow

Like · 1 Like

Figures 8.12 – 8.21 Car tracks

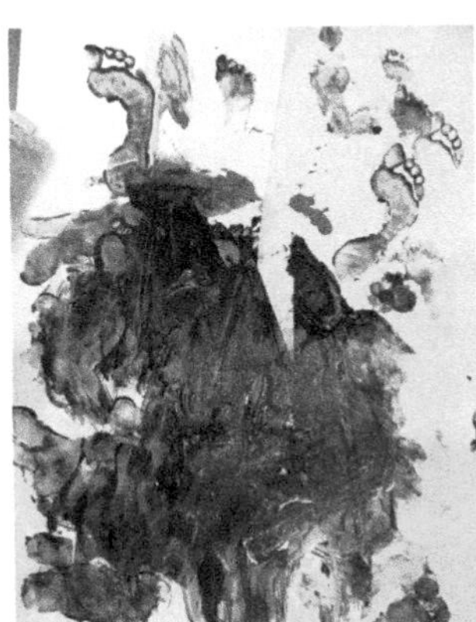

(Continued)

(Continued)

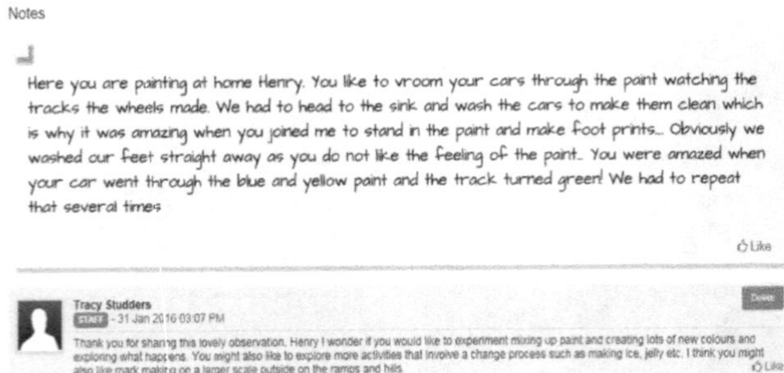

Notes

Here you are painting at home Henry. You like to vroom your cars through the paint watching the tracks the wheels made. We had to head to the sink and wash the cars to make them clean which is why it was amazing when you joined me to stand in the paint and make foot prints.. Obviously we washed our feet straight away as you do not like the feeling of the paint. You were amazed when your car went through the blue and yellow paint and the track turned green! We had to repeat that several times

Like

Tracy Studders
STAFF - 31 Jan 2016 03:07 PM

Thank you for sharing this lovely observation. Henry I wonder if you would like to experiment mixing up paint and creating lots of new colours and exploring what happens. You might also like to explore more activities that involve a change process such as making ice, jelly etc. I think you might also like mark making on a larger scale outside on the ramps and hills.

Like

Figures 8.22–8.26 Car tracks at home

Through Tracy's online observations I was able to see such significant moments in Henry's experiences at the nursery and how their relationship was developing, how curious he was to explore the new environment and how engaged he was in the new challenges Tracy was creating for him.

Notes

Henry you had a great first visit to our Forest School today By using dry sticks and dipping them into puddles we were able to see how deep they were You enjoyed collecting the fir cones in your bucket and found a great stick which you took home with you I could see high how your well being was as you were humming a little happy tune (dah de dah de dah) as you explored the forest You really liked the tyre swing spinning round and round and round 'again again' you said each time it slowed down When I told you it was nearly time to go you replied' I'm not ready yet' I wasn't ready either we were all having a great time but we will go back again

Like

Felicity Norton

Tracy Studders

Figures 8.27–8.34 At forest school

Whilst working full-time I am still able to share in my son's day by sitting with him during the evening and looking through photographs, watching videos and reading observations posted online. Sharing these moments as a family is magnificent.

Tracy's passion and interest in my son, which as a parent are so vitally important, are evident through every observation. Her obvious interest and curiosity in him shine through and I feel safe and secure that my son is in a truly wonderful environment that allows him to express who he is and his family worker revels in and celebrates who he is.

(Continued)

(Continued)

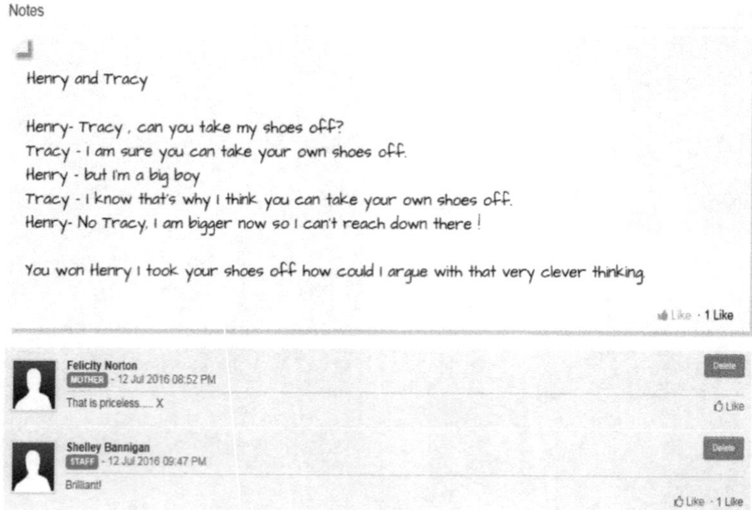

Figure 8.35 Quote of the day

Case study

LOGAN'S STORY

A case study of transition from nursery to primary school

(a continuation of Leanne's Story in Chapter 3 written from the organisation's perspective)

Logan is the younger of two children. He lives at home with his mother Leanne and his sibling and visits his father most weekends. Logan attended the Pen Green Centre from approximately 18 months when he was in the nurture group; the nurture group has a 2 children to 1 staff member ratio which means staff can be highly responsive and where necessary pick children up from home. Logan then transitioned into nursery and had the same family worker as his sister had had previously. Prior to Logan starting nursery, Tracy (his family worker) made connections with Logan in nurture group, she also invited Logan to come and spend some time in nursery with her. Tracy also visited Logan at home to get to know him in his family context. Logan was offered five mornings in nursery, an increase from the two mornings he had attended in nurture group.

Coping with separation

Soon after starting nursery Logan's attendance began to deteriorate. Tracy spoke with Leanne about this and asked if she could help her in any way. Leanne explained that she still struggled to get up in the morning and often had things to do and she just took Logan with her or Logan was playing happily at home. Tracy spoke about the importance of regular attendance and the opportunities in nursery for Logan to develop friendships. Logan was still struggling to separate from Leanne and settle into nursery and his irregular attendance did not help. Tracy and Leanne agreed to a change of start time so that Logan could attend more consistently and build up trust with adults and his peers. Tracy also committed to providing familiar toys and activities for Logan on arrival and support for both Leanne and Logan.

Logan took time to adjust to his new routine of coming into nursery mid-morning, he would often observe and not really participate with others. Tracy described Logan as needing time to emotionally self-regulate and plan with his family worker what he would like to do. At times he would become upset and angry, as he was struggling to cope and wasn't able to articulate his feelings; Tracy made herself available to Logan at these critical times. After a few months Logan settled into nursery, however when he had periods of absence, he would still struggle to separate from his mother and these transitions still needed to be handled with sensitivity. Tracy used video vignettes to show Leanne how Logan settled and what he had chosen to do when he was in nursery. She also took time to talk to Leanne and to encourage her to attend regularly.

Planning for transition to school

Logan was offered a place in the primary school his sister attended and the school were aware of the attendance issues. Tracy arranged to take Logan into school to help familiarise him with his new environment. Logan was not always keen to visit school and this may have been because he was anxious to be in nursery when his mother returned.

Tracy suggested to Leanne that she and Logan participated in the summer enrichment project in nursery during the summer holidays. This project involved nursery children, their siblings and parents, nursery staff and primary school teachers in shared outings, focused interventions in nursery and a support group for parents to talk about their hopes and fears for their children starting school. Leanne thought this was a great idea and committed to attending all the sessions.

During the summer transition project, Leanne spoke honestly and openly with Logan's class teacher. Angela, the Head of Nursery, brokered this conversation. Leanne told the class teacher about her own childhood and what she

(Continued)

(Continued)

thought Logan might find difficult when he started school. Leanne spoke proudly about Logan's interests, what he enjoyed doing at home and his amazing knowledge of numbers. She also spoke about the strong relationship he had with his father. Leanne did express her anxiety about how Logan would separate from her each morning. The class teacher said that this information was really helpful and that she would offer support when necessary.

Baseline assessment in school

Six weeks after starting school, Logan's class teacher made the judgement that he was not in line for a good level of development on his baseline assessment. She said that Logan was really struggling with personal, social and emotional development and his attendance was already starting to slip. Logan was also considered to be 'non-compliant' at times. On his way home from school Logan visited staff in nursery on a weekly basis and he proudly shared what he was learning at home and in school. He was confident and competent in literacy and maths and demonstrated real skills in these areas. Nursery staff regularly reminded Leanne about the importance of getting Logan to school on time and reminded her about how much his absences affected his personal, social and emotional development. They also congratulated Leanne on how well Logan was doing in school. Logan was by now making a good relationship with his class teacher, however she was leaving the school at the end of his first term.

At the beginning of the spring term, the head of Pen Green nursery met with Logan's new class teacher to talk about Logan's learning and development. The class teacher said that Logan had excelled in specific areas and that he was now working with a year 1 class for some literacy and maths sessions. She said that because of his 'immaturity' Logan still struggled with personal, social and emotional development. By the summer term he was joining a year 2 class for literacy and maths and Logan had achieved a 'good level of development' overall.

By the end of his first year in school Leanne told us that she was very proud of Logan and that he comes out of school most days wanting to share with her what he has learnt. Leanne reflected 'he has got so much knowledge already and he always wants to know more. I think he is really clever. His dad has worked so hard to support him with homework and to teach him things, he does loads of things with him'.

How did Pen Green nursery support Logan's transition to school?

- Logan's family worker visited him at home on a regular basis and was a constructive critical friend to the family.
- His family worker planned experiences in nursery based on Logan's interests at home.

- His family worker built an open and trusting relationship with Logan's mum.
- His family worker planned individual transition arrangements based on her intimate knowledge of Logan.
- The class teacher was invited to an open evening in nursery to meet the family worker and look through documentation.
- The class teacher was invited to visit nursery to see Logan.
- The class teacher visited Logan at home.
- The family worker kept an open dialogue with the receiving class teacher.
- The family worker negotiated additional visits to school to help build up Logan's confidence.
- His family worker had daily dialogue with the parent.
- We built up video documentation of Logan's time in nursery.
- The family engaged in summer enrichment days – transition project.
- The class teacher engaged in the transition project.
- The nursery staff had difficult conversations with Leanne about attendance.
- The nursery staff brokered conversation between the parents and class teacher.
- The nursery staff continued to support Logan and mum after he went to school.
- The nursery staff maintained a dialogue with the class teachers over the whole of the child's first year.

When reflecting on this case study we calculated the costs of our interventions on behalf of a child that was no longer attending our nursery; clearly they were high. However the consequences of not intervening could have been catastrophic.

Increasingly the documentation that we produce at Pen Green contributes to the wider debate between:

- parents and early years educators;
- parents, early years educators and primary school colleagues;
- parents, early years educators and politicians and policy makers;
- parents, early years educators and Ofsted teams.

As an integrated centre for children and families we continue to develop our work with local parents, children and the wider community, but at the same time we keep a sharp focus on the really critical issues in early childhood education at every level.

Suggestions for your own practice

- Setting up a system to observe each child in your setting makes planning for learning possible.
- Think about the information you gather from parents/carers – does it help your team plan for individual children and small groups of children – are you able to extend across all areas of learning?
- Reflect on the way you document children's learning – is it a process shared daily/regularly with parents? How could you make it as current as possible, and how do you make it possible for all the important adults in a child's life to stay involved?
- Think about whether each child leads their own exploration of the curriculum and how you might follow their lead?

Key points

- An equal and active dialogue can be developed between workers and parents as part of a democratic process of parental engagement.
- The model we have called 'The Pen Green Loop' illustrates the two-way process of dialogue between worker and parent.
- Examples of documentation are illustrated, including one from a secure online learning journal.
- An example of a challenging but successful transition from nursery into primary school.

Recommended reading

Carr, M. and Lee, W. (2012) *Learning Stories*. London: Sage.
Freire, P. (1996) *The Pedagogy of the Oppressed*. London: Penguin.

Websites

Let the Children Play: www.letthechildrenplay.net/2013/03/be-reggio-inspired-documentation
Educational Leadership Project: www.elp.co.nz

9

Sharing knowledge with families in a 'drop-in' provision within an integrated centre for children and families

Sandra Mole

Introduction

The Family Room at Pen Green provides a drop-in space for parents/carers and their children, all day and every day. Very few demands are made on the parents using that space. Some carers might access the room every day. Others might pop in once a week or once in a while. Consequently, parents or carers with a wide range of needs use the space. Workers have to be adaptable and aware of the needs of each family. This chapter focuses on two families, who are very different but have both benefited from the PICL approach.

My role as a family worker in the family room

Together with my colleague Caroline, I am a family worker in the Family Room, a community drop-in resource which can be accessed before, after or instead of groups or nursery at Pen Green. The role is quite unusual because we support families in their everyday lives as well as in their interactions with each other, at the same time as providing a safe and welcoming drop-in space for young children.

When studying the family worker role within Pen Green, Alaide Santos (1992) a Brazilian postgraduate student, recognised:

> the skills certainly include being able to build up trusting relationships with people and be engaged in therapeutic tasks such as counselling and support. Besides these, (she has to) be able to have a good understanding of parents' needs and develop work to meet those needs. Certainly she has to be very open-minded, flexible and aware of any parent coming into the Family Room. It means not being judgemental and having the ability to approach everyone.
>
> (Santos, 1992: 45)

As family workers in an open access drop-in space, we aim to build powerful relationships by increasing the parents' confidence, celebrating children's achievements and fostering a belief in each individual's abilities: 'relationships do not just happen and often involve considerable risk. Learning to trust the other person involves being prepared to rely on their judgment and actions' (Gilchrist, 2004: 63). It is our job to inspire citizenship and a sense of community, increase awareness of adults' political voice, challenge inappropriate behaviour, acknowledge and contain emotions and build upon existing skills and attributes: 'The combination of informality with very serious, but still informal, work carried out there with parents, make it [the Family Room] a special place' (Santos, 1992: 105).

The Family Room was part of the original conceptualisation of the Pen Green Centre. Staff believed that there would always be families that were just not ready for formal groups and needed 'a place to be', a safe and accepting place. Conradson reminds us 'there are few which seek to provide a place for people to relate to others and simply be' and 'the significance of such places for marginalized citizens should not be underestimated' (2010: 521).

Ethical considerations

When deciding to write about families for this chapter it was extremely important to me that I remain ethical and ensure families have consented and are fully informed of the implications of appearing in a book. I hoped, in writing this chapter, to start a dialogue about some of the transformational work that occurs on a daily basis in the Family Room. I had problematised the Family Room in my Master's dissertation and was very aware, as Holman (1987) stated, that parents can become 'objects of research' and can be placed in an inferior position, in which they are expected to *supply* information but *not to obtain any*. The principle of doing no harm underpinned the choice of participants and the ways that the interviews were co-constructed in each of these case studies. Each 'case' was chosen not to represent a shared problem but because 'in all it's particularity *and* ordinariness, this case itself is of interest' (Stake, 2000: 437).

It should be noted that Corby is a relatively small town and just changing the names of participants would not be enough to ensure their anonymity, so family composition and other details have been changed to make each case study less recognisable.

I feel incredibly privileged to have the opportunity to produce two case studies with families. I focused on how adopting the *PICL approach* with parents who were not able to access Pen Green's PICL groups had increased their involvement in their child's development and learning. The case studies were written and then revisited so families could reflect on their experience of being involved and what had happened since the interviews: 'Sometimes in-depth knowledge of an individual example is more helpful than fleeting knowledge of a larger number of examples. We gain a better understanding of the whole by focusing on a key part' (Gerring, 2007: 1).

Case study

DYLAN, SHELLEY, SCOTT AND ANNA'S STORY

Family context

Dylan is a 2-year-old boy who came into the Family Room once a week with his paternal grandmother Shelley. Dylan's parents, Scott and Anna, both work full-time; Dylan is cared for by various other family members during the week.

Involving Dylan's parents in his learning

Dylan seemed tired and withdrawn each time he came into the Family Room and would be somewhat distant from the other children. We felt concerned about his low levels of well-being and involvement (see Chapter 4 for definitions of the concepts of 'Well-being' and 'Involvement'). Dylan would choose to sit on the adult chairs or curl up in the corners, anything to be away from the busy flow of the room. Dylan had a grubby, well-loved, bear that Shelley objected to him dragging everywhere but it was the only thing that he seemed to value. Often Dylan would switch off from the commotion of the room and somehow manage to fall asleep, for a couple of hours at a time.

Caroline and I reflected deeply about Dylan, acknowledging that his behaviour was painful for us to bear. We felt more confident working with loud, aggressive or energetic 2-year-olds but felt a sense of loss when trying to cater effectively for the needs of a toddler who was so quiet and withdrawn.

As our relationship grew with Shelley, we began talking to her more about Dylan and his father Scott. Both of Dylan's parents worked full-time and Dylan was cared for by various family members during the week. Shelley shared with us that Dylan refused to sleep in his own bed and did not have any sort of routine; she believed his parents were often exhausted. Dylan insisted on staying up with his mummy and daddy when they got home from work and would only go up to bed when they did, insisting on being alongside them in their bed. Any attempts to get him to sleep in his own very well-decorated and well-equipped bedroom would result in a night of tears and tantrums and ultimately end in him being allowed back into the parental bed. Shelley despaired that his mother gave in and felt she was 'spoiling' him. We now understood why he might be so tired during the day after a disturbed night.

Each Tuesday we would think carefully about what resources we could put out that might be attractive to Dylan, enticing him away from the chairs or corners, but we could find nothing that held any interest for him for more than a couple of minutes.

(Continued)

(Continued)

He showed extremely low levels of involvement.

Table 9.1 Involvement Scale going from low to extremely high

Extremely low	The child hardly shows any activity: • no concentration: staring, daydreaming; • an absent, passive attitude; • no goal-oriented activity, aimless actions, not producing anything; • no signs of exploration and interest; • not taking anything in, no mental activity.

> If you are involved, you feel appealed by the activity, you are truly interested and driven to engage in it. You cannot achieve a high level of involvement if you do things only because others ask or force you to. The motivation must come from within. (Laevers, 2011)

We worked hard with Shelley to think more creatively about how we could cater for Dylan's needs. At times this was challenging; Shelley believed that a quiet and unobtrusive child was something of a bonus and an opportunity to socialise with the other adults in the room. When we spoke about drawing Dylan into play in the Family Room she believed we were trying to discourage the use of his beloved bear and suggested we just take it away from him. Naomi Eisenstadt, whose thesis on the 'Moorlands Drop In' in Milton Keynes is one of a very few reports about community drop-ins, reflected that 'the real challenge is to share knowledge in ways that build confidence in both parents and children' (Eisenstadt, 2011: 157). We spoke with Shelley about the importance of 'transitional objects' to young children (Winnicott, 1991: 5); both family workers and grandparents needed to acknowledge the comfort that Dylan was gaining from something so familiar that reminded him of the comfort and security of his home and was enabling him to maintain contact with his parents during their working hours.

Dylan began relating to us individually to a small degree. He was able to use our names and from the safety of the adult chairs would allow us to read a story or offer small world figures. Gradually he began joining in with some of the activities on offer in the Family Room.

We believed that the environment was improving for Dylan when he sat and painted with the other children. His well-being appeared to be higher than before and he cheerily described who he had painted in his picture. As he told Caroline about 'mummy's yellow hair' he began crying, sobbing in fact, and was quickly inconsolable and asking for his mother. Shelley was quick to offer a cuddle and tell him not to worry, trying to distract him, but Dylan rejected her soothing and his distress was palpable. Goleman reflects on how 'Everyone in a child's day offers a model, for better or for worse, of how to handle distress'

(Goleman,1996: 174); sometimes as adults we respond to children with affection because we cannot bear to see their grief.

Caroline, who had been in a reflexive practice staff study group called The Emotional Roots of Learning which is led by the Northern School of Child and Adolescent Psychotherapy, knelt down beside him and said 'it's ok to miss your mummy and daddy and it's ok to cry'. She went on to tell him 'my children miss me when I have to be at work and I miss them too. We don't have to be brave all the time'. Dylan became quiet as he listened to her, and then began smiling.

Caroline later shared with me that before undertaking the Emotional Roots course she would have probably used techniques like Shelley's to get Dylan to stop crying and distract him by getting him to think about something other than his parents. The power and impact of naming and acknowledging the emotion he was feeling were visible to all of us. Laevers (2011) talks about the basic needs of well-being.

The basic needs

1. Physical needs (need to eat, drink, move, sleep, etc.).
2. The need for affection, warmth and tenderness (being hugged, physical contact and vicinity, receiving and giving love and warmth).
3. The need for safety, clarity and continuity (need for a more or less predictable environment, need to know where you stand, what is allowed and what is not allowed and being able to count on others).
4. The need for recognition and affirmation (feeling accepted and appreciated by others, meaning something to others, being part of a group and belonging).
5. The need to experience oneself as capable (feeling that you can do something yourself, master something, experience how to push the limits of your capabilities, experience success).
6. The need for meaning and (moral) values (feeling a 'good' person and feeling connected with others and the world).

After this we realised that it was important to attempt to build a stronger relationship with Dylan's mother and father as well as his grandmother Shelley. We were used to making connections with families and we knew and understood the value of home visiting to build children's resilience: 'through contributing to the development of support networks and building relationships with families, early years centres can help provide a foundation for future resilience' (Kirk, 2003: 96). But we

(Continued)

(Continued)

were mindful about how we might need to carefully broach the subject with Shelley. We did not want to do anything that might imply we wanted to undermine her or go behind her back; she was a very proud and loving grandmother. She had also suggested that Dylan's parents might not want to be seen as parents who were not coping or required support. As Quinton reminds us 'understanding "support" includes understanding how being given support makes people feel' (2004: 24).

We spoke with Shelley gently about how making contact with Dylan's parents and home visiting would help us better plan for Dylan's learning and development. We asked her whether, as Dylan's grandmother, she felt it would be appropriate for us to meet his parents and see Dylan in his home context: 'Given the crucial impact of early experiences on children's continuing development and well-being, the importance of these new relationships cannot be over-stated' (Brooker, 2010: 194). Shelley agreed to ask Scott and Anna but was keen to defend their position as working parents. We had a heartfelt discussion about the pain that juggling work and young children can bring to any couple.

Shelley rang us the following day to excitedly tell us that Dylan's parents would really appreciate a home visit and passed on their thanks. The visit was arranged for the following Wednesday. When Dylan came in to the Family Room he talked about how we were coming to his house and which toys he would be showing us. He told every person that came into the Family Room that day 'Sandra and Caroline are coming to my house tonight'.

Dylan and his parents warmly welcomed us to their home. Dylan took great pleasure in introducing his daddy, pets and mummy to us. We talked with his parents about the importance of parental involvement and the child development frameworks we used to plan for children's learning. It was clear that Dylan was a very treasured little boy.

In the Family Room we usually encourage parents to keep folders about their children's learning, supporting them with resources and new information. There was not a folder for Dylan. He only came in once a week, had only recently started engaging with other children and the activities in the room and was there with his grandmother. We realised this was a huge error on our part and talked with his parents about developing a two-way communication process where we could send home pictures and observations from his time in the Family Room and they could feed back and provide their own pictures and observations at home. We took pictures with the family to go into the folder. It felt important that Dylan should have pictures of his mummy, daddy and pets to be able to look through and connect with whilst in the Family Room.

During the first home visit Dylan took delight in showing us his bedroom and garden and displayed extremely high well-being. Scott and Anna both talked openly about being working parents and how tough this can be. We enquired about Dylan's weekly routine and realised that he was being cared for by up to six different family members each week. Although Shelley had him every Tuesday much of the other caring was less predictable, and often arranged at the last minute. We also discussed the sleeping routines that Shelley had shared with us; Scott and Anna were both happy to continue with Dylan sharing their bed despite their lost sleep as they felt that he was only 2 years old and seeking comfort and contact from parents who he missed during their long days at work.

We discussed with Dylan's parents other opportunities for Dylan that were available at Pen Green, and later completed a nursery application form. We visited Dylan at home about every three weeks and observations were forthcoming on both sides. Shelley felt that Dylan became much more involved in Family Room life and was more lively and engaged when in her home.

When Dylan was ready to begin nursery we were able to negotiate sessions which would fit around Scott and Anna's working patterns so that life could become more predictable for Dylan. We shared his file with his new family worker. We could confidently describe what activities Dylan enjoyed and how he played with resources. During his nursery settling-in period Anna and Scott took it in turns to be with him in nursery and worked together to ensure a smooth transition for him.

When reflecting back on what difference this made to the family Scott and Anna wanted to share that the pressure of full-time work meant that childcare was a constant stressor; they were so happy to see Dylan that they did not want to spend time with him enforcing strict bedtimes or ordinary routines. Once they tracked how a week of childcare looked for Dylan they appreciated why he was always clinging to them and they were keen to get more structure in place so they could reap the benefits of a working life without so much emotional turmoil. Initially they had thought that family care was better for him than nursery care but when they saw how fractured it actually was for Dylan, they were happy to introduce him to the setting. They were reassured that he would be eligible for a free entitlement of 15 hours. With him in nursery during set hours they could tailor their working hours around him and this allowed for much more satisfactory time together. The impact on Dylan's well-being was clear for all the important adults in his life to see and he has since made a smooth transition into school where he continues to grow and develop.

Case study

LEE, DENISE, JACOB, KELLY AND BEN'S STORY

Family context

Lee, the youngest of Denise's four children, was two when I first met him. Given a discretionary place in our Baby Nest (education with care provision for children from 9 months to 3 years) because of his family circumstances, he had

(Continued)

(Continued)

a diagnosis of global development delay and Hyporeflexia (below normal reflex responses). Denise's story involves social workers, drugs, grief, poverty, domestic abuse, debt, housing problems, support, integrated practice, relaxation and fun; she could be described as loud, aggressive, kind-hearted, generous and determined.

When I first met Denise she had just ended a period of involvement with social services. She had used the Family Room occasionally, and was being supported by the local family support charity, Home Start. Two of her children were at primary school, one was in the Pen Green nursery, and Lee attended the Baby Nest at Pen Green twice a week.

Lee's additional needs affected his joints and core strength. He would spend many afternoons asleep in a pushchair. Denise was very nervous about rough play, fearful that he would be hurt. She did not want him to use the soft room or run around in the garden. When Lee used the Family Room he would amuse himself with small toys but often chose not to engage in messy activities with the rest of the children in the room.

Involving Denise in Lee's learning

After about a month of knowing Denise and Lee, I needed to complete a child study for my MA and seized the opportunity to get to know both of them better. I was mindful of what Holman (1987) refers to as 'research from the underside':

> research is associated with power because it can be the key to information which others do not possess and because the publication of that information can influence the decisions which determine how resources are distributed and how services are shaped.
>
> (Holman, 1987: 671).

I wanted the experience to be enriching for us all. Easen and colleagues (1992) reflect that 'parents can be very effective partners only if professional workers take notice of what they say, how they express their needs, and if parents' contributions are treated as intrinsically important'.

I was aware that Denise was disappointed to not be able to join the PICL group at Pen Green; a weekly group during which parents watch recordings of their children in nursery and reference their learning to the frameworks discussed in Chapter 4. At the time Lee was not yet in nursery and the group had already been running for two terms for children in his year group.

Although I had been a parent at Pen Green and volunteering and working for a decade, my previous academic studies had been in law and business so I needed to learn about the child development theoretical frameworks being used by staff alongside Denise.

Genuinely believing that parents are children's first and most enduring educators my child study was about Denise being able to capture and reflect back on her little boy's play. Involving his siblings, too, allowed us to see who touched his life and who or what was significant to him.

The first week we began the study happened to be half term so each time Lee came into the Family Room he was accompanied, in an already very busy and chaotic setting, by his older siblings. Denise told me 'he's ball daft, that's all he wants to play with'! We filmed Lee baking with his brother and sister and ended up with hours of footage, which was interesting socially, but we both felt we could not link what we were seeing with any of the theoretical frameworks we had been reading about.

The next time I filmed Lee, Denise had nipped out for a smoke. Lee quickly became inconsolable and Caroline and I took it in turns to comfort him. We did not have a sound knowledge at this time of his interests but by chance, we suggested he draw mummy a picture and he calmed down and sat at the table. He chose my biro and some paper and he began mark making. Since he looked involved in the task I filmed him, however when we sat and watched the film we noticed he was displaying a low level of involvement. Although he was mark making his eyes were scanning the room and every time someone entered the Family Room he looked up hopefully. As soon as Denise returned he glanced at his picture before discarding it and running to her for comfort; quiet and compliant behaviour soon revealed itself to me as aimless and uninterested.

After a few weeks of working alongside each other Denise invited me home for tea and this was the beginning of a strong working relationship between her family and me in my role as family worker. I left the Centre with Denise, Lee and Ben and went to collect the older two children from school. After this we all walked home together chatting about the day, the weather and generally getting to know each other better. Once at their home I gave each child a disposable camera so they could record each other and talked with them about studying Lee. They excitedly told me about his love for balls and set off to record everything he did.

While waiting for his dinner he began playing with a football in the living room. This involved running in and out, in and out, of the room kicking the ball while beaming. When watching it back Denise and I could see that although this was tremendously annoying in a home with three siblings, he was highly involved. He had chosen the activity himself, set his own rules and was intrinsically motivated.

She complained that he was never interested in the big toys she bought him so when I visited the home I asked his sister to show me his favourite toys. She pulled out two bead mazes, a spinning top and another football. It would seem that whether consciously or not, Denise was providing resources to support and extend his rotation schema (Athey, 2007).

(Continued)

(Continued)

When it was time to go into the kitchen for dinner Lee sat on the floor with his spinning top, he was keen to show me just how fast it could go and got to the stage of thumping it down and resting his forehead on it as it span wildly. Watching the video vignette later Denise noticed he was completely absorbed and how much pleasure he was getting out of the experience. Over the next couple of months, during which we both filmed Lee many times, he consistently showed a strong rotation schema.

The final piece of filming I did was again a time when Denise had gone out for a smoke. This time he was playing with two Duplo figures, whilst sitting inside the empty Duplo box. He was talking to each figure; he was so relaxed and self-assured that, when reaching over the edge of the box for another figure, he fell, quickly regained his balance and continued playing. He was so highly involved that he failed to notice when Denise came back into the room.

Once the child study had been submitted Denise was keen to continue observing Lee in this way so we began keeping folders of all the children in the Family Room, much like the Celebrations of Achievement documentation used in the nursery and Baby Nest. Daws found that:

> people who are properly listened to and appreciated for who they are and what they have to face may then be able to take on the ideas about themselves ... then start thinking for themselves and perhaps create some of what was missing.
>
> (1999: 278)

Because we wanted to see the child reflected through the eyes of their parents we left the folders to the parents, supplying cameras, taking it in turns to record children, printing pictures and ensuring there was a ready supply of paper and glue. Denise was the most dedicated author and took great pride not only in recording information about Lee, but also in the aesthetics of the folder itself. Being able to study her child in this way gave her the confidence and language to have a deeper dialogue with Lee's Family Worker when he began attending nursery.

Like his mother, Lee became more confident and involved in activities; he grew verbally and physically. With so much knowledge we were all able to find more appropriate resources that would challenge and excite him. One rainy day, Denise and Lee set up a bowling alley in the Family Room that proved to be a great hit with all the children, and other parents.

Having completed the child study with me, and maintaining a folder of Lee's achievements for a year, Denise enrolled in our volunteer course. She successfully completed it and began volunteering in a number of groups and cooking in the Family Room on a weekly basis. By the time it was Lee's time to go to school we had very little involvement with the family; in the Family Room they were growing in confidence. As Kirk points out:

> coping successfully with transitions throughout life, such as school entry, moving homes or entering employment, requires being able to establish positive relationships with authority and negotiating with a wide range of people to acquire appropriate supports. Parents who use early years provision will have already rehearsed many of the skills they need to manage changes, including the development of formal and informal support networks.
>
> (Kirk, 2003: 96).

If we meet in the street now Denise will excitedly tell me about how well Lee is doing at school and that he is now working in line with his peers. His love of balls has remained a constant. He now plays for a local football team and was chosen to be a mascot for Leicester City, just weeks before they won the Premier League:

> Families matter, most of all to children ... children's needs are best met by supporting their families within the community. (Phelan, 1983: 37)

Learning from the two case studies

In both case studies I have tried to illustrate the value of meeting parents 'where they are' whether physically, as in the case of Dylan's parents, or emotionally in the case of Lee's parents. It is widely accepted that children can counter some of the effects of multiple disadvantage if they have parents who are involved in their education. As early years educators, the onus must be on us to make this a possibility. As a Family Worker, I am only contracted to work 9.00 a.m. to 3.00 p.m. but, like most who choose this profession, I have a commitment to the families far beyond the working day.

Dylan was part of a large, loving family, all of his material needs were catered for handsomely but he was getting lost in a complicated system of adults, working hard to provide for him financially. His grandmother was always open with us but we noted the void created by the missing voices of his parents. It took a great deal of tact to broach the idea of meeting with them but the relationships that developed as a result of adopting a PICL approach meant that Dylan could share all he did when apart from his parents and share what he had done with his parents when he was with us.

As an adult and a child, Denise had belonged to a family that had been referred to many services duty bound to 'fix' whatever problem was their specialism. She was suspicious and wary of me. I was required to prove myself as someone trustworthy and reliable. I believe that the PICL approach allowed us to begin a dialogue about Lee, which then grew to embrace everything her family were experiencing. Munro points out 'the quality of the relationship between the child and family and professionals directly impacts on the effectiveness of help given' (Munro, 2011: 23).

Whether or not parents have the academic language that professionals often favour, or the means to illustrate links to the Early Years Foundation Stage curriculum, they will have noticed their children's schemas, levels of well-being or involvement and what intrinsically motivates them. Through choices of toys, outings and provision of resources most families will be supporting these interests already. Quinton states 'parenting is something that parents do, not something that parents have. Variation in what they do reflects what they have in the way of resources and support as well as their skills and characteristics' (Quinton, 2004: 27).

Introducing the well-being scales to Dylan's parents meant they had a powerful tool with which they could initiate a richer dialogue with Shelley to consider how their son may be feeling and what steps needed to be taken to ensure a gentle transition into her care. Denise felt very differently as being a part of a family who until recently had been teetering on the brink of social care and having often experienced social exclusion, she felt the well-being scales were somehow judgemental and prescriptive. Looking at his schemas, however, meant we could both focus on how he was playing with the resources he was being offered in a positive manner and consider together how we could extend his learning.

Offering each of the parents the opportunity to document their findings in a portfolio acknowledged the unique insight they had into their child's learning and gave them the chance to frame that knowledge in the same manner that professionals do. Hughes and MacNaughton point out that 'practitioners legitimise their own practice within the language game' (2000: 253) and reflect that the 'ideal speech about the child would be discourse between parents and staff that would be genuinely open, free from the distortions, habits and traditions associated with the structured inequalities' (2000: 249).

We worked with Dylan's parents for just over six months and Denise for just over two years.

Suggestions for your own practice

- Consider how you engage with all parents.
- Spend time thinking about how you use language and then how you explain the child development frameworks that you are sharing with parents.
- Outstanding practitioners will accept and respect the cultural and social context within which each family is located. Freire (1970) encourages us to be 'really human, empathetic, loving, communicative, and humble'.
- Is it possible for you to home visit the children you work with?

Key points

- Meeting parents 'where they are', not where you would like them to be.
- How we introduce the key concepts to parents as a shared language.
- The transformational nature of the PICL approach.
- Sharing knowledge and resources.
- How much time we need to work with families to effect changes in relationships and attitudes (ours as well as the parents').

Recommended reading

Freire, P. (1996) *Pedagogy of the Oppressed*. London: Penguin.

Holman, B. (1983) *Resourceful Friends – Skills in Community Social Work*. London: The Children's Society.

Holman, B. (1987) 'Research from the underside', *British Journal of Social Work*, 17(6): 669–83.

Websites

Laevers (2005) Well-being and Involvement in Care Settings: A Process-oriented Self-evaluation: www.kindengezin.be/img/sics-ziko-manual.pdf

10

The impact on parents' lives

Annette Cummings

Introduction

This chapter gives an account of how I, formerly a parent at Pen Green and now a teacher in the nursery, initially got involved in the research project in 1996–7. It also describes two stories of nursery parents' different experiences of being involved in a study group and one child's experience of her mother being involved over a period of one to three years during the late 1990s, with an update of where they are in 2016.

My account

As a family worker at Pen Green, I have experience of co-leading a research and development study group that focuses on parents' involvement in their children's learning. As a group leader, I have found the group absorbing, thought-provoking and enlightening. It has been wonderful to watch the parents grow in confidence and knowledge as the year progresses. It is also fascinating to listen to the parents' views and comments on how their children engage in play at home. Each parent brings to the group a wealth of knowledge of their own child, which helps to provide a more holistic approach to the child when it comes to planning provision for the nursery (see Chapter 8). Throughout the time that I have been running the group, I have become very interested in the way that the parents' involvement with their children's learning project has had a knock-on effect in relation to the parents' own personal growth and development.

Getting involved in my own children's learning

One of the reasons that I really enjoy co-leading the Parents' Involvement in Their Children's Learning (PICL) group is that it was because of my involvement with my own children's learning that I felt impelled to go back to university to do a post-graduate teachers' certificate in education. When my eldest child started at the Pen Green nursery in 1993, the research and development work at the centre was in its early days. Even then, all the nursery parents had a chance to go to a training session on schemas, which was led by Tina Bruce, an education consultant and author of several books on early childhood education.

At this time, I knew nothing about schemas, but I did know that the things Alexandria was doing at home were driving me mad. Alexandria, who was aged 3 at the time, had a favourite game, hide-and-seek. She used to get inside the duvet cover and do the press studs up, or get inside the curtain lining. She always wanted to dress up and put make-up on. Meanwhile, my younger child, Olivia, who was aged 16 months, used to empty tins out of the kitchen cupboard, put them into her pram and wheel them around the house. Between both children, I thought I would go crazy.

I went along to a child development session, at the Pen Green Centre, when Alexandria was attending the nursery, and I found the whole thing mind-blowing. Everything fell into place. Alexandria was displaying typical 'enveloping' behaviour and Olivia was 'transporting'. I was hooked. It all seemed so simple. The schema training helped me to understand my children better and also helped me to make extra provision at home to help them extend their play.

When Olivia showed signs of an 'enveloping' schema, I just took it in my stride. I knew exactly how to support her in her play and bought her Polly Pocket dolls, which would incorporate both schemas (enveloping and transporting).

Olivia always displayed her cluster of schemas that include enveloping and transporting. On a holiday to Minorca, when Olivia was about 7, she wanted to pack her own hand luggage. When we reached our apartment, she disappeared into the bedroom and reappeared five minutes later. I thought nothing of it until I went to hang the clothes up in the wardrobe. When I opened the wardrobe door, there were 37 teddy bears staring at me. Olivia could not stop laughing. She thought it was very funny that nobody knew she had transported them all the way to Minorca from her room at home.

The parents that I work with (Figure 10.1) in the research group have had similar experiences. For example:

- Louise has two children, Sean and James, and is married to Scott. Sean started nursery in 1996 and left to go to school in 1998 when James, his younger brother, started using the nursery. Both children have had the benefit of attending nursery for two full years, which seems to us, at Pen Green, to be ideal. Louise attended the PICL study group for four years.

- Eloise is married to Dave, and they have two children, Beccy and Jessica. Eloise went to the PICL study group every week for three years. Beccy spent a year at the nursery and Jessica was full-time in the nursery for two years. I interviewed Beccy for this 3rd edition.
- Dave is married to Tracey and they have two children, Lorin and Ross. Both parents attended the PICL group. When Lorin moved on to school, Ross was in the nursery. Dave attended the PICL study group for two years.

Figure 10.1 A family in the research group: Eloise and Dave with Beccy and Jessica

Starting the group

All new parents, both mothers and fathers, are encouraged by their family worker to join a research study group when their child starts nursery. They are normally introduced to the programme on an initial home visit well before the child comes into the nursery. As a teacher in the nursery, I always talk to the parents to explain how valuable it is for us to have information on what their child is doing at home, and I explain how that information is used in the nursery. I also explain that learning about why your children do certain things can help in terms of what you provide for them in the home. It can also increase your understanding of the way that children think. Parents are very interested in what their children are learning, and most of our parents have some link with the research project through attending the PICL study group, keeping a diary, or coming to the key concept training sessions in the first term (see Chapter 4).

Some parents find going to a group difficult to handle, and sometimes it is the thought of their own literacy skills that comes to the fore. Their anxieties about writing often date back to their own experiences of schooling. This literacy issue is sensibly dealt with by staff so that most parents can feel comfortable about attending. The staff explain that, although some parents in the group will want to keep diaries, there is no need to write anything down if parents are reluctant writers. All parents can discuss their children's interests and development orally in a supportive small group setting. Sometimes parents have low self-esteem, so gentle encouragement is needed to get them to attend the group. I always tell the parents that joining the group is also a good way to make new friends, because, as parents, they all have at least one thing in common, their children.

Case study

LOUISE'S STORY

Louise's feelings on starting the group

Sean was 3 and had started nursery, and I decided to become involved in the PICL group. I had already been at the centre doing lots of other parent groups and I really enjoyed the centre. It gave me something to do during the day and somewhere where I could learn. So I started attending the PICL group and I really enjoyed it. It just broadened my horizons as to what Sean was doing.

Sean was really boisterous as a toddler; he was very physical. He was always into climbing, running around, hiding and running away. I had to run a lot after him and be behind him a lot of the time, as he was always doing dangerous things. James, my other little one, does exactly the same. I found Sean quite hard. Being your first child, I always felt as if wherever I looked it was always Sean that was, you know, mucking about, as they say, or running about or throwing things. He used to throw everything. He used to be quite rough with other children, which was really hard. When Sean started nursery, and I had the opportunity to join the PICL group and learn something about why he was doing these things, I thought 'brilliant'. It was an ideal opportunity to give him everything I could, you know, from learning myself. The PICL group really opened my eyes as to why Sean was doing these things.

Going to the group itself was about making new friendships and also just about being able to get things off your chest and being reassured as to why the children were doing things, rather than bottling everything up – talking to people who understood as well, you know. The nursery staff who run the group could help you out.

Finding out about schemas

When I first went to the group, it was just brilliant knowing why he was doing things, especially the throwing, because he used to throw everything, and obviously that was his trajectory schema. They told me that he was going on to

(Continued)

(Continued)

learn about areas and everything to do with mathematics and things, and I was thinking, 'Wow,' and it took a little while to sink in, really. But then, as I went to the group, I learnt more and more why he was doing things at nursery, and it was relatively easy to see what he was doing at home. Sean used to flood my bathroom; he liked to see the water overflowing. Before, I was getting really angry because it was, like, so-called naughty things he was doing. Obviously, it still is a bit naughty sometimes, because you don't want your bathroom soaked or whatever, but why he was doing it was because he was learning. I used to try and think of alternative things for him to do, which wasn't wrecking my house and being dangerous. One thing he used to love was glass – he loved to see it smashed, which was really out of order. So I took him to the bottle bank, you know, hoping it would satisfy his need, but it wasn't enough; he still used to go on about glass. So at the PICL group, which was a lovely group, we talked about it. You felt as if you could go in and tell the group what they were doing, getting worries off your chest, and you'd be reassured why he was doing things. So then the staff at the PICL group suggested I get some ice cubes. So in the summer I used to freeze loads of ice, and let him go out in the garden with a big bucket and a hammer. He loved the banging and he used to smash all the ice everywhere, all along the path and that. It seemed to satisfy his need and then he sort of went on to something else.

I found the group really helped me in finding ideas for things for Sean to do that were interesting and safe.

Louise on being part of a group

I suppose the big thing I got out of the group was that what the boys were up to was OK. It boosted my confidence as a parent just knowing it was OK. I used to feel, a lot of the time, that Sean was the only one in the whole world that was doing these things, and I got to realise that he wasn't. Everybody else was able to share their anxieties as parents, and it made me feel a whole lot better. Because, a lot of the time outside of the group, I'm really honest about what they do, and sometimes I used to think that maybe I said too much. I sometimes felt as if other parents wouldn't say the things I said, they only said all the good things, and that used to make me feel even worse. So going to the research group was about sharing, and everybody in the group is the same, they used to share their anxieties, and it just helped us to understand that it was OK.

Louise – what it's meant to be part of the group

Coming to the group really helped my confidence in wanting to learn more about the children, and now I've gone on to run a group myself to do with babies.

It's called 'Growing Together', and it focuses on under-nursery-age children where parents can come and learn, from a really early age, why children are doing things. I really enjoy doing it because it's sort of an extension of me being involved with the PICL group as a parent. Now I'm helping to run this one, and it's really gone well. I found being in the role of the teacher strange at first because you feel a bit – well, you've always been to groups as a parent, but I want them to learn what I've learnt through the group. I'm really enthusiastic about, you know, letting them see what I've learnt through the group, how it's opened my eyes as to why my children are doing the things they do, and, you know, just finding that understanding. The group's helped my confidence. My boys come first, and being their advocate, going to school, and being able to talk to their teacher has been important.

When Sean started school, there was a bit of a problem. I sort of had a word with the teacher about it, and I wouldn't let it go. It was to do with his baseline assessment. I knew exactly why Sean hadn't done very well in baseline, because it takes Sean a few months, the person he is, to settle into change, to feel comfortable, to do his best. So I went in and explained that to the teacher. Now, you know, after a couple of months, he's coming out with flying colours. So, you know, I've followed it through with Sean, and the group has made me a lot more confident to speak to teachers. Like I say, when I had Sean, I really wanted to learn about children's development because you have a baby and it's a whole new world. I didn't really know anything about how children learn. I wanted to do something for myself so I did my diploma in child day-care by correspondence. Then I went on to do the Confident Parent, Confident Children Open University group at Pen Green. Then I went on to do the PICL group, and since then it's really taken off. I really enjoy working with children. I now work in a playgroup at the sports centre. James goes to school in September, so I think that's a turning point for myself. I always thought I'd like to be at home with the children when they're small, but when they do go to school, then it's time for me. I'm halfway-knowing what I'd like to do, and, you know, I was just thinking about whether to do my NVQ when James goes to school in September.

What next for Louise?

After Louise left school at 16, she went straight into an office, carrying out general administrative duties, and was amazed that she lasted in the job for eight years! When Sean was born, it was time for Louise to move on. She did O-level psychology and typing at the local college and eventually got a job at the local sports centre, working at reception and then moving on to working in the crèche.

At this point in her life, Sean had started attending nursery at Pen Green. Louise with her new baby James continued to use the baby groups at Pen Green

(Continued)

(Continued)

and then embarked on the Open University group, Confident Parents, Confident Children. Attending all these groups and courses made Louise want to gain more knowledge and insights into her children's learning. It was at this point that she joined the PICL group. From there, her career has snowballed. She has had paid employment from the centre, working in the kitchen and in the office. She is now a course leader of the 'Growing Together' group, paid for by the local college. This group is a research group concerned with supporting parents with babies and toddlers who want to understand more about their infants' learning and development.

Since Sean has moved to primary school, Louise has been a volunteer in the classroom, and her husband Scott has recently become a school governor. Louise completed her NVQ level 3 and worked as a member of supply staff in the nursery for some time. Subsequently, she became a full-time member of the nursery team.

An update in 2016 – Louise

Since 1999, Louise's learning journey into education has opened many doors of opportunity. After realising that her passion was working with children and families, she became a Family Worker in the nursery. Since then Louise has developed into a very skilled and sensitive practitioner, describing herself as 'calm, sensitive and organised'. She enjoys the complexities of working with families alongside building trusting relationships with children and colleagues.

Louise's practice has been enriched through CPD. In 2011, she began a foundation degree in Early Years Education from which she graduated with a first class honours degree. She then progressed to BA level, graduating with another first class degree in 2015. Louise described her time as a student as 'challenging but satisfying', a thought reflective of her passion for working with families, as well as a desire to develop and extend her practice. Louise has also contributed to articles in Nursery World magazine and has spoken at national and international conferences.

Louise is now one of the pedagogical leads in the nursery, a role she has aspired to for some time. She believes that the 'intimate model of working with children and parents' she experienced with her own children at Pen Green has helped her to succeed in this role. By engaging parents and successfully supporting her colleagues, she continues to develop her leadership skills. Louise has now set herself the challenge of undertaking a teacher training programme in the near future.

Sean and James both view Louise as a learner and achiever. They have attended both of her graduation ceremonies and have told her they are 'very proud of her'.

Likewise, Louise is proud of her sons. James is exploring further avenues with his future career and will be supported by his mum to achieve his goals. Being practically natured, James has a skill for DIY and enjoys solving hands-on problems. He is also a very good cook and can always 'throw a meal together' using his creativity. Sean was a high achiever at GCSE level and has now gone on to a happy and successful role as a care worker.

Figure 10.2 Louise, a Senior Family Worker at Pen Green

Case study

ELOISE'S AND BECCY'S STORY

Eloise was apprehensive but joined the group anyway and found some benefits from regular attendance. For example, attending the group gave her the confidence to talk to her children's teachers. Both daughters have done well but her older daughter, Beccy, has done very well educationally. Beccy has obviously been well supported by both of her parents, which we do not see as a coincidence. Beccy was excited to tell her story for this edition of the book.

An update in 2016 – Beccy and her family

Eloise has always been an advocate for her children as they progressed through the school system. Beccy (Becky changed the spelling of her name when she moved to

(Continued)

(Continued)

secondary school), her older daughter, stated that 'my parents have supported me all through the school system and I have been lucky'. When Beccy left Pen Green nursery she moved to the local primary school alongside the friends she had made in nursery. She was very happy there and still has a strong bond with the friends she made. Beccy then transitioned to secondary school and set her sights on going to university. She did very well at her GCSEs and A-levels and achieved her goal of attending university on a four-year degree programme. Part of the course was a year away teaching English in a primary school in France.

With Eloise working at the centre for a number of years, the family still have close ties to Pen Green. When being interviewed, Beccy said that she has felt 'connected' to Pen Green throughout her life. At age 16, Beccy became involved with the summer play scheme provision and after-school club at the centre, a role she really enjoyed. She mentioned that the role 'felt comfortable' as she knew a lot of staff already. Building up relationships with children was a key element of this role, something Beccy took in her stride. She particularly liked working with the most disadvantaged and challenging children, as it was an opportunity to understand the complexities they faced at home. Beccy continued to work at the centre when home from university and in 2012 was also involved in a research project. As part of this project Beccy came back into nursery and was filmed. There are still images of Beccy around the centre as a child and as a young adult.

In 2001, Beccy told her mum that she wanted to be a teacher. By the end of 2016, Beccy will be well on her way to fulfilling this dream. She graduates this July with an honours degree and has just registered with a local teaching school to start ITT in September.

Figure 10.3 Beccy in 2016

Case study

DAVE'S STORY

Dave's feelings about starting the group

I started with the PICL group a month after Ross started nursery. He has been coming to nursery for roughly 18 months and I have been doing the PICL group for much the same time. I went along mainly to get involved with knowing why Ross was doing certain things, because when our daughter was coming up to 7, she came through the nursery, and there were things she did, playing at home, that would drive me mad. My wife Tracey was involved with the nursery anyway, coming to baby groups and groups with Lorin before. She would say, 'She's doing this because of this and this is her schema', and I didn't know anything about what she was going on about.

I was interested to come along when Ross came to nursery because I was now on permanent night shift, whereas before I used to work a double day shift, 6–2 or 2–10, so I couldn't get involved. I wanted to come along and find out why Ross was doing certain things and how he could be encouraged. We found that Lorin was always encouraged, with drawing and painting and writing and even with simple maths, at nursery. Now, at school, she is in the top group in the class, she reads really well, better than some children I know who are a lot older, and she writes and spells words that my boss at work would struggle with. She's really doing very, very well, so I was encouraged to come along to these things, to the group, to find out how I could help Ross in the same way as Lorin had benefited.

Also, going to this group, I have managed to find out about things that my child does that I was not particularly pleased with or happy about. We used to be a bit wary of Ross bouncing around, jumping off the furniture. Now, rather than tell him off all the time, we realise the only thing we can do is make what he does safer, so my sister-in-law bought him a trampoline for his birthday. He used it a lot, rather than the furniture, which is encouraging. He bounced around on the trampoline until he became, not bored with it, but he'd bounced enough, and now it's in the playhouse in the garden, and if they're out in the garden in the summer, he'll bounce on it again.

Finding out about schemas

I'd spoken to Tina Bruce on a number of occasions on study days, and I've always found what she had to say really interesting, because you look at your children and you don't realise the hidden things, their ways of thinking. Before the schema training, I would have spent all this money on toys that he wouldn't play with,

(Continued)

(Continued)

whereas now I know I would have saved myself a lot of money, and I've bought him boxes, some wooden boxes, anything to put things in and move them about because he's into this enclosure schema. We've learnt that you don't have to spend a lot of money on expensive toys that they're not going to play with. At Christmas this year, through the PICL group, knowing that Ross was into dressing up (envelopment schema), we bought him a dressing-up Buzz Lightyear wings, mask and helmet. A lot of our friends spent hundreds of pounds on their children, but, with Ross, he had nearly everything he wanted. He was really excited about everything he got, and he plays with everything. Not just like Christmas Day and Boxing Day and it's all forgotten, he's still playing with everything we bought him now, and I think we'd have struggled to spend £50 on him this Christmas. I've gained a lot of new learning talking with Tina and finding out how she gets her ideas and things, and I've borrowed a book by Tina, from Trevor the head of centre, and I've been taking it to work with me, and it's fascinating – it's really good.

Ross has been interested in Sellotaping things, connecting things together with Sellotape, tying things, making up parcels. He's forever bringing us things in paper stuck with Sellotape and saying, 'I've brought you a present', so one of the staff suggested we buy him a Sellotape dispenser. Because he's got little hands, he can't peel the Sellotape off the roll, and they've got one at nursery and he knows how to use it. So we bought him a big Sellotape dispenser, some paper, pens and bits for Christmas. It was the best present we could have bought him at the time, this Sellotape dispenser, and the Sellotape was all over the house. But whereas a lot of parents would have been annoyed at the Sellotape stuck to the doors and wrapped around the chair legs and things, we know why he does it. It's made our life a lot calmer.

Dave on being part of the group

If there's something that we don't particularly like him doing at home or something I am worrying about, I felt I could talk about it in the group. For instance, Ross had a dummy, and I used to say, he was nearly 4 at the time, and he still had this dummy stuck in his mouth. I mean, I criticise people for saying, I don't like my son playing with prams or I don't like my son playing with dolls or dressing up and all this, and I criticise people for that, yet I could see myself doing much the same thing and saying the same things about his dummy. I used to talk about it at the PICL group, I used to come to it and say, 'Look, what am I going to do about it, this dummy?' and lots of the parents were saying, you know, that they had to leave it for Santa. One of them said that her son buried it in the garden and things like that. We went on holiday, and for the whole fortnight Ross had it stuck in his mouth. I used to get really worried, thinking, 'Oh, what's he gonna do, he's got all these dummies, and people are gonna think, look at the size of that kid with that dummy.' The week after we came home, I was at the point of thinking, 'Oh, no.' I was gonna hide them or throw them all out and just tell him they'd gone. But one night he was going to bed, he had his dummy, and he just said to me, 'I don't like the taste of this.' I said, 'Well, we've only got two or three, try this one. I'll run it under the tap.' He replied, 'No, I don't like the taste of that one.' I said, 'We haven't got any more.' He replied, 'I don't want one then.' He put these three dummies on his chest of drawers in the bedroom and went to bed. That was the end of it, he never had them again, and afterward I kept thinking all this fuss I've made, and people would have been thinking, 'Oh my God, here he goes again about this bloody dummy.' But all this fuss I'd made, at the end of the day, he was the one who instigated finishing it, and we've learnt, a lot of the time, from the group, a lot of the parents had said that he'll give it up when he wants to, and I was thinking, 'When will that be?' But I didn't mind going to the PICL group and saying, 'Look, I'm really concerned about this', even though, in a way, I was being very similar to the ones who say, I don't like him playing with prams, or I don't like him doing this. I could see that I was along those lines, but I didn't mind saying it because I felt really strongly about it.

Dave on what the group has meant to me and the future

The group helped me as a parent. I think it's great because I work permanent night shifts, and it's horrible to say, but it's more like a social event. I mean, you come and chat with other parents, and it's always good to come. I love it, I love coming to the group. We have a chat and a laugh. I've learnt so much more about my children, and I've learnt how to encourage them to learn through playing and what they're getting out of what they do. Apart from my own children, I've never had that much experience with younger children, so I started helping at the nursery: through my involvement with the PICL group, I've become more involved with Pen Green than my wife is. She's done her A-Level English here, but I've also done parent interviews for the Sure Start Project and I've interviewed to appoint new staff. I've personally gained a lot from it. I mean, I sort of found out now I've got other career opportunities, really, as well as developing various skills like visiting other people in their houses and doing interviews. I've had training. I've helped out with interviews for staff at Pen Green as well, which I never have been asked to do anywhere, really, other than at work, and I also found that, in my opinion, my input has been valued, and that's something that helps everybody's self-esteem and personal development. One of the senior members of staff asked if I'd ever considered working with children as a career, which I hadn't. I'd never really thought it was a viable career opportunity, really, until I sort of looked into it, and then I thought maybe I could do the NVQ through gaining experience working with the Pen Green nursery children.

(Continued)

(Continued)

What next for Dave?

Dave left school at 17 and went on to a building site. He then worked as a painter and decorator for two years before moving into warehouse management.

Dave is on the road to a new career through coming to the centre and joining different groups. He has now enrolled in the Wider Opportunities Programme, a European Social Fund employment scheme run by staff at the centre. He is attending a course called 'Introduction to Childcare', which is a preparation course for the NVQ in childcare.

Dave works as a volunteer in the Pen Green nursery on a Thursday afternoon and now has paid work supporting a child with additional needs in the nursery every afternoon at story time.

Dave got involved with the Sure Start programme's parent-led needs assessment (Pen Green Research Base Report, 2000), interviewing parents on a range of issues. This was paid work, and he has been approached to do follow-up interviews this summer. Although Dave still works night shifts as a warehouse manager, his new career in childcare could not be further from the career he planned when he left school.

An update in 2016 – Dave

Dave enjoyed supporting his children at nursery and in 1999 was interested in looking into a career in childcare. As he looked further into the profession he realised that he would have to take a pay cut of around £10,000 per annum. This was the deciding factor and he reluctantly decided to stay with his employer. He has been with the same company since and his career has progressed and he holds down a very responsible job. However there were some benefits to working constant nights as it allowed him to come off shift, take the children to school, pick them up at the end of the day and read a bedtime story to them before going back out to work. This was very important to him as a father to the children.

Tracey, who also attended the PICL group, began working as a teaching assistant to the Special Needs Co-ordinator at a local secondary school. She then trained and qualified as a HLTA and spent lots of time in the classroom. This gave Tracey plenty of hands-on experience and she realised that she could be a teacher. Tracey then worked as an unqualified teacher in the humanities department in the school for a number of years. She then left to undertake a BA in Learning and Teaching. Following this, she continued to teacher training level and completed the GTP teacher training, meeting her goal of becoming an NQT. Tracey is now qualified as a full-time teacher in a Corby primary school. Ross has been equally academically successful. At secondary school, he was awarded a special prize voted for by all the teachers in recognition of his all-round attributes. On leaving school, he was awarded a full scholarship with an accountancy company called KPMG. He is paid to train, and is currently residing between Exeter University where he is studying and Birmingham, where one of the offices of the company are located. On completion, the five-year course will provide Ross with a degree in accountancy as well as other professional qualifications. In addition to his academic success, Ross has taught himself how to play a range of musical instruments including the guitar, drums and keyboard and has recently begun playing the ukulele. His efforts have proved worthwhile and he has just been offered his first 'gig' in Exeter which he excitedly awaits. Ross's love of superheroes, which we documented when he was at nursery, has never left him and he is still an avid collector of Star Wars memorabilia. This strong link to his early years is also evident in his remaining friendships with children that he met at nursery. He continues to visit them in London. Dave's daughter Lorin has recently given birth to her first child which has made Dave and Tracey proud first-time grandparents who are excited about the future.

Figure 10.4 The Freeman family

Reflection

This chapter demonstrates the importance of parents being involved in their children's learning and that it has beneficial effects for all concerned. Involvement with their children's learning from an early age seems to have given the parents the confidence and the resources to ensure that their children succeeded in the education system. They are the best advocates for their children and felt able to challenge and to ask questions when they felt that the system had let them down in some way. Being involved in their own children's learning has also inspired Louise and Tracy to develop a love of learning that was never nurtured in their own school experiences. They have both recognised that they can make a difference in other children's lives and have chosen careers that reflect this.

The benefits for the children have been measured in the fact that they are confident and competent young adults with bright futures ahead of them. They have been supported by their parents through school and have developed a sense of themselves as successful learners who can succeed and achieve in life. These young people are the next generation of parents who hopefully will be advocates for their own children in the future:

> Parents and carers of young children in whatever family configuration or circumstance thus have an absolutely vital role in education for they are the most significant reference point with regard to children's identity, learning stance, the scaffolding of understanding of learning outcomes.
>
> (Pollard, 1996: 307)

Suggestions for your own practice

- Try to see things from the parents' viewpoint.
- Recognise that parents have expertise when it comes to their own children.
- Offer a warm and welcoming space to hold any groups or meetings for parents.
- Offer times for groups or meetings that reflect the working patterns of the parents.
- Find out from the parents how they see the role of the school in the education of their children.

Key points

- Parents are their children's first and most enduring educators.
- In our experience all parents are interested in being involved in some way with their children's learning
- Our task is to make it possible for the parents to become involved.
- Talking with other parents increases confidence.
- Children can succeed in the education system when their parents are involved and interested.

Recommended reading

Blanden, J. (2006) '"Bucking the trend": what enables those who are disadvantaged in childhood to succeed later in life?' Department of Work and Pensions Working Paper No 31, Corporate Document Services, Leeds.

Whalley, M., Arnold, C., Lawrence, P. and Peerless, S. (2012, December) 'The voices of their childhood: families and early years' practitioners developing emancipatory methodologies through a tracer study', *European Early Childhood Education Research Journal*, 20 (4): 519–35.

Websites

Pen Green: www.pengreen.org
Research Gate: www.researchgate.net/publications

11

Working in groups with parents of young children

Growing together at the Pen Green Centre

Jo Benford and Colette Tait

Introduction

'Growing Together' are a series of three groups, which run each week for parents with children from birth to three years of age. These groups evolved as the result of the three-year research project 'Parents' Involvement in Their Children's Learning' (PICL). In the PICL project, workers from the nursery met alongside parents whose children attended the nursery. The workers and parents watched video vignettes of the children in the nursery and workers shared theoretical frameworks with parents (see Chapter 4). Parents were able to share their specialised knowledge about their own child, and together workers and parents could dialogue and try to understand each child's development. The discussion generated in these study groups informed the nursery planning session on a weekly basis, and also impacted upon what the parent provided for the child in the home.

How growing together evolved from PICL

After the PICL study groups had run successfully for three years we wanted to try and extend this work. We wanted to set up a study group for parents with younger children (from birth to three years). We wanted to provide a forum in which parents and workers could study the younger children's development, once again using video material and the four key concepts that we had successfully used in the PICL project:

- Involvement (Laevers, 1997).
- Well-being (Laevers, 1997).
- Schema (Athey, 1990).
- Pedagogic Strategies (Whalley and Arnold, 1997a).

This is how Growing Together began, but there was a big difference – parents were going to attend the group sessions *with* their children.

When we initially developed Growing Together, we spent some time thinking about what our aims were.

Subsequently, we came up with a list of aims for the Growing Together group.

- To give parents a chance to play with their child.
- To help parents to understand more about their relationship with their child.
- To dialogue with parents about their child's development.
- To encourage reflective parenting (through reflecting on video material).
- To facilitate parent-to-parent support (we have found that close and supportive relationships between women occur at Growing Together).
- To validate the feelings women are experiencing when they are suffering from PND.
- To encourage helpful attachment experiences through video feedback and discussions.

Once the group had been set up it became apparent that something was missing. The four key concepts were very useful in terms of child development. However, as parents were sometimes bringing very young infants we felt it was critical to look closely with the parents at the relationship between them and their child. Because of this we found it useful to draw on some psychoanalytic theory:

- Holding (Winnicott, 1965).
- Containment (Bion, 1962).
- Attachment (Bowlby, 1991 [1969]).

The psychoanalytic theory

Holding

The concept of holding describes the emotional holding parents can give their baby by holding them in mind (Winnicott, 1965).

So when, for instance, you put your baby to bed and leave the room, they understand that you are still there for them – you are not abandoning them. They have learnt to believe this from the way you have responded to them *both* physically and emotionally since birth – they understand that you are holding them in mind.

Understanding the concept of 'holding' also has an impact on the running of the group. We have planning and reflection time each week; we do this to try and keep links between the weekly sessions, therefore holding parents and children 'in mind'. If a parent hasn't attended Growing Together for a couple of weeks then we will phone them. Once again, we believe that this process of giving time to 'thinking about' and 'making contact' lets parents know we are thinking about them even though we haven't seen them – thus holding them in mind.

Containment

The concept of containment describes the parent taking in the baby's distress, understanding it and responding so that the baby feels emotionally looked after, contained (Bion, 1962).

So, for instance, when a child is grieving (and they could be grieving about something that appears very small to us – losing a toy, or grieving over the death of a pet) a parent who is able to 'contain' their child will allow them to express all the range of emotions they are feeling – their feelings won't be dismissed and the adult won't deny the child is having those feelings.

In terms of practice, we try to ensure the provision is regular and reliable, so that parents and infants can feel secure in the setting. We also try to ensure that the sessions are not cancelled or moved to a different place and that there is a continuity of workers. Again, we believe that this structure in the provision helps parents feel emotionally contained.

Attachment

The concept of attachment describes how adults and children form and develop reciprocal relationships (Bowlby, 1991 [1969]). Colwyn Trevarthen refers to attachment as 'developing companionship' (2001).

The language of Attachment describes this concept in terms of a child, the 'care seeker' who looks for her 'care-giver', when she is aroused by anxiety caused by too much distance. It is a spatial theory revolving around the idea of proximity to one's carer/loved one. This mechanism is mobilised when a young child is experiencing stress, which she is unable to cope with herself, as she has no capacity yet for emotional self-regulation. For example, if an infant or young child cannot see her care-giver, then her 'world' feels extremely unsafe and the child will show considerable distress in order to generate the care-giver's response to recreate safety for the child. Soothing language, look and touch from the care-giver will reduce the child's distress and high cortisol levels, so she returns to a state of managing her world.

Following Bowlby's ideas, a child can only explore her world, and play is her main form of doing that, if she is feeling nurtured and cared for sufficiently – which is why Attachment is so important in a setting like Pen Green and specifically in Growing Together groups:

> A securely attached child will store an internal working model of a responsive, loving, reliable care-giver, and of a self that is worthy of love and attention and will bring these assumptions to bear on all other relationships.
>
> (Holmes, 2001: 78)

What's happening now?

At Pen Green we currently run two Growing Together sessions each week. These sessions are run as drop-in groups for parents with children aged from birth to three years of age. We use theoretical concepts to underpin our practice and we aim to encourage positive parent/child relationships. Each group lasts for an hour and a half. The two groups happen at Pen Green; up until recently we also had a group running at a community centre in an area of the town where there are areas of high deprivation. The room we are based in at Pen Green, and the room at the community centre, are not purpose built – they are multipurpose rooms, and quite a lot of time and effort goes into setting up those rooms. During the rest of the week the room at Pen Green is a community drop-in. It is a familiar space to many of the children and families who attend Growing Together.

In Growing Together we need to get the balance right. We need appropriate play provision for the children, as well as a warm and welcoming atmosphere for their parents. We do this by ensuring that the provision remains constant for the children; there is always sand, water, dough, a train set, trucks, and some dressing-up resources. We also set up a baby area with a large mirror, treasure baskets and cushions for the infants. Among all this play provision we have adult-sized chairs for the parents, and we always ensure that we offer parents a warm drink on their arrival.

All three groups are highly staffed by workers with different backgrounds and skills: child development, psychotherapy, parent support, and health. Generally you could expect between 8 and 18 parents with children to attend any one session, making the ratio of workers to families quite high. This enables workers to get to know families well, and provide a consistent and supportive atmosphere. Although the groups are 'drop-in' groups for anybody to attend we do try to encourage members to attend regularly as this type of continuity helps to provide a safe and secure environment for both parents and children.

Crèche provision

We are also able to offer a crèche for the Growing Together groups that occur at Pen Green. This means that a parent with a child three years or older, could put that child into the crèche, and then attend the Growing Together session with their younger child. In some instances, parents with two children aged from birth to 3 have come along to two different Growing Together sessions and put each child in turn into the crèche. This means that a parent can have some 'one-to-one' time with a child if they desire.

What makes Growing Together different from other toddler drop-in groups?

During the sessions we film parents, children and workers, using an iPad. We may film a child at play, or a parent/child interaction. We then view the film we have just made. One of the workers and the parent who has been filmed will watch the video material together, and discuss it. The video can be watched at normal speed, and also one frame at a time, so you can get a really close-up, 'in-depth' look at what has gone on.

At this point the worker may introduce some theory (either from child development or psychoanalysis – the seven key concepts) if it feels appropriate. By discussing theoretical concepts with parents we are able to begin to dialogue; we have a shared language with which to discuss the video material. The parent is then able to select a sequence of still images from the video material, and choose some language to accompany the images.

At the end of the session the parent is able to take away a copy of this 'portfolio'. We believe this process encourages reflective parenting and positive experiences.

Lili's portfolio

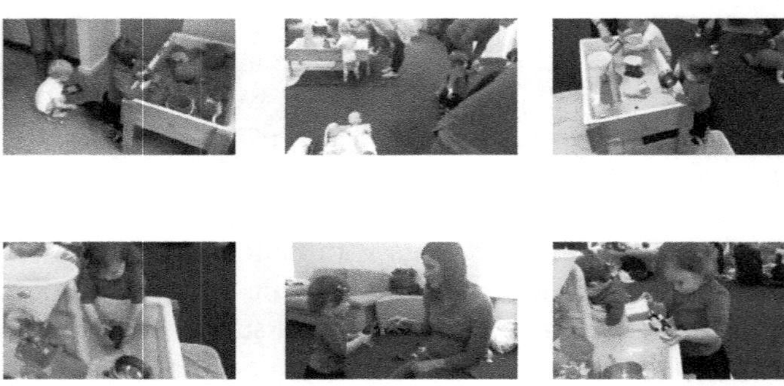

Lili at Growing Together 20/03/2015

Lili is very interested in covering things, she likes to feel textures. She tries to take things apart to figure out how it is made. She is just starting to ask other people for help, like with needing her hands washing, (picture 2). She is coming out of her comfort zone. She is starting to use her imagination, such as when we were feeding the animals, (picture 5). She often has two toys to play with now.

Figure 11.1 Lili's portfolio

Throughout the discussion about this piece of video the worker, alongside Julia, Lili's mum, would have thought about how deeply involved Lili was; what her well-being was like, and what Julia's role was in terms of supporting Lili's play. Julia was able to sit alongside Lili, encourage her and provide appropriate language to support her play. The final wording on the portfolio comes directly from Julia.

This is the kind of informal way in which we would begin to introduce these concepts to parents attending Growing Together. In the following section we introduce two families, using case study material, to illustrate how they have used the Growing Together groups, and how the concepts shared in Growing Together have impacted on them.

Case study

EMILY AND SOPHIE'S STORY

This case study focuses on Emily and Sophie who have been coming to Growing Together for seven months. At this time, Sophie is 2 years and 4 months old, and Emily is 19 weeks pregnant. In this case study we tell you a story, which took place over a four-week period for Sophie and Emily. For each week we report:

- the events that happened;
- Emily's feelings, in Emily's own words;
- how the concepts of Holding and Containment influenced our responses as workers towards Emily and Sophie.

Holding

The concept of holding describes the emotional holding parents can give their baby by holding them in mind (Winnicott, 1965).

Containment

The concept of containment describes the parent taking in the baby's distress, understanding it and responding so that the baby feels emotionally looked after, contained. (Growing Together Booklet, 2000. See Bion, 1962.)

(Continued)

(Continued)

Week 1

Events

It was midway through the Growing Together session, and each session lasts for an hour and a half. Sophie was busy playing with the tunnel. Emily stood up, and without saying anything to Sophie she walked towards the door, to go to the toilet.

Sophie looked up and saw her mum, Emily, moving towards the door. She began to cry. Emily heard her, turned and went back to Sophie, picking her up and taking her to the toilet with her, without speaking to her.

Emily reflected on how she felt when this happened.

Emily's Feelings

> I felt upset that Sophie was upset. I felt guilty that I was leaving her ... I also felt pissed off that I never got a minute to myself. The biggest feeling was guilty, but it made me feel so special. I felt really needed. Although it was hard most of the time I felt really needed.

Holding and Containment

We have a reflection and planning time each week – keeping links between sessions, holding parents and children in mind. This week in our reflection time we thought about how upset Sophie was when she realised Emily was about to leave the room.

Week 2

Events

Once again, Sophie was playing when Emily stood up and walked towards the door. This time she actually left the room. Almost immediately Sophie began to cry. Tracy G. (a worker) went over to Sophie and told her where Emily had gone. Sophie continued to cry. She asked Sophie if she wanted to go and find Emily. She said yes and lifted her arms up. Tracy G picked her up and carried her out of the room and waited outside the toilet. Sophie was still crying. She talked to Sophie about her mum being behind the door in front of them, and Sophie began to settle and stopped crying. Emily came out of the toilet and took Sophie from her arms, saying 'it's really difficult to leave her, she's like this all the time'. Sophie appeared pleased to see Emily.

Emily's Feelings

> When I came out of the toilet I felt awful – I felt wretched. I was thinking you might think I am a bad mother. I thought, you might think I was doing something wrong, because why would she cry like that? But I thought, well you might see what it is like for me. I was envious towards other parents – I didn't know anyone who had a clingy child like Sophie. I would compare her to other children.

Holding and Containment

At the end of the session, during reflection time, Tracy G explained the event to the team. We talked about strategies we could use in future weeks to support Emily and Sophie. The weekly sessions provide a setting for Emily where she can feel 'held', if we are able to support her and listen to her.

During the session Tracy G was able to contain Sophie's feelings by noticing her distress, understanding it, and providing her with help and comfort. Allowing Emily to talk about her difficulty in leaving Sophie was also a form of containment for her.

Week 3

This week we had an outside consultant, Penny Lawrence, in the session. Penny was gathering video material for a video that is part of a Growing Together Training Pack, and she filmed what happened this week when Emily left the room.

Events

This week's events mirrored the events from Week 2. Emily left the room. Sophie pointed towards the door and started to cry. Sophie walked to the door and tried to open it. I (Colette a worker) responded to Sophie by going over to her, crouching down and asking Sophie if she wanted to go and find her mum.

Figure 11.2 Colette asks Sophie if she wants to find her mum

(Continued)

(Continued)

Sophie lifted her arms up and I carried her out of the room, to wait outside the toilet. Sophie calmed much more quickly this week. While standing outside the toilet I spoke to Sophie about how her mum was behind the door (in a similar way to that in which Tracy G had, the previous week).

Figure 11.3 Colette speaks to Sophie about her mum being in the toilet

Emily came out of the toilet and once again took Sophie into her arms. As we went back into the group room I said to Emily, *'it might be helpful to tell Sophie where you are going ... she may still get upset, but at least she will know where you are'*. Emily didn't respond.

Figure 11.4 Emily takes Sophie into her arms

Emily's Feelings

> I felt awful still, I felt guilty for leaving her ... but I never got a minute to myself ... I knew she (Colette) was right (to say about telling Sophie where I was going), my mum had said it as well.

Holding and Containment

I (Colette) was able to contain Sophie's feelings. I responded to Sophie's distress in an almost identical way to the way in which Tracy G had responded to Sophie the previous week. The reflection and planning time each week enabled us to keep links between the events that were happening, and hold both Sophie and Emily in mind.

Between Weeks 3 and 4 Emily had reflected on what her own mum and I had suggested. She had decided to try telling Sophie where she was going when she was about to leave her. We saw Sophie behaving very differently on Week 4 to the way she had behaved in previous weeks.

Week 4

Events

Sophie was playing with the train set. Emily told Sophie that she was going to the toilet. Emily left the room, and Sophie continued to play with the train set, without becoming distressed. Sophie left the train set and walked over to Tracy G(worker) and took her hand. She said 'lady come'. She pulled at Tracy G's hand. Tracy G stood up and Sophie, still holding her hand, led her to the door. Sophie led Tracy G to the toilet door and then said 'mummy in there'. Sophie did not cry. Emily came out of the toilet and asked if Sophie had been crying. Tracy G explained what had happened.

Emily's Feelings

> This week I told Sophie I was going to the toilet. I said to her, 'mummy's going to the toilet and I will be back in a minute'. I thought 'I wonder if she will come wandering out?' I'd thought about it and tried it during the week and it had been working. When I came out of the toilet and saw you standing there and you told me she had fetched you and hadn't cried the biggest thing I felt was relief. What I was doing was working – I was getting somewhere with her.

Holding and Containment

At this time Tracy G talked to Emily about the concepts of 'holding and containment', in relation to what had happened for her and Sophie over the last four weeks.

It would appear that through this process Emily had begun to reflect on one aspect of her relationship with her daughter Sophie. She had begun to tell Sophie when she is about to leave her for a few moments, and to reassure her that she will return. As a result of this, Sophie appears to have come to some understanding, over time, that when Emily leaves the room she is not abandoning her, but that she will return shortly. Sophie is safe and secure in this knowledge, and Emily is much happier too.

(Continued)

(Continued)

Emily reflected once again

> It's changed my life ... I don't know why I didn't do it sooner, and now I do it all the time. Now I can leave her, I tell her where I am going. Before when she was clingy she would cry when I got back, but now she is happy and everything is normal. (Emily talked to us about how her relationship with her partner has changed, but most of all how Sophie's relationship with her dad had changed.) Now Alan takes her up to bed and reads her a story. He enjoys it, it is his special time. He now feels more bonded with her. It is lovely, I sit and watch *Eastenders* in peace or eat a bar of chocolate on my own ... I was worried about how demanding she was especially when the new baby arrives. I feel a lot more relaxed about the baby ... everyone has commented on it, my mum, Alan's mum, Alan.

Case study

HEIDI, ETHAN AND LEAH'S STORY

This case study is about Heidi who attended Growing Together for several years before becoming a worker within the group.

Heidi first came to Growing Together four years ago when her son, Ethan, was three weeks old. There was building work being undertaken at the Centre at the time and the group was being housed in a temporary mobile:

> The group was in the mobile when I first came ... it was just nice to get out. We were filmed, it was lovely ... it made me feel special about him. I knew one of the group leaders as she worked in the nursery and so it made it easier for me to come ... there was a friendly face, somebody who knew my name and my history already.

Heidi continued to attend the group regularly and two years later had a baby girl, Leah, and continued to come to Growing Together.

To begin with Heidi joined the group to:

> socialise with other mothers ... to get out of the house and meet with other people in the same position as me. As Ethan got older and began to get interested in things in the group I found myself playing more and more with Ethan ... and then when he got older I had more time again to talk with other people at the group.

Heidi talked about the filming that happens in Growing Together: 'the filming is really good, and looking back is really good. Ethan and Leah both like to look at the pictures and show their Dad what they are doing'.

Ethan's interests

Ethan spent a lot of time both at Pen Green and at home playing with train sets. Heidi reported that Ethan loved watching Thomas the Tank Engine videos, and playing with his 'Thomas' crane. He had enjoyed watching the video and seeing the crane being used to pick 'Thomas' up when he was derailed! Heidi had also taken Ethan on a trip to see Thomas the Tank Engine, and had taken him on a train.

Ethan loved playing with the train set at Growing Together and returned to it week after week.

Ethan's portfolio

Figure 11.5 Ethan involved with the train set

During the discussion with Heidi about the video of Ethan playing with the train set she commented:

> I knew that Ethan liked playing with certain things, trains being the number one thing, but I didn't realise the significance of what he was doing in terms of schemas. I just thought he enjoyed playing with trains, but when you watch the video and do it frame-by-frame you can see his expressions, his concentration and how involved he is.

(Continued)

(Continued)

Heidi was also fascinated by the things she spotted in the video, that perhaps were missed in the session: 'You also catch the little bits ... like when he puts the two opposing magnets together and then he does it again'.

Figure 11.6 Ethan propelling the engine around the track by utilising the opposing magnetic forces

Heidi appreciated watching the film alongside a worker and learning about different theoretical frameworks:

> you've got someone there to look at it with you who knows about these frameworks. I could then look for different things and think about why he was doing particular things. You then use that way of thinking to look at how he is playing in other areas.

Myke, Ethan's dad, was able to see what Ethan was doing at Growing Together. Heidi reported that previously Myke sometimes thought that what Ethan was doing was intended to 'wind him up', but then through being introduced to schemas he said that he understood him more and looked at what he was doing differently.

Heidi said, when thinking about schemas:

> It's a compulsion to do it and to stop them would be bad for the child. I think for Myke to not say no to him and watch what he's done has been

good as he's seen how much he's progressed ... I think Myke enjoyed it too – hearing and seeing what Ethan was doing, and it helped him to play the way Ethan wanted to play. As adults you think things should be done a certain way, but once you understand, you go with what the child wants to do.

Leah's experience

Leah was a very contented baby and for about a year Heidi brought both Ethan and Leah to the group.

Figure 11.7 Heidi brought both Ethan and Leah to the group

Heidi was able to take Leah along with her to spend time with Ethan, and was also able to leave Leah with friends in the group if she wanted to spend some time alone with Ethan.

As Leah got older she used the group very differently to Ethan. She tended to move around the room, accessing all the provisions. Leah also spent a lot of time watching people. On this occasion when Leah was filmed she was engaging in a social interaction with other adults who attended the group. Leah was 18 months at this stage, and had been interested in trying to get dressed herself for some time. She spent a lot of time trying to put a doll's sock on and off her foot (Figure 11.8).

(Continued)

(Continued)

Leah's portfolio

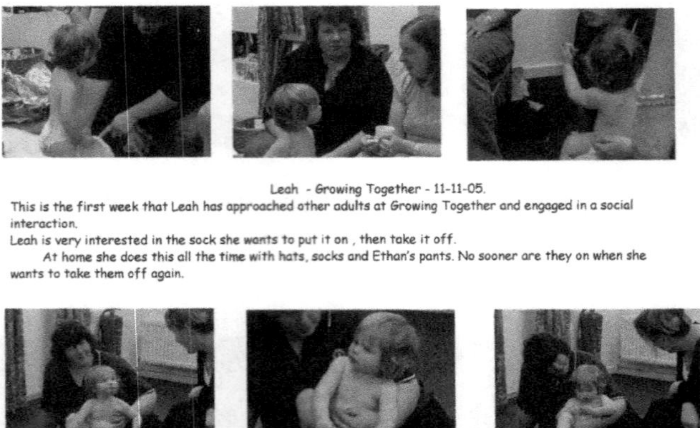

Figure 11.8 Leah engaging with social interaction

Through watching the film and then taking stills, Heidi says, '... this makes you realise you've got to be aware of what you're doing and how what you are doing really affects your children'.

Moving on

Leah was offered a place in the Pen Green nursery when she was 2 years old. In our reflection time at the end of one of the sessions we spoke together about the possibility of asking Heidi to become a worker in the group. There has been a long history at Pen Green of asking parents who have used groups effectively to then become group leaders, with appropriate support and training. We all thought that this was a really good idea, and soon afterwards approached Heidi:

> When they first asked me I was apprehensive. I thought I'd really like to do it but was worried about how it would be, being in a different role.

Heidi has been working in the group for six weeks now and says:

> I still find it strange because when I was group member I didn't interact with all the people in the group so don't feel able to easily approach everybody now, but am aware that my responsibilities have changed.

> I really like interacting with the children in the group – I had a lovely time at the sandpit with Ethan and Liam making sandcastles. They were reacting to me, laughing and really engaging with me ... they wanted me to be involved in their play ... it was lovely.
>
> I'm enjoying what I'm doing.

Finally ...

Growing Together is a drop-in group, running each week, in which parents can gain emotional support and spend time with their child. The group seeks to encourage positive parent–child relationships, and uses video material to encourage 'reflective parenting'. We have found that both the child development concepts and the psychoanalytic concepts are useful concepts to share with parents. This sharing of concepts is instrumental in building up a shared language with which to discuss both children's development and parent/child relationships. The psychoanalytic concepts also impact on the running of the sessions. Spending time as a staff team planning and reflecting each week helps us to keep links across the weeks, and therefore we are more able to support parents and children effectively.

Suggestions for your own practice

- To consider how you are currently working alongside families with children under three to support their developing relationships.
- To consider how using video as a reflective tool can help you to know and understand the parent/child relationship more deeply.
- To identify ways to have an open and honest dialogue with parents about their relationship with their child.

Key points

- The setting up of Growing Together was to give parents of younger children opportunities to focus on their relationship with their child.
- Growing Together is a drop-in group for parents/carers of children from 0–3.

(Continued)

(Continued)

- We create a 'holding' environment by having the same provision each week.
- We use iPads to film one family each week and to reflect on the film with the parent/carer and produce a portfolio that same day.
- As a staff team, we value the time spent reflecting on what has happened for parents that week in a pre-brief and de-brief. These are essential parts of the whole process.

Recommended reading

Jordan, B. and Henderson, A. (1995) 'Interaction analysis: foundations and practice', *The Journal of the Learning Sciences*, 4(1): 39–103.

Ogden, T. H. (2004, December) 'On holding and containing, being and dreaming', *The International Journal of Psychoanalysis*, 85 (6): 1349–64.

Websites

Anna Freud Centre: www.annafreud.org

12

Developing PICL in primary schools, children's centres and in childminder settings

Kate Hayward, Tracey Cotterell, June Smith, Andrea Layzell and Julie Denton

Introduction

This chapter looks at how the Pen Green 'Parents' Involvement in Their Children's Learning' (PICL) approach has been developed in different contexts following PICL training. The essential elements of a whole team approach, a focus on beliefs and values about working with parents, and the sharing of video observations and frameworks in an equal and ongoing dialogue to analyse children's learning with parents are explored. While each case illustrates the principles of PICL in practice, the approach encourages context-specific developments.

Challenging a traditional view of involving parents

by Kate Hayward

In the previous edition of this book (Whalley et al., 2007) I wrote a chapter about my experiences of attending the Parents' Involvement in Their Children's Learning (PICL) training programme at Pen Green. I challenged myself at the time, working as a Reception teacher in a primary school, to go 'beyond the reading record', the only means of regular communications between teachers and parents, and to engage in day-to-day dialogue with parents about their children's learning. This involved sharing video observations and spending time listening to parents' observations and stories about what their child was learning at home. I learned so much more about the children than I ever could as a class teacher on my own and working with the children and their families in this way was much more fun. All the adults and the children were connected and supported. As Chris Athey said, 'the effect of participation can be profound' (Athey, 1990: 66).

As a Pen Green PICL trainer for some years now I regularly hear participants say at the beginning of the training, 'well our parents are not interested' or 'it's all very well but we don't have the time to talk with parents and parents don't have the time to talk with us'. Often I think this stems from a traditional view of parental involvement where the practitioners are expecting parents to conform to what they have on offer, and then seem to blame the parents when these approaches do not work. If we think for a moment about the experience of a parent on their way to and from work, there will be little time for a chat at dropping off or picking up times. Faced with a blank sheet to write about 'family voice' or an official looking book to record what your family do together at home, it is understandable that parents sometimes shy away from participating in these attempts to engage them, at the risk of being labelled as 'not interested'.

The PICL training challenges participants to accept that if the methods they are using to involve parents are not working, then they need to change their approach. The advent of online electronic documentation-sharing platforms has gone a long way to breaking down some of the barriers to engagement, in that parents can respond to exciting documentation in their own way and in their own time, in a format that makes sense to them. Suddenly, practitioners are realising that parents are interested and know a lot about their children that the staff can benefit from knowing. In addition, within the PICL approach, sharing videos and frameworks for thinking about children's learning gives the opportunity to deepen the documentation and dialogue about the learning. If a dialogue can be maintained, either face-to-face or via electronic communication, then both parents and workers can share, celebrate and extend the learning that is happening both in the setting and in the home.

What does the PICL training entail?

This training programme has been developed at Pen Green from a research project on parental involvement (Whalley et al., 2007), and it consists of two days' initial training followed by a programme of work in one's own setting and a child study. A further third day of training is included at the end of the programme to help participants reflect on how to continue to develop partnership work with parents.

PICL Programme

Training at Pen Green

Two days' training on:

- the principles that underpin our work with children and families and the 'Pen Green Loop' of communication between workers and parents and parents and workers;

- four frameworks for understanding learning:
  1. Involvement (Laevers, 1997).
  2. Well-being (Laevers, 1997).
  3. Schemas (Athey, 2007).
  4. Pedagogical Strategies (Lawrence and Gallagher and The Pen Green Team, 2015).

Development work in your setting

- Audit of current practice in terms of involving parents.
- Action plan for organisational changes to improve involvement of parents.
- Report on organisational changes and outcomes.

Work with a family to analyse their child's learning

A child study using video to observe and analyse a child's learning in partnership with their parents, using the four frameworks studied.

A third day at the end of the programme where the project work is shared and developed by participants during which they reflect on the process and plan future development work.

Throughout the programme the emphasis is on the 'developmental partnership' (Easen et al., 1992) between parents and staff. It is about building a relationship of trust, through different models of engagement that suit the family. The use of video is key to the engagement and is a vehicle for initiating and sustaining a dialogue about the child's interests and play at home. The frameworks provide a shared dialogue about learning, which enables parents and staff to respect one another and deepen their thinking about the child.

Reflections on your own practice

- Is there a true sharing of knowledge about each child in your setting (i.e. an equal dialogue where both the view of the parent and the view of the practitioner are heard and acted upon)?
- Does the parent's knowledge about their child enable practitioners to act differently and better support the child in their learning?

(Continued)

(Continued)

- Is the parent able to challenge practice and do practitioners change what they do in response to this challenge?
- Do practitioners share knowledge and have discussions about the child's learning with both parents and all the key adults in children's lives?

Developing the PICL Licence

As practitioners attended the PICL training, Local Authorities and regional organisations began to express an interest in training networks of settings in PICL, across a geographical area. Pen Green became engaged in extending the PICL work to many different areas across the country. Some of this training came within nationally funded DfE projects such as the ELP and Parents as Partners in Early Learning (PPEL) programmes (see the Bradford case study in this chapter), in other areas a whole training programme was funded to enable connected settings or whole staff teams to work on the PICL approach together (see Haven Nursery School and Children Centre case study in this chapter).

As the work developed, excellent examples of PICL in practice were recorded, in many different contexts, in settings where staff were working with families in diverse communities. Staff were very excited about the approach and were keen to take the work further in their area. In response to this, Pen Green created a licensing arrangement whereby participants who had completed the whole PICL programme, and who met certain quality criteria, were supported in offering the PICL training themselves to colleagues in their locality.

What does a PICL Licence entail?

The PICL Licence is issued for one year and enables accredited PICL trainers to offer up to 60 places on PICL training, usually in three events (20 people per event). We recommend that people attend the training in pairs from each setting so that a total of 30 settings are trained within one year. All the materials and support required to offer the training are provided.

To be a PICL accredited trainer you need to:

- complete the PICL programme;
- write up the project work with a staff team;
- write up the child study and effectively analyse and share the child study video (we encourage PICL trainers to develop their own materials, with permission from families, so that they can use their child study video in training and, if possible, to involve the parents who worked with them in the training too);

- attend a 'training of trainers' event where the Pen Green philosophy on adult learning is explored and techniques for supporting reflection and self-critique are developed;
- read and discuss the literature on a child-centred (social-constructivist) view to children's learning, the theories of Involvement and Well-being (Laevers, 1997), schemas (Athey (2007), pedagogy (Pen Green Centre, 2016), and parental involvement (Whalley et al., 2007).

Throughout the licensing agreement there are quality control measures that are put in place which include:

- on site visits by a moderating tutor during a day 1 or 2 and a day 3 training event;
- evaluations sent to Pen Green for each event;
- follow-up phone calls to participants;
- moderation of materials produced by participants through the licensing agreement.

Developing PICL in primary schools, children's centres and childminder settings

The following four case studies illustrate how PICL has been developed in a range of settings in different parts of the country. The first case illuminates the work undertaken in a primary school and children's centre following the PICL training at Pen Green. The second documents a nursery school and children's centre's journey with PICL from whole team training to training across their area through a PICL Licence. The third case discusses how the PICL approach was developed across a network of settings within a Local Authority through different initiatives, and the fourth illustrates the power of this work through a sensitive case study by a childminder working with one family.

Case study

1. BADOCK'S WOOD COMMUNITY PRIMARY SCHOOL AND CHILDREN'S CENTRE, BRISTOL

by Tracey Cotterell

Badock's Wood Community Primary School took Southmead Children's Centre on as part of their organisation in 2012. The school and Children's Centre is in the north of Bristol where 61 per cent of the population are identified as meeting the 30 per cent most deprived criteria. The vision of our head, Zak Willis, was to create 'an all-through provision that oversaw care and learning for children and

(Continued)

(Continued)

families'. I joined as the Assistant Head for the school, Centre Lead for the Children's Centre and Lead Teacher in April 2014. Although these are a lot of hats to wear and many balls to juggle this does give me the benefit of being able to see the organisation from many different viewpoints.

I soon discovered that Badock's Wood, as a whole, was indeed passionate about working with families. However the effectiveness of this 'partnership' was debatable. There was no disagreement that 'parents and professionals can help children separately or they can work together to the greater benefit of the children' (Athey, 1990: 66). With no home visits at this point in the Children's Centre and parents rarely completing the 'wow sheets' to go in the learning journals, it would be hard to say that the voice of the parent at this time was very loud or even being heard. So were we working in an effective partnership?

Pen Green training

Having decided that developing our partnership with parents was central to our work we needed to work on how to take this forward. We had already sent two staff on training for MCLV (Making Children's Learning Visible) so the 'Pen Green Way of Working' had drawn us in. The follow-up was to involve our parents more effectively in children's learning and so following the success of the MCLV we budgeted for two staff to go on the training for PICL at Pen Green. However, as with many settings, staff can move on and there is a probability of losing momentum or becoming a lone voice in a large organisation.

We decided that we needed to send a larger team. The professional dialogue then keeps bubbling away instead of going 'off the boil' and the potential of creating a bigger buy-in simply made this the right choice for us. It also gave us a buffer should there be any change in staffing. We therefore sent four staff on PICL training at Pen Green. It was important to send a decision-maker (me) along to ensure that there wasn't the need to re-sell on returning from the training. We also sent two of our room leaders, one from our pre-school and one from the 2-year-olds room and our SENCo. This mixture gave us staff on the front line working every day with the children and senior leaders. The four of us went on the first two initial days of training where we went through the negotiation exercise of why we should work with parents. We all returned, enthused, to the centre. We wanted to start these groups in the Children's Centre first and then roll it out to the Early Years department in the school too.

Why work with parents? Negotiation exercise back at the Children's Centre

After a brief summary of the thinking behind PICL and the Pen Green Loop, we ran the negotiation exercise, during an inset day, along the same lines as we'd experienced at Pen Green. We had a mixture of room leaders and keyworkers from our educare rooms, family support team, front office and admin staff as well as our leadership team. Everyone had to write down four reasons, on four separate pieces of paper, about why they felt that working with parents was important.

There were many reasons written down for this and all were valid, ranging from 'to build a picture of the child' to more specific reasons such as 'because they know their child best and work with them the longest, and so their knowledge is powerful to us'. The surprise for everyone was that we then asked them to get into pairs and negotiate which four they would keep and which ones they would jettison. No one liked throwing away their ideas. This got harder when pairs had to pair up to make groups of four people and come up with just four reasons for working with parents. We had quite a divide between those who thought that the fact that parents 'love' their children is important and those who felt that that was not a reason for working with parents. This is still an ongoing dialogue.

Whalley and Chandler (2001: 75) suggest that 'the relationship between the professional and the parent carer is also influenced by our beliefs about what working together in partnership really means'. In our family support rooms there has been a history of not having adult comfy chairs to sit on. When this was questioned, the response was because parents *'need'* to be playing with their children and they can't if they sit on comfy chairs and chat to adults. The unpicking of this boiled down to the thinking that parents *'need'* to be told, they *'need'* to be shown. This seemed like a partnership out of kilter, and a lack of recognition of the expertise of the parents about their children. This felt uncomfortable for all of us. It had become a way of working with no one questioning it. If we were to build on sound foundations then we had to challenge the beliefs and values held about working in partnership with parents before moving on.

The barriers to working with parents did boil down to the obvious one of 'there is no time' to ones which seemed to be based on myths that have become 'truths' – for example we heard many times that this community is 'a proud community, they won't listen to us', a phrase that perhaps infers we are the experts. Had we fallen into a trap of thinking that apathy was the problem for us to help solve with our parents, when it is more likely to be poverty (Whalley and The Pen Green Team, 2001: 5)?

How are we taking this forward?

The discussions around why we work with parents automatically took us onto 'how' we do this. We introduced the idea of PICL and the frameworks for analysing learning during an inset day and through regular staff meetings. The next step was to organise starting it, so after finding a time (removing the barrier of no time) to talk to parents we sent out invitations to all parents and put it into our newsletters.

(Continued)

(Continued)

We were both surprised and disappointed that we only had a few replies and only a couple of parents turning up to talk to us. We tried changing the time of the session, but this time no one turned up! It would be easy at this point to give up and say that the parents were not interested in these sessions, fulfilling the thought that this is apathy and nothing else.

However we knew through talking to individual parents that they were interested, so we had either put a barrier in the way inadvertently or we had failed to remove a barrier. Perhaps we had started our groups with a perception of a 'done to' attitude rather than making it explicit that this would be a true partnership involving 'power-sharing, a recognition of parents' equally valuable knowledge and expertise and an understanding of the real pressures that young families face' (Whalley and The Pen Green Team, 2001: 5).

We reflected on this as a team and came up with many ideas. We tried to put ourselves in their shoes and recognised how daunting it is to come along to a group session for the first time, especially when you don't know anyone, and you only have a little information about what will happen. This takes a lot of confidence and everyone's time is valuable. The easiest option is simply not to come. We decided that we would focus on children whose families were eligible for the Early Years Pupil Premium. We had a chat with each parent, asking them to come along. The personal touch of inviting them individually seemed to work. This meeting allowed us to discuss any potential barriers such as childcare, which we addressed with a crèche. We then met them on the day in the reception area and walked in with them. These sessions are now off the ground and flying. We have a mixture of mums, dads and grandparents. We follow the needs and interests of the parents, much as we do with following children's interests. We have a theme for each session, such as Levels of Involvement, but we ensure that there is time to simply talk. This has raised discussions about having a weekly coffee morning where anyone can pop in and talk to each other or any of us; we have been asked if we can invite the police in for a session so that children can see that the police are there to help, and not just there when things go wrong. We could not predict any of these conversations. This only comes with time to listen and mutual respect.

Case study

MIA'S STORY AT FOREST SCHOOL

After the first two days training at Pen Green we all had to choose a family each to work with at the centre through the use of video footage. We are rolling Forest School out across the centre and the school. Our first practitioners to be working towards this qualification need an experienced Forest School practitioner on each of their sessions. I go on these weekly sessions as the support for the practitioner leading the session. This is ideal for me, having time to stand back and observe during the sessions and enjoy the interactions. I chose a family with a child (Mia) on one of these sessions. I needed to build a trusting relationship with her mum, Sophie. This didn't take long because Mia dragged her over to me every time she saw me with the same question 'Are we going on Forest School today?' We put up a display of Forest School photographs after each session, which drew all the parents in, and with their permission we put these onto the screen in the reception area of the centre. This prompted lots of discussion and many opportunities to talk.

Figure 12.1 Mia

Figure 12.2 Mia and a friend

Armed with a series of stills from video footage for my first meeting with Sophie and with a focus on Involvement levels, this revealed how the knowledge and expertise of a parent can simply sideswipe you. I had assumed that Mia had low

(Continued)

(Continued)

involvement levels when she was 'looking into space', but Sophie told me that this was her 'mascara face'! Sophie pulled the face for me; eyes wide open, head tilted down slightly and mouth slightly open; I immediately recognised the expression! This is when she is fascinated by something and focused. How wrong could I be! This helped me recognise this sign of Involvement and build on her engagement more appropriately in her learning on Forest School. Sophie is one of our first parents in our first PICL group.

We knew through conversations with parents and through replies to our questionnaires that parents wanted to work as closely as possible with us and to talk about their children. We still have 'wow' notes and drop off and pick up times are still valuable, but they are enhanced through having more time to talk and listen to our parents. If this is to work then as a team we need to continually reflect on why we are working with parents so that we all move from 'being largely compensatory to participatory' (Pugh, 2001: 147).

PICL is the start of our team truly listening to parents and working in partnership to help their children at the beginning of their journey for lifelong learning.

Case study

2. HAVEN NURSERY SCHOOL AND CHILDREN'S CENTRE, GOSPORT

by June Smith

Whilst attending a residential at Pen Green as part of a Master's module on Working with Families, I was privileged to hear a parent talk passionately about the difference PICL had made to her life, and her children's. Despite facing a series of challenges within her family life, she spoke eloquently about how her family worker and the PICL group had helped her to identify and support her children's schema, thereby also helping her to understand and manage what she had previously considered their 'naughty behaviour'.

This was certainly a 'light bulb' moment for me and caused me to question our approach to working with families, both in the nursery school and how 'parenting support' was provided by Family Support Workers in the Children's Centre.

On my return to the Centre, I related my experience to colleagues in the Senior Leadership Team and received an enthusiastic and positive response. We agreed unanimously that PICL was definitely the way forward for our Centre! Through staff meetings and Inset we then provided opportunities for all staff to reflect on the *true* quality of our interactions with parents. As a staff team, we were confident of positive relationships within the Centre, particularly between parents and key persons. We thought about the daily conversations with parents at the beginning and end of nursery sessions – discussion predominantly around children's welfare (eating, sleep, behaviour, etc.). We enjoyed high levels of parental involvement, particularly in respect of supporting events, fundraising activities, etc. However, what we wanted to improve was 'engagement' – parents contributing to their children's learning in the nursery and practitioners having a better understanding of the child's life and interests outside the nursery. In other words we realised that our relationships with parents should be more 'doing with' and less 'doing to'.

What PICL did for us as an organisation

In order to build the PICL approach into our nursery practice, we changed the routine and timing of sessions, allowing 15 minutes at the beginning of every session when children could go off and play in the nursery rather than being restricted to their family areas for registration. This enabled parents and key persons to have quality conversation time without distractions and PICL training gave practitioners the confidence to focus conversations on children's learning.

Duncan's story: 'Can you see me?'

Hannah, a key person in the nursery, related a conversation she had with a parent about her child's enveloping schema – climbing into boxes, covering himself with blankets and folding his finished paintings in half. The next day Duncan's mum, Michelle, explained how she had completely re-arranged her lounge furniture to clear a space in the middle of the room for several empty cardboard boxes. Instead of struggling with challenging behaviour at home, she was delighted to tell Hannah 'that was the best afternoon we have had for ages'!

She took a photograph to share with nursery staff on her child's online journal.

Staff responded with a comment that they had been playing hide-and-seek in the forest, which Duncan had said was his 'favourite game'.

Linking the principles of PICL with the sharing of video clips and observations on a web-based facility for sharing learning journals has resulted in a significant increase in parental contributions to children's electronic profiles.

(Continued)

(Continued)

Figure 12.3 Duncan

The Children's Centre staff also used the online learning journal linked to the PICL approach to record and share observations in groups and drop-ins such as Stay and Play.

Case study

ARCHIE, JAMES AND TOBY'S STORY: WEAVING IT IN

Several boys developed a fascination for using the masking tape from the creative studio, to the extent that it was becoming quite a challenge to manage their sometimes boisterous 'enthusiasm' for sticking it everywhere, and frustrating for children who needed it for their modelling! After discussing this with parents and learning that parents were also interested in how to support their children more effectively, we decided to extend the boys' schema by providing opportunities to fix and join in the nursery. A trolley was resourced with a range of materials, including various kinds of sticky tape, string, wool, fasteners, etc. and a piece of trellis erected in the creative studio.

Figure 12.4 Toby shows great concentration as he weaves into the weaving board

Apart from basic safety rules regarding the dangers of putting string etc. around necks, the children were able to follow their own interests and ideas and the results were recorded through photos and video, which were used in subsequent PICL training sessions to illustrate a child's high level of involvement and well-being when their schema is supported.

Archie shows a real interest in using the weaving board during play to learn time. He confidently interlinks the wool through the spaces on the board, up, down and through the other sections to weave the pieces together. James joins Archie and they work together to fill the gaps, respecting each other's work space and helping one another. Archie is aware that he needs to use the resources carefully: 'I can't pull it too tight otherwise the string will snap'.

(Continued)

(Continued)

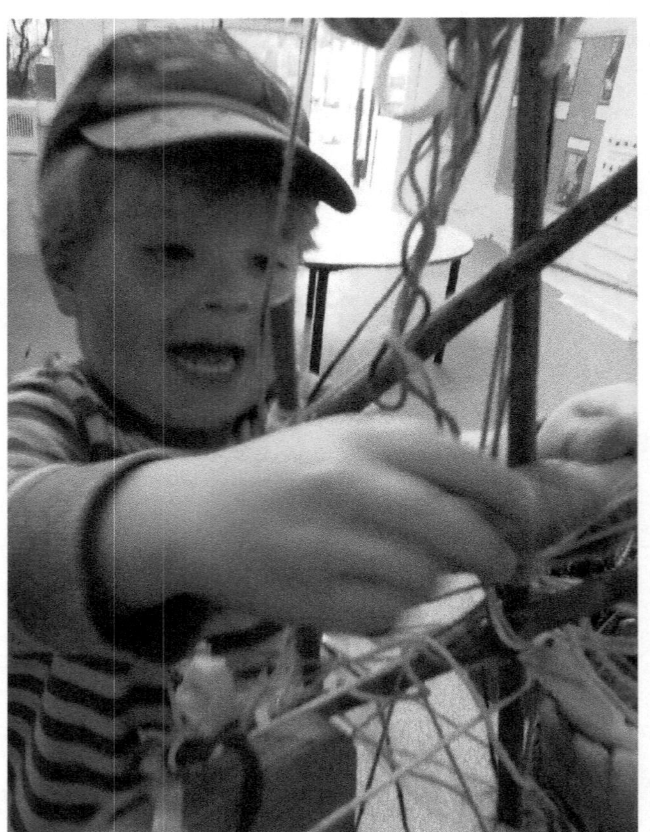

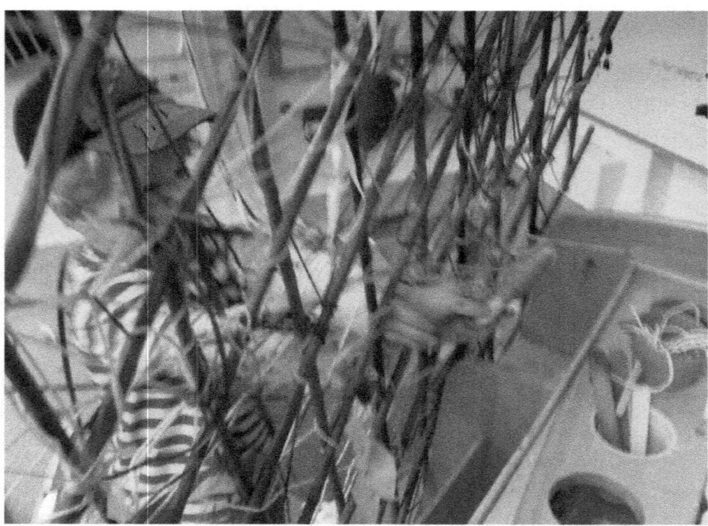

Figures 12.5–12.7 Archie

Reply from Archie's mum:

Scarlett Martin, 19 December 2014

This is lovely. Nice to see the boys working together and Archie understanding the materials.

Reply from key person Hannah Mitchell, 19 December 2014

He really enjoyed this activity and his concentration was amazing considering how busy the Hive is with all of the children learning and playing.

Going beyond our own Centre

This period of reflection within the Centre coincided with my growing involvement with the Gosport Education Improvement Partnership (GEIP). This is a group of schools within the Borough of Gosport working collaboratively with partner organisations to raise standards and improve outcomes for children, young people and families. As Head of a Nursery School, I represented Early Years on the GEIP Management Group and was involved in the strategic decision-making process. At that time the group was debating what strategies would be most effective in addressing the issues of low aspirations for the children of Gosport, an issue which featured in the Local Strategic Plan. Based on

(Continued)

(Continued)

the positive impact of introducing the PICL approach within the nursery, I put forward a proposal that early investment in parental involvement training for staff in all Gosport early years settings and reception classes could have long-term benefits for all children and families in the Borough.

The GEIP Management Group unanimously supported the proposal and approved funding to enable PICL training to be delivered across the area under licence.

If this was to be effective, it was agreed that all settings within the private, voluntary, independent and maintained sectors should be invited to participate.

It was also suggested that communication and working relationships between preschools and schools would benefit if staff from settings who shared the same site, or worked in close proximity to each other, attended the training together and worked collaboratively on the child study project. An initial cohort of 26 attended the three-day training, and four practitioners from this original group were nominated to undertake the training to become PICL trainers/facilitators, including:

a head of nursery;

a nursery SENCO;

a Reception Teacher;

a Deputy Manager in a PVI setting.

It was felt that the varying backgrounds and experience of this mix of trainers reflected the underlying principle of the GEIP to foster a collaborative approach to improving outcomes for children across all phases of education. It was also hoped that by representing all sectors of early years provision within the training team, we would avoid the risk of any practitioners feeling excluded because it was 'just for schools' or 'just for preschools'.

Three cohorts were trained under licence and, as we had hoped, each group included practitioners from PVI and maintained settings including private day nurseries, preschools, naval settings and Opportunity Groups, Reception classes (teachers, teaching assistants and one headteacher!), special schools and children's centres (including crèche staff and family support workers). This rich mix of participants encouraged stimulating discussions during the training, as participants were given the opportunity to increase their understanding about practice in different settings and how the PICL approach could 'work for them'. After the initial two days' training, participants were encouraged to stay in touch through regular network meetings at the Centre. Some practitioners found these particularly helpful when carrying out their child study for day three and were able to share the challenges and successes of introducing PICL into their settings.

Case study

3. A LOCAL AUTHORITY DISSEMINATING PICL IN BRADFORD

by Andrea Layzell

Over a period of about four years, more than 280 early years practitioners, registered childminders, family support workers, teachers and advisory staff attended the Parents' Involvement in Their Children's Learning (PICL) programme in Bradford, West Yorkshire.

Bradford is a metropolitan district in the north of England, with a diverse population of over half a million. The PICL programme was made widely available, with staff from the authority facilitating the learning under licence from Pen Green. The framework was specifically named in the local quality support programme as a way for practitioners to evidence a commitment to effective working with parents.

Parental participation had long been a priority for the early years service, and Bradford had received funding from the Department for Children, Schools and Families (DCSF), under the then Labour government, to develop parents' participation in children's learning through the PPEL project. The national PPEL project was specific and time limited, running between 2006 and 2007, and hinged locally on providing resources such as IT and video equipment that supported access to Pen Green's training of practitioners in the 'Parents' Involvement in Their Children's Learning' (PICL) programme. I worked alongside Pen Green in the initial training programme, providing facilitation and funding for equipment. Soon after I worked for the local authority as the project co-ordinator of the local pilot of the national Two Year Old Offer (2YOO), and held the remit to support the extension of the work of the PPEL project and the PICL training. Senior officers in the authority, including Robin Naylor, the then Head of the Early Years and Childcare Service, recognised that parents taking an active role in their children's learning should be a key element of any strategy that hoped to improve outcomes for children, so the two pieces of work linked together very well.

Working with families facing economic disadvantage

The widely accepted view, evidenced in the Effective Provision of Pre-School Education (Sylva et al., 2004), that parents, by participating in their children's learning and development, have the power to make significant differences to children's achievement, was recognised in Bradford. In a context of a community with higher than average levels of disadvantage, active participation by parents

(Continued)

(Continued)

was seen as highly desirable. The PPEL project was part of the wider work in the district to improve the educational achievement of the children of the city, where low levels of qualification and high levels of poverty and disadvantage were driving much of the work to improve outcomes for children and families. The District's needs assessment in relation to child poverty, produced in August 2007, describes how one in three (31.4 per cent) children were living in poverty in the District, almost 41,000 children, compared to the figure in England as a whole, where one in five children were living in poverty (Department of Services to Children and Young People, 2010). In this authority area 18 per cent of the adult working age population, approximately 52,000 people, had no formal qualifications.

Background to Pen Green's work in Bradford

In 2007 the two national projects of PPEL and Early Learning Partnership Project (ELPP) resulted in a programme of work across the Local Authority District that focused on the parents of young, particularly disadvantaged, children being involved in their children's learning and early education.

There is clear evidence of the importance of the role of the parent being embedded in policy and practice from the earliest days of the authority's Early Years and Childcare Service. Some of the service's significant pieces of work and initiatives in the early 2000s had parental involvement at their core, for example:

- Engaging parents in early work on language development.
- Promotion of the Reggio 'whole community' approach to early childhood development.
- A locally focused Single Regeneration Budget (SRB) Early Start programme, (a European funding stream utilised to deliver a time limited, target driven, early intervention programme).

> The movement from shallow to deep learning can be best characterised as the growth of personal understanding, of ownership and the movement away from dependency. (West-Burnham and Jones, 2007: 48)

There was a consistent and steady demand in the district for places on PICL training, and feedback received after courses was overwhelmingly 'good' and 'very good'.

I contacted practitioners who had attended the PICL programme and many participants indicated in the returned research questionnaire that they had attended PICL training on the recommendation of others, or that their managers had required them to attend, both possible indicators of high expectation. Their completed questionnaires, responses and interviews confidently recorded their self-assessment of the impact on their own skills and confidence. Many of the practitioners interviewed described the transformational impact of the programme on their work with families:

'I found the PICL training totally inspiring and motivational. I LOVED it' Childminder

'... helps Early Years Practitioners to understand children better'

Family Support Worker

'More child-initiated "work" occurs and is followed up by more practitioners'

Foundation Stage Co-ordinator

'Staff are better tuned to children's learning'

Deputy Head of Nursery School and Children's Centre

'Parents are more engaged with A's learning style, meaning A's well-being is increased. She has also begun talking!'

Assistant Head Primary School

'... surprised at how readily the concepts were understood by the parents'

Teacher in Children's Centre

One such practitioner was Julie Denton, a childminder working in Bradford in 2007, who still works as a childminder in the district – see below.

Case study

4. USING THE 'KNOWLEDGE-SHARING' APPROACH IN A CHILDMINDING SETTING BY JULIE DENTON

I became a registered childminder eleven years ago, prior to which I worked as a mental health nurse for many years. Building relationships has been an important aspect of my working life, so naturally it remained so as I built my childminding practice, and considered the relationships I had with the families who used my service.

At the time when I was first introduced to PICL I worked with one part-time assistant. This enabled us to provide our service for a larger group, of up to six early years children, during a couple of days of the week. We did this to provide flexibility for our parents, some of whom were healthcare shift workers. Since this

(Continued)

(Continued)

time the service has expanded and I now work with four part-time assistants, providing our service for 22 families. The children are aged between 9 months and 12 years, and have various patterns of attendance.

I attended the PICL training that was offered in Bradford, initially disappointed that I couldn't obtain a place on the training that was so over-subscribed, but I was lucky to be offered the opportunity on an extra course, added due to demand.

At the time that this opportunity became available I was at a point of searching for ways to evaluate my provision. I wanted to know if we were providing the very best we could for the children and families. How could I tell? I had implemented diaries, shared photos and files of achievements for the children, I felt that I talked to the parents as much as I could, and believed I had a good relationship with them, but how could I improve? I was a bit stuck.

The PICL course was illuminating. It offered the opportunity to study four frameworks. These were Schema (Athey, 1990), Well-being and Involvement (Laevers, 1997) and Pedagogic Strategies (Pen Green, 2005). We explored our values in relation to the significance of parents, and working with parents to support the child. I found this approach fitted comfortably with the principles I already held, of recognising and supporting the child's interests in order to facilitate learning opportunities, and of developing strong relationships with parents.

Laevers' frameworks of 'Involvement' and 'Well-Being' are robust and accessible, and provide a valuable opportunity to reflect on and assess my provision. I was initially sceptical about schema theory, but I stayed open-minded. I began to use video, which is an element of the course, and I was amazed. I saw schematic learning everywhere in my setting! This was a real eureka moment for me, I now feel much more able to consider each child's individual interests and plan opportunities to stimulate these interests further.

I conducted a child study (an aspect of the PICL course), which brought everything to life. Reflecting upon this, I now see that it was a transformational point in my practice. I found the frameworks affirmed my values and beliefs, and offered me the opportunity to deepen my ways of working with parents. I have continued to work in this way, focusing on developing a dialogue with parents in which we can share our knowledge of the child. This is supported by Easen et al. (1992) who suggest that within this partnership the parent and practitioner roles are equal: the practitioner offers 'general' child development theory, whilst the parents contribute their 'personal theory' regarding the child, who they know better than anyone else.

Two of my colleagues, locally based childminders, completed the PICL course at a similar time and together we formed a peer support group. We met approximately once every six weeks with the aim of sharing good practice, focusing on working with parents and the frameworks. We shared video footage, which we analysed together, creating an opportunity to explore our ideas and learning in a safe environment. We were able to celebrate and share our successes, and help each other to unpick any difficulties we encountered in working in this way. Since this time the group has separated, the other ladies have moved to working in different environments as pre-school practitioner and after-school club leader. Jo, the pre-school practitioner, continues to use the frameworks and partnership approach within her new role, demonstrating that this is a way of working that can be used within changing contexts.

I also act as a peer support provider within my local authority. I was recently asked to provide support for a childminder who had expressed an interest in developing her understanding of, and confidence in, working with parents. She felt she had a good relationship with the parents but wanted to work in a more focused and professional way. We explored using the frameworks within her practice, supported by video footage, to explore the child's learning with the parents. We both enjoyed this opportunity to work together, and as a result we are in the process of forming a group of interested practitioners. We aim to focus on working with video and the frameworks, and explore our approach to working with parents within our settings.

I would like to share with you a case study that demonstrates how working in a respectful and reciprocal partnership enabled me to support a child, and her parents, whilst they were undergoing a difficult period of transition.

Case study

AMY'S STORY

Amy attends my setting for two days per week. When she was 26 months-old her sibling Jack was born. Their mother Eleanor had a difficult labour that resulted in her being unwell for several weeks. During this time we noticed that Amy's behaviour changed whilst with us. Previously she had been settled and showed high levels of well-being, and deep involvement in her play. However she became suspicious and guarded, inflexible in her play, at times hostile and a little aggressive towards the other, usually younger, children. The frameworks of Well-being and Involvement illustrated consistently lowered measurements in both aspects. Eleanor recovered and was able to bring and collect Amy again, but I found myself worried about her too; she seemed tired, tense and flat in her mood.

I felt it was important to offer opportunities for these concerns to be explored, with a view to supporting a positive way forward, so Eleanor and I arranged to meet. During this meeting Eleanor was able to share her own feelings of concern; she had experienced patterns of behaviour at home which mirrored the way I described Amy was acting in the setting. Eleanor was emotional at the beginning of this meeting, describing her worries and

(Continued)

(Continued)

her feelings of being overwhelmed, without ideas for a way forward. She felt guilty that things were not as she wanted them to be.

Reflecting on this meeting we believe it had both a cathartic and supportive focus. We reviewed the scales of Well-being and Involvement together, which acted as an indicator, confirming that we needed to act. This was an empowering process for us both.

We continued to meet regularly, including with John, Amy's father. We spent time reviewing and discussing video footage of Amy that I had recorded in the setting. Eleanor's Health Visitor supported her at home and my local Quality and Inclusion Officer joined us for some of the meetings, helping us with techniques to encourage wanted behaviours. We focused on Amy's interests and established a consistent approach between home and setting, whilst continuing to monitor Amy's Well-being and Involvement. This was made much easier because we had a shared language; we could describe behaviours in terms of the frameworks without risk of appearing judgemental or using emotionally loaded language.

Whilst there have been ups and downs we gradually saw Amy's levels of Well-being and Involvement rise. She became happier at home and in the setting, and learned to cope better with her new sibling and the changes within her family. Amy is now 46 months-old, she attends my setting with Jack, towards whom she is particularly supportive and enjoys an affectionate relationship.

I asked Eleanor how she felt the frameworks had supported us during this time. She wrote:

> By having the frameworks in place we were able to identify Amy's needs more quickly and precisely and thus provide appropriate, focused provision and care to support her Well-being.

In order to genuinely share perspectives both Amy's parents and I had to be prepared to take some risks. For me there was anxiety that Eleanor and John might feel I was intruding too deeply and I might cause offence. I also had to consider that Amy was unhappy in my setting. I needed to examine my own practices and be prepared to articulate and potentially change the ways I had been working. Eleanor and John also took risks as they were prepared to share some very personal experiences, fears and concerns, trusting that I would treat these sensitively, appropriately and not make judgements.

By taking these risks we built a trusting relationship in which we could talk honestly and deeply about our concerns, and celebrations. We were able to share genuine perspectives and knowledge of Amy, at home and in the setting, and formulate interventions that supported both Amy and her family.

Concluding remarks

These four very rich accounts illustrate the transformational nature of the PICL approach, which can be adapted and used in any setting. The idea that parents are the first 'port of call' when it comes to getting to know children, comes through each account in different ways. Laevers' concepts of 'involvement' and 'well-being', as well as the work on 'schemas' and 'pedagogic strategies', have been very helpful to our practice in engaging families in dialogue as well as in professional development opportunities for other professionals.

Suggestions for your own practice

- Challenge yourselves about the way you involve parents – is your approach working for every family?
- Think about the PICL approach detailed in these case studies and how you could deepen and sustain the dialogue with families about their children's learning.
- Could you use video to share clips of each child when they are deeply involved in their learning both at home and in the setting?

Key points

- PICL training is about challenging your practice in relation to involving parents – if what you are doing is not working then you need to change what you are doing.
- PICL training can enable a whole staff team to work effectively and reflectively – constantly improving their practice through working as co-educators with parents.
- Once you have completed the PICL training programme you can become an accredited trainer and work with Pen Green in offering PICL training under licence.
- The PICL approach is supported when a network of settings work together and share developments in practice.

Recommended reading

DCSF (2010) *Aiming High For Children, Three Years On*. Crown Copyright 2010.

Early Learning Partnership Parental Engagement Group (2010) *Principles for Engaging with Families: A framework for local authorities and national organisations to evaluate and improve engagement with families*. London: National Children's Bureau. Available at www.socialserviceworkforce.org/system/files/resource/files/engaging_with_families_0.pdf (accessed 23rd January 2017).

Pugh, G. (2001) *Contemporary Issues in the Early Years: Working Collaboratively for Children*, 3rd edn. London: Paul Chapman Publishing.

West-Burnham, J. and Huws Jones, V. (2007) *Spiritual and Moral Development in Schools*. London: Network Continuum Education, p. 48.

Postscript

Developing a sustainable approach

Margy Whalley

Transferring and using knowledge that derives from existing best practice is often problematic (Fullan, 2002); however practitioners and parents at Pen Green, working in collaboration with early years educators in many local authorities, have been able to develop a pedagogically grounded 'learning focus' (Jackson, 2001). This approach is described as the Parents' Involvement in Their Children's Learning (PICL); a knowledge-sharing approach. We have had the pleasure of working with and training staff teams in many early childhood settings across the UK where practitioners are recognising the importance of children's learning in the home and the role their parents take on as co-educators in collaboration with practitioners in the settings.

We now need to embed this approach; educators in *all* early childhood settings and schools have to become cultural brokers and mediators recognising the strength and commitment of parents and realising the talents of parents and children (Feinstein and Sabates, 2007). Early years practitioners have to develop a shared language with parents and a shared understanding about how children develop and how children learn, both at home and in the nursery. It is vital that practitioners listen to and understand parents' own theories about the development of their child. It is also essential that nursery staff share with parents their theoretical and practice-based understanding of children drawn from their observations of the child in the nursery setting. Developing this shared language requires consummate skill and continuous professional reflection and dialogue. It takes time to develop reciprocal ways of working and to build on what the community has to offer. Working in this way will transform children's life chances.

Chris Athey, in her last years as mentor to Pen Green team, described the Parents' Involvement in Their Children's Learning programme at Pen Green in this way:

> I cannot think of any other project, involving so many people in so many different roles, which functions as Pen Green is doing within a coherent and internally consistent view of education ... the PICL programme reflects a set of consistent values based on mutual respect. The focus is on co-operation. Competition is confined to individuals trying to get better at what they are doing which is helping children to become successful and autonomous learners ... Pen Green is revolutionary in its insistence on identifying and articulating positive learning for individual children and involving parents and extending those aspects in an educationally worthwhile direction.
>
> (Chris Athey, 2001, personal correspondence)

Today, as the third edition goes to press, there are many practitioners and parents working within the same democratic paradigm and developing creative and challenging co-educational partnerships. However, the early years phase is experiencing unprecedented turmoil. We used to talk about the 'great under fives muddle' in the 1960s, when early years services were often fragmented, underfunded and neglected. Now after a tsunami of national interest and investment early childhood services are facing drastic cutbacks. Much of Labour's heritage has been privatised and the rest reduced to a residual service for the most vulnerable. The onus is on all of us working within the sector to engage with politicians and policy makers in the spirit of collaboration. We must insist that they understand, as we do, that nursery schools and children centres are part of our UK heritage, that children have a right to these outstanding services. We have to get them to recognise that the silver bullet to really achieving the best outcomes for all children is for us to work as co-educators with their parents. Working in this way, we can oppose the injustices of inequality.

> In the Pen Green paradigm, involvement begins and ends with an aspiration to equality. There is no pretence, nor any passing the buck. Staff are the experts on children in general: carers are the experts on the particular child. Their pooling of knowledge makes the chance of engendering progress for the child so much more likely. The attitude is 'we can help each other'. Carers' perspectives are respected and needed.
>
> (Fletcher, 2014: xiiii)

References

Abbott, D. (1998) *Culture and Identity*. London: Hodder & Stoughton.

Allen, G. (2011) *Early Intervention: The Next Steps. An Independent Report to HM Government*. London: Cabinet Office.

Allman, P. (1983) *The Nature and Process of Adult Development*. Buckingham: Open University Press.

Anderson, K. (1987) 'Beginning where we are', in S. Anderson, S. Armitage, D. Jack and J. Wittner (eds), *Oral History Review*, 15: 103–27.

Arnold, C. (1990) *Children Who Play Together Have Similar Schemas*. Corby: Pen Green Centre.

Arnold, C. (1997a) *Understanding Young Children and their Contexts for Learning and Development: Building on Early Experience*, Unpublished MEd thesis, Leicester University.

Arnold, C. (1997b) 'Sharing Ideas with Parents About How Children Learn', in M. Whalley (ed.), *Working with Parents*. London: Hodder & Stoughton.

Arnold, C. (1999) *Georgia's Story*. London: Paul Chapman.

Athey, C. (1990) *Extending Thought in Young Children: A Parent–Teacher Partnership*. London: Paul Chapman.

Athey, C. (2007) *Extending Thought in Young Children: A Parent-Teacher Partnership* (2nd edn). London: Paul Chapman.

Arnold, C. and the Pen Green Team (2010) *Understanding Schemas and Emotion in Early Childhood*. London: Sage.

Audit Commission (1994) *Seen But Not Heard: Developing Community Health and Social Services for Children in Need*. London: HMSO.

Bakhtin, M. (1986) *Speech Genres and Other Late Essays*, C. Emerson and M. Holoquist (eds). Austin: University of Texas Press.

Ball, C. (1994) *Start Right: The Importance of Early Learning*. London: RSA.

Barber, M. (1996) *The Learning Game*. London: Victor Gollancz.

Barrett, H. (2009) 'We need to talk about parenting programmes', *Working with Parents: A 'way of working' or a 'delivered formula'?* The Pen Green Centre for Children and their Families and National Children's Bureau International Conference, Corby, England, 9 November.

Bartholomew, L. and Bruce, T. (1993) *Getting to Know You*. London: Hodder & Stoughton.

Bertram, A.D. (1995) 'Adult engagement styles and their use in staff development'. Paper presented at the 5th European Early Childhood Educational Research Association Conference, Sorbonne, Paris.

Bertram, A.D. (1996) 'Effective early childhood educators'. Unpublished PhD thesis, Coventry University.

Bertram, A.D., Laevers, E. and Pascal, C. (1996) 'Grasping the quality of adult–child interactions in early childhood education settings: the adult style observation schedule', in S. Rayna, F. Laevers and M. Deleau (eds), *What are the Educational Objectives for Pre-School Education?* Paris: Nathan.

Bertram, T. and Pascal, C. (2000) *Early Excellence Centres: First Findings Autumn 1999*. London: DfEE.

Bettelheim, B. (1990) *Recollections and Reflections*. London: Thames & Hudson.

Bion, W. (1962) *Learning from Experience*. London: Heinemann.

Blakemore, C. (1998) Unpublished paper at Pen Green Centre Conference on Giving Children a Sure Start, November, Corby.

Blanden, J. (2006) '"Bucking the trend": what enables those who are disadvantaged in childhood to succeed later in life?'. Working paper no. 31. London: Department for Work and Pensions.

Bowlby, J. (1991[1969]) *Attachment and Loss*, vol. 1. London: Penguin.

Bredekamp, S. and Shephard, L. (1989) 'How best to protect children from inappropriate school expectations, practices and policies', *Young Children*, 44 (3): 14–34.

Bright, J. (1998) 'Provision for young children'. Implementation paper for the Cross-Departmental Review of Provision for Young Children, 26 February.

British Educational Research Association (BERA) (2011) *Ethical Guidelines for Educational Research*. London: BERA. Accessed on 17/03/17 www.bera.ac.uk/wp-content/uploads/2014/02/BERA-Ethical-Guidelines-2011.pdf.

Brooker, L. (2010) 'Constructing the triangle of care: power and professionalism in practitioner/parent relationships', *British Journal of Educational Studies*, 58 (2): 181–96.

Bruce, T. (1997) *Early Childhood Education*, 2nd edn. London: Hodder & Stoughton.

Bruce, T. (1999) 'Seminar on pedagogic architecture'. Unpublished paper presented at Pen Green in October.

Bruce, T. (2005) *Early Childhood Education*, 3rd edn. London: Hodder Arnold.

Bruce, T. and Meggitt, C. (2002) *Child Care and Education*. London: Hodder & Stoughton.

Bruner, J. (1977) *The Process of Education*, 2nd edn. Cambridge, MA: Harvard University Press.

Buber, M. (1970) *I and Thou*, W. Kaufmann (trans.). Edinburgh: T & T Clark (1923).

Burk-Rodgers, D.B. (1998) 'Supporting autonomy in young children', *Young Children*, May, 75–80.

Carr, M. (2001) *Assessment in Early Childhood Settings: Learning Stories*. London: Paul Chapman.

Carr, M. and Lee, W. (2012) *Learning Stories: Constructing Learner Identities in Early Education*. London: Sage.

Ceppi, G. and Zini, M. (1998) *Children, Spaces, Relations: Meta Project for an Environment for Young Children*. Milan: Reggio Children, Somus Academy Research.

Chandler, T. (1997) 'Daring to care – men and childcare', in M. Whalley (ed.), *Working with Parents*. London: Hodder & Stoughton.

Chandler, T. (2005) *Pedagogy and leadership. Research Bursary on Leadership*. Unpublished paper, Dartington.

Concise Oxford English Dictionary (2011) 12th edn. A. Stevenson and M. Waite (eds). Oxford: Oxford University Press.

Conradson, D. (2010) 'Spaces of care in the city: the place of a community drop-in centre', *Social & Cultural Geography*, 4 (4): 507–25.

Dahlberg, G. (1998) Seminar held at the Thomas Coram Foundation, London, unpublished.

Dahlberg, G., Moss, P. and Pence, A. (1999) *Beyond Quality in Early Childhood Education and Care: Modern Perspectives*. London: RoutledgeFalmer.

David, T. (ed.) (1994) *Working Together for Young Children*. London: Routledge.

Daws, D. (1999) 'Parent-infant psychotherapy: remembering the Oedipus complex', *Psychoanalytic Inquiry: A Topical Journal for Mental Health Professionals*, 19 (2): 267–78.

Department of Education and Science (DES) (1990) *Starting With Quality*. London: HMSO.

Department of Health (1991) *The Children Act 1989: Guidance and Regulations, 2, Family Support, Daycare and Educational Provision for Young Children*. London: HMSO.

Department of Services to Children and Young People (2010) 'Ending child poverty: everyone's business.' Available at http://observatory.bradford.gov.uk/resource/view?resourceId=2091 (accessed 11/04/16).
DCSF (2010) *Aiming High For Children, Three Years On*. Crown Copyright 2010.
DfEE (1996) *Early Excellence – A Head Start for Every Child*. London: Labour Party.
DfEE (1997) *Excellence in Schools*, DfEE in 3681. London: HMSO.
DfEE (1998) *Meeting the Childcare Challenge*. London: HMSO.
DfEE (1999) *Sure Start: A Guide for Trailblazers*. London: DfEE.
Drummond, M.J. (1989) 'Early years education: contemporary challenges in early childhood education', in C.W. Desforges (ed.), *British Journal of Educational Psychology*, Monograph Series No. 4.
Drummond, M.J. (1993) *Assessing Children's Learning*. London: David Fulton.
Duranti, A. (2010) 'Husserl, intersubjectivity, and anthropology', *Anthropological Theory*, 10 (1): 1–20.
Dweck, C. (2014) 'Carol Dweck: the power of believing that you can improve', [Video file]. Accessed on 10/07/16 www.ted.com/talks/carol_dweck_the_power_of_believing_that_you_can_improve/transcript?language=en
Easen, P., Kendall, P. and Shaw, J. (1992) 'Parents and educators: dialogue and developing through partnership', *Children and Society*, 6 (4): 282–96.
Edwards, C., Gandini, L. and Forman, G. (1998) *The Hundred Languages of Children: The Reggio Emilia Approach – Advanced Reflections*, 2nd edn. London: Ablex.
Eisenstadt, N. (2011) *Providing a Sure Start*. Bristol: The Policy Press.
Epstein, D., Elwood, J., Hey, V. and Maw, J. (1998) *Failing Boys*. Buckingham: Open University Press.
Epstein, J.L., Elwood, J., Hey, V. and Maw, J. (1996) *Partnership 2000 Schools Manual*. Baltimore, MD: Johns Hopkins University.
Feinstein, L. and Sabates, R. (2007) *The Public Value of Adult Learning*. London: CFWBL.
Field, F. (2010) *The Foundation Years: Preventing Poor Children Becoming Poor Adults*. The report of the Independent Review on Poverty and Life Chances. London: HM Government.
Fletcher, C. (1999) 'Home and school myth: parents don't care', in R. O'Hagan (ed.), *Modern Educational Myths*. London: Kogan Page..
Fletcher, C. (2014) 'Preface: a review of the Pen Green research paradigm', in E. McKinnon (ed.), *Using Evidence for Advocacy and Resistance in Early Years Services*. London: Routledge.
Flyvbjerg, B. (2006) 'Five misunderstandings about case-study research', *Qualitative Inquiry*, 12 (2): 219–45.
Freire, P. (1970) *Pedagogy of the Oppressed*. Harmondsworth: Penguin Books.
Freire, P. (1996) *Pedagogy of the Oppressed*. London: Penguin Books.
Fuerst, J.S. and Fuerst, D. (1993) 'Chicago experience with an early childhood programme: the special case of the Child Parent Centre Program', *Educational Research*, 35 (3): 237–53.
Gallagher, T. and Arnold, C. (in press) *Working With Children 0–3 and their Families*. London: Routledge.
Gardner, H. (1991) *The Unschooled Mind*. London: Fontana Press.
Gaunt, C. (2016) 'Interview – Dr Margy Whalley and Barbara Riddell', *Nursery World*, 25 January.
Geertz, C. (1973) 'Thick description: toward an interpretive theory of culture', in *The Interpretation of Cultures: Selected Essays*. New York: Basic Books.
Gergen, K. (2009) *Relational Being*. Oxford: Oxford University Press.
Gerring, J. (2007) *Case Study Research: Principles and Practices*. New York: Cambridge University Press.
Ghedini, P., Chandler, T., Whalley, M. and Moss, P. (1995) *Fathers, Nurseries and Childcare*. European Commission Equal Opportunities Unit/Early Childcare Network.
Gilchrist, A. (2004) *The Well-Connected Community*. Bristol: Policy Press.
Gilkes, J. (1987) *Developing Nursery Education*. Milton Keynes: Open University Press.

Goffman, E. (1963) *Behaviour in Public Places: Notes on the Social Organization of Gatherings*. New York: Free Press.

Goldschmied, E. (1991) 'What to do with the under twos. Heuristic play. Infants learning', in D. Rouse (ed.), *Babies and Toddlers: Carers and Educators. Quality for Under 3's*. London: National Children's Bureau.

Goleman, D. (1996) *Emotional Intelligence*. London: Bloomsbury.

Greenfield, S. (1997) *The Human Brain: A Guided Tour*. London: Weidenfeld & Nicolson.

Haggerty, M. (1996) *Using Video to Work With Te Whaariki*. New Zealand: Wellington College of Education.

Handy, C. (1997) *The Empty Raincoat*. Reading: Arrow Books.

Harcourt, D. and Keen, D. (2001) 'Learner engagement: has the child been lost in translation?', *Australasian Journal of Early Childhood*, 37 (3): 71–78.

Hargreaves, D.H. (1996) 'Teaching as a research-based profession: possibilities and prospects', Teacher Training Agency Annual Lecture, April.

Harlen, W. (1982) 'Evaluation and assessment', in C. Richards (ed.), *New Directions in Primary Education*, London: Falmer Press.

Haw, K. and Hadfield, M. (2011) *Video in Social Science Research: Functions and Forms*. London: Routledge.

Hayward, K., Fletcher, C., Whalley, M., McKinnon, E., Gallagher, T., Prodger, A., Donoyou, H., Potts, J. and Young, E. (2013) 'The architecture of access: a grounded theory on the nature of access to early childhood services within a children's centre derived from nine parent voices', *European Early Childhood Research Journal*, 21 (1): 94–108.

Hobbs, R. (1998) Team building for staff at Pen Green Centre, Internal Training Session.

Holman, B. (1987) 'Research from the underside', *British Journal of Social Work*, 17: 669–83.

Holmes, J. (2001) 'The search for the secure base', *Attachment Theory and Psychotherapy*. Suffolk: Bruner-Routledge.

Holt, J. (1967) *How Children Learn*. Harmondsworth, Middlesex: Penguin Books Ltd.

Hoyuelos, A. (2013) *The Ethics in Loris Malaguzzi's Philosophy*. Reykjavik: Isalda.

Hughes, P. and MacNaughton, G. (2000) 'Consensus, dissensus or community: the politics of parent involvement in early childhood education', *Contemporary Issues in Early Childhood*, 1 (3): 241–58.

Isaacs, S. (1936) *Intellectual Growth in Young Children*. London: Routledge and Kegan Paul.

Jackson, D. (2001) 'The creation of knowledge', Networks Collaborative Enquiry for Schools and System Improvement, Paper presented to CERI/OECD/DFES/QCA/ESRC Forum on Knowledge Management in Education and Learning, 18–19 March 2002.

Jordan, B. and Henderson, A. (1995) 'Interaction analysis: foundations and practice', *Journal of the Learning Sciences*, 4 (1): 39–103.

Kendon, A. (1990) *Conducting Interaction: Patterns of Behavior in Focused Encounters*. Cambridge: Cambridge University Press.

Kendon, A. (2004) *Gesture: Visible Action as Utterance*. Cambridge: Cambridge University Press.

Kirk, R. (2003) 'Family support: the role of early years' centres', *Children and Society*, 17: 85–99.

Kress, G. and Van Leeuwen, T. (2001) *Multimodal Discourse: The Modes and Media of Contemporary Communication*. London: Arnold.

Kvale, S. (1996) *InterViews*. London: Sage.

Laevers, F. (1994a) *The Leuven Involvement Scale for Young Children*, LIS and YC manual and videotape, Experiential Education Series 1, Leuven, Belgium, Centre of Experiential Education.

Laevers, F. (1994b) 'The innovative project: experiential education 1976–1995', *Studia Pedagogica*, 16: 159–72.

Laevers, F. (1995) Lecture at EEL, Worcester College of Higher Education, September.

Laevers, F. (1996) 'The Leuven Involvement Scale for Young Children LIS-YC', Manual and Video Tape, Experimental Education Series No.1, Leuven, University of Belgium: Centre for Experiential Education.

Laevers, F. (1997) *A Process-Orientated Child Follow Up System for Young Children*, Centre for Experiential Education, Leuven, Belgium.

Laevers, F. (2011) 'Experiential education: making care and education more effective through well-being and involvement', J. Bennett (topic ed.), in R.E. Tremblay, M. Boivin, R. De V. Peters, R.G. Barr (eds), *Encyclopedia on Early Childhood Development* [online]. Montreal, Quebec: Centre of Excellence for Early Childhood Development and Strategic Knowledge Cluster on Early Child Development, pp. 1–5. Available at: www.childencyclopedia.com/documents/LaeversANGxp1.pdf (accessed 8 January 2016).

Lawrence, P. and Gallagher, T. (in press) 'Pedagogic strategies': a conceptual framework for effective parent and practitioner strategies when working with children under five, in T. Gallagher and C. Arnold (ed.), *Working with Children 0–3 and their Families*. London: Routledge.

Lawrence, P., Gallagher, T. and The Pen Green Team (2015) '"Pedagogic strategies": a conceptual framework for effective parent and practitioner strategies when working with children under five', *Early Child Development and Care*, 185 (11–12): 1978–94.

Lee, V. and Das Gupta, P. (1995) *Children's Cognitive Language Development*. Milton Keynes: Open University Press.

Linell, P. (2009) *Rethinking Language, Mind, and World Dialogically*. Charlotte, NC: Information Age Publishing.

Litowitz, B.E. (1997) 'Just Say No: Responsibility and Resistance', in M. Cole, Y. Engestrom and O. Vazquez (eds), *Mind Culture and Activity*. Cambridge: CUP.

Mairs, K. (1990) *A Schema Booklet for Parents*. Corby: Pen Green Centre.

Mairs, K. and The Pen Green Team (2013) *Young Children Learning Through Schemas: Deepening the Dialogue about Learning in the Home and in the Nursery*, C. Arnold (ed.). London: Routledge.

Malaguzzi, L. (1993) 'For an education based on relationship', *Young Children*, 11: 9–13.

Malaguzzi, L. (1998a) *The Hundred Languages of Children*. London: Ablex.

Malaguzzi, L. (1998b) 'History, ideas and basic philosophy: an interview with Lella Gandini', in C. Edwards, L. Gandini and G. Forman (eds), *The Hundred Languages of Children: The Reggio Emilia Approach – Advanced Reflections*. London: Ablex Publishing Corporation.

Malcolm, A. (1993) 'Fathers' involvement with their children and outside work commitments', unpublished study submitted as part of the Diploma in Post-Qualifying Studies.

McKinnon, E. (2005) 'Family life and family services – putting the jigsaw together'. Symposium paper presented at the European Early Childhood Research Association's Annual Conference, Dublin, September.

McKinnon, E. (2014) *Using Evidence for Advocacy and Resistance in Early Years Services*. London: Routledge.

McNeill, D. (1992) *Hand and Mind: What Gestures Reveal About Thought*. Chicago: The University of Chicago Press.

Meade, A. (1995) *Thinking Children*. Wellington: New Zealand Council for Educational Research.

Mezirow, J. (1977, October) 'Perspective transformation', *Studies in Adult Education*, 9: 153–64.

Miller, R.L. (2000) *Researching Life Stories and Family Histories*. London: Sage.

MODE (2012) *Glossary of Multimodal Terms*. https://multimodalityglossary.wordpress.com/ (accessed 18 June 2015).

Moir, A. and Moir, B. (1999) *Why Men Don't Iron: The New Reality of Gender Differences*. London: HarperCollins.

Moss, P. (1992) 'Perspectives from Europe', in G. Pugh (ed.), *Contemporary Issues in the Early Years*. London: Paul Chapman in Association with the National Children's Bureau.

Moss, P. and Penn, H. (1996) *Transforming Nursery Education*. London: Sage

Munro, E. (2011) 'The Munro Review of Child Protection: Final Report, A Child-Centered System', DoE.

Nash, J.M. (1997) 'Fertile minds', *Time Magazine*, 3 February.

Norris, S. (2004) *Analyzing Multimodal Interaction: A Methodological Framework*. Abingdon: Routledge.

Norris, S. (2011) *Identity in (Inter)action: Introducing Multimodal (Inter)action Analysis*. Berlin/Boston: de Gruyter.

Nucci, L. and Smetana, J.G. (1996) 'Mothers' concepts of young children's areas of personal freedom', *Child Development*, 677: 1870–86.

OECD (Organisation for European Co-operation and Development) (1997) *Parents as Partners in Schools*. Paris: OECD.

Ofsted (2009) *Pen Green Inspection Report*. London: HMSO.

Oliver, C., Smith, M. and Barker, S. (1998) 'Effectiveness of early interactions'. Paper for the Cross-Departmental Review of Provision for Young Children.

Olson, D. R.,and Bruner, J. S. (1996) 'Folk psychology and folk pedagogy', in D. R. Olson and N. Torrance (eds.), *The Handbook of Education and Human Development*. Oxford: Blackwell.

Pascal, C. (1996) Lecture at Pen Green Centre. Unpublished.

Pascal, C. and Bertram, A. (1997) *Effective Early Learning*. London: Hodder & Stoughton.

Pen Green (2005) 'Adult pedagogic strategies', updated by Pen Green Team, unpublished.

Pen Green (2013) 'Pen Green Evidence-Based Practice: Making Children's Learning Visible', C4EO Validated Local Practice Submission Form, Available at: http://archive.c4eo.org.uk/themes/schools/vlpdetails.aspx?lpeid=451 (accessed 17 March 2017).

Pen Green Centre (2016) *Adult Pedagogic Strategies: Professional Development Learning Materials*, Unpublished Document, Pen Green Centre, Corby, Northants.

Pen Green Centre/DfEE (1999) 'Autumn term evaluation project: pedagogic architecture'. Unpublished paper.

Pen Green Research Base Report (2000) 'Parent-led needs assessment'. Unpublished internal document.

Phelan, J. (1983) *Family Centres: A Study*. London: The Children's Society.

Piaget, J. (1962) *Play, Dreams and Imitation in Childhood*. London: Routledge and Kegan Paul.

Podmore, V., May, H. and Carr, M. (2001) *The Child's Questions: Early Childhood Folio 1/*, NZCER

Pollard, A. (1996) *The Social World of Children's Learning*. London: Cassell.

Pugh, G. (2001) *Contemporary Issues in the Early Years: Working Collaboratively for Children*, 3rd edn. London: Paul Chapman Publishing.

Pugh, G., De'Ath, E. and Smith, C. (1994) *Confident Parents, Confident Children*. London: National Children's Bureau.

Pushor, D. (2007) 'Parent engagement: creating a shared world', Research paper: Ontario Education Research Symposium.

Quinton, D. (2004) *Supporting Parents – Messages from Research*. London: Jessica Kingsley Publishers Ltd.

Ramaekers, S. and Suissa, J. (2011) 'Parents as "educators": Languages of education, pedagogy and "parenting"', *Ethics & Education*, 6 (2): 197–212.

Reddy, V. (2008) *How Infants Know Minds*. Cambridge, MA: Harvard University Press.

Rinaldi, C. (1998) 'Projected curriculum constructed through documentation – Progettazione: an interview with Lella Gandini', in C. Edwards, L. Gandini and G. Forman (eds), *The Hundred Languages of Children: The Reggio Emilia Approach – Advanced Reflections*. London: Ablex.

Rogers, C.R. (1983) *Freedom to Learn for the 80s*. London: Merrill.

Rutter, M.L. (1997) 'Nature–nurture integration: The example of antisocial behavior', *American Psychologist*, 5 (4): 390–98.

Rutter, M. and Rutter, M. (1992) *Developing Minds*. Harmondsworth: Penguin.

Rutter, M. (1997) 'An update on resilience: conceptual considerations and empirical findings', in S.J. Meisel and J.T. Shonkoff (eds.), *Handbook of Early Child Intervention*. New York: Cambridge University Press.

Ryle, G. (1949) *The Concept of Mind*. London: Hutchinson.

Santos, A. (1992) 'Nursery education in context – a case study of a combined nursery centre in England'. Unpublished MPhil dissertation, Cranfield Institute of Technology.

Schütz, A. (1966) 'The problem of transcendental intersubjectivity in Husserl', in *Collected Papers III*. The Hague: Nijhoff.

Scott, P. (1996) 'He has seen the future and it gets harder: profile of Charles Handy', *Times Educational Supplement*, 29 November, p. 4.

Schwandt, T. (1999) 'On understanding understanding', *Qualitative Inquiry*, 5 (4): 451–64. doi: 10.1177/107780049900500401.

Schwandt, T. (2000) 'Three epistemological stances for qualitative inquiry: interpretitivism, hermeneutics and social constructivism', in N. Denzin and Y. Lincoln (eds), *Handbook of Qualitative Research*. Thousand Oaks, CA/London: Sage. pp. 189–214.

Shaw, J. (1991) 'An investigation of parents' conceptual development in the light of dialogue with a community teacher'. Unpublished PhD thesis, University of Newcastle-upon-Tyne.

Singer, E. and de Haan, D. (2007) *The Social Lives of Children: Play, Conflict and Moral Learning in Day-Care Groups*. Amsterdam: SWP.

Smiley, P.A. and Dweck, C. (1994) 'Individual differences in achievement and goals among young children', *Child Development*, 65: 1723–43.

Smith, T. (1990) 'Parents and pre-school education', in N. Entwistle (ed.), *Handbook of Educational Ideas and Practices*. London: Routledge.

Smith, T., Smith, G., Coxon, K., Sigala, M., Sylva, K., Mathers, S., La Valle, I., Smith, R., Purdon, S., Dearden, L., Shaw, J. and Sibieta, L. (2007) National Evaluation of the Neighbourhood Nurseries Initiative (NNI) Integrated Report, http://webarchive.nationalarchives.gov.uk/20130401151715/http://www.education.gov.uk/publications/eOrderingDownload/SSU-2007-SF-024.pdf

Stake, R. (2000) *The Art of Case Study Research*. London: Sage

Stimson, J. (1995) *Worried Arthur*. Loughborough: Ladybird.

Strauss, A. and Corbin, J. (1990) *Basics of Qualitative Research*. London: Sage.

Streeck, J., Goodwin, C. and LeBaron, C. (eds) (2011) *Embodied Interaction: Language and Body in the Material World*. Cambridge: Cambridge University Press.

Sylva, K. (1994) 'A curriculum for early learning', in C. Ball (ed.), *RSA Start Right: The Importance of Early Learning*. London: RSA.

Sylva, K. (1999) 'Linking quality processes to children's developmental outcomes'. Keynote Lecture, Warwick Conference, April.

Sylva, K., Melhuish, E., Sammons, P., Siraj-Blatchford, I. and Taggart, B. (2004) 'The Effective Provision of Pre-School Education (EPPE) Project. Final Report'. London: DfES Publications.

TES (2000) 'Early years shops save money', *Times Educational Supplement,* 25 February, p. 11.

Trevarthen, C. (2002) 'Learning in Companionship', *Education in the North: The Journal of Scottish Education*, 10: 16–25.

Trevarthen, C. (2015) Unpublished data. Pen Green Steering Group viewing, 10 March.

Trevarthen, C. and Hubley, P. (1978) Secondary intersubjectivity: confidence, confiding and acts of meaning in the first year', in A. Lock (ed.), *Action, Gesture and Symbol*. London: Academic Press, 183–229.

Trevarthen, C. and Schögler, B. (2007) 'To sing and dance together: from infants to jazz', in S. Braten (ed.), *On Being Moved: From Mirror Neurons to Empathy*. Amsterdam and New York: John Benjamins Publishing Company.

Vygotsky, L.S. (1978) *Mind in Society*. Cambridge, MA: Harvard University Press.

Weinberger, J. (1996) *Literacy Goes to School – The Parents' Role in Young Children's Literacy Learning*. London: Paul Chapman.
Wells, G. (1986) *The Meaning Makers: Children Learning Language and Using Language to Learn*. Portsmouth, NH: Heinemann.
West-Burnham, J. and Jones, V. (2007) *Spiritual and Moral Development in Schools*. London: Bloomsbury/Network Continuum Education.
Whalley, M. (1992) 'A question of choice', unpublished MA thesis, Leicester University.
Whalley, M. (1994) *Learning to Be Strong*. London: Hodder & Stoughton.
Whalley, M. (1996a) Unpublished paper for EECERA Conference, Lisbon.
Whalley, M. (1996b) *Confident Parents, Confident Children: Group Leader Notes*. Milton Keynes: Open University Press.
Whalley, M. (1997a) 'Parents' involvement in their children's learning', Conference paper, November.
Whalley, M. (1997b) *Working with Parents*. London: Hodder and Stoughton.
Whalley, M. (1998) 'Getting fathers involved', *Basic Skills Magazine*, March/April, pp. 25–8.
Whalley, M. (1999) 'Leadership in early years settings', unpublished PhD thesis, University of Wolverhampton.
Whalley, M. (2005) 'Developing leadership approaches for early years settings: leading together', PowerPoint (Accessed on May 2015 www.ncsl/.org.uk/media/f58/76/community leadership-together-Whalley.ppt#262).
Whalley, M. (2006) 'Leadership in integrated centres and services for children and families – a community development approach: engaging with the struggle', *Childrens Issues, Journal of the Children's Issues Centre*, 10 (2): 8.
Whalley, M. (2007) *Involving Parents in Their Children's Learning,* 2nd edition. London: Paul Chapman.
Whalley, M. (2014) 'Introduction: the Pen Green Research, Training and Development Base' in E. McKinnon (ed.), *Using Evidence for Advocacy and Resistance in Early Years Services*. Abingdon: Routledge
Whalley, M. and Arnold, C. (1997a) 'Effective pedagogic strategies', *TTA Summary of Research Findings*. London: TTA.
Whalley, M. and Arnold, C. (1997b) 'Parental involvement in education'. Paper for Teacher Training Agency.
Whalley, M., Arnold, C., Lawrence, P. and Peerless, S. (2012) 'The voices of their childhood: families and early years' practitioners developing emancipator methodologies through a tracer study', in *European Early Childhood Education Research Journal*, 20 (4): 519–35.
Whalley, M., Arnold, C. and Orr, R (2013) *Working with Families in Children's Centres and Early Years Settings*. London: Hodder.
Whalley, M. and Chandler, T. (2001) 'Parents and staff as co-educators – 'parents' means fathers too', in M. Whalley and the Pen Green Team (eds), *Involving Parents in Their Children's Learning*. London: Sage/Paul Chapman.
Whalley, M. and the Pen Green Team (2001) *Involving Parents in Their Children's Learning*. London: Sage/Paul Chapman.
Whalley, M. and The Pen Green Team (2007) Training Materials given out when participants attend the three day PICL course for practitioners, Pen Green Research Base, Corby, Northants.
Whalley, E. and Whalley, P. (1996) *Making schemas easy to understand*, Briefing paper for a conference at Pen Green Research, Development and Training Base, Corby, Northants.
Whitaker, P. (1986) 'A humanistic approach to teacher in-service education', *Self and Society*, 4 (6): 276–81.
Winnicott, D.W. (1965) 'The theory of the parent–infant relationship', in D.W. Winnicott (ed.), *The Maturational Processes and the Facilitating Environment*. London: Hogarth Press.
Winnicott, D.W. (1991) *Playing and Reality*. East Sussex: Brunner-Routledge.

Index